The Multichannel Challenge

The Multichannel Challenge

Integrating customer experiences for profit

Hugh Wilson, Rod Street and
Lindsay Bruce

ELSEVIER

AMSTERDAM • BOSTON • HEIDELBERG • LONDON • NEW YORK • OXFORD
PARIS • SAN DIEGO • SAN FRANCISCO • SINGAPORE • SYDNEY • TOKYO
BUTTERWORTH-HEINEMANN IS AN IMPRINT OF ELSEVIER

Butterworth-Heinemann is an imprint of Elsevier
Linacre House, Jordan Hill, Oxford OX2 8DP, UK
30 Corporate Drive, Suite 400, Burlington, MA 01803, USA

First edition 2008

British Library Cataloguing in Publication Data
A catalogue record for this book is available from the British Library

Library of Congress Cataloging in Publication Data
A catalog record for this book is available from the Library of Congress

ISBN: 978-0-7506-8711-9

For information on all Butterworth-Heinemann publications
visit our web site at books.elsevier.com

Typeset by Charon Tec Ltd (A Macmillan Company), Chennai, India
www.charontec.com

Printed and bound in Slovenia

08 09 10 11 10 9 8 7 6 5 4 3 2 1

Contents

List of Figures

List of Tables

Acknowledgements

As consultants and in our work with IBM and Cranfield Customer Management Forum we have been privileged to work and write with many extremely learned and talented people. We acknowledge that there are many parts of this book that rely on work we have done with them, and on their work that they have shared with us to allow us to build upon it. In particular, we thank the following for their contributions to our research and writing. This book is the richer for their input and for their kind permission to use work we have done together.

Kevin Bishop, Vice President for NE Europe for IBM.com, who contributed material on the coverage model for IBM.

Professor Elizabeth Daniel of the Open University and Professor John Ward of Cranfield School of Management, whose collaborative research with the authors produced the pensions channel curve diagram and the prioritisation of multiple projects matrix, both in Chapter 6 and the insurance company market map in Chapter 4.

Alex Garrett, a business writer, who assisted the authors in the research of the GM/Vauxhall case study discussed in Chapters 2 and 7, as well as the IBM case study in Chapters 4 and 5.

Matt Hobbs of IBM's Global Business Services, who contributed much of the material on building a full financial case used in Chapter 6.

Jennifer Love, formerly of IBM Global Business Services, who contributed much of the material on metrics and measurement used in Chapter 8.

Dr Stan Maklan of Cranfield School of Management, who contributed significantly to the BT case study discussed in this book and who kindly allowed the authors to use his Infinite Innovation Inc. examples.

Dr Brian D Smith of PragMedic Ltd, who, with the authors, conducted the consultancy project that produced the export consultancy segmentation map in Chapter 4.

Malcolm McDonald, Emeritus Professor of Marketing at Cranfield, whose vision and support helped to establish the Cranfield Customer Management Forum.

Moira Clark, Professor of Strategic Marketing at Henley Management College and formerly Senior Lecturer at Cranfield, for her many contributions to our thinking on how to create profitable relationships in a multichannel world.

The former Cranfield students whose theses helped us to develop and road-test many of our tools and ideas, including Hester Stuart, Janet Thomson, Ben Knighton, Turab Hasan, Rita Madaleno, Hrishikesh Mehta, Claudine Epper, Roopalee Dave, Charlene Kosgey, Susan Edwards-Aisuebeogun and Namrita Sehgal.

We also thank the numerous others at Cranfield, at IBM and in the companies with whom we have collaborated over a number of years to develop the ideas in this book.

Foreword

Good. It is well past time that 'channel management' should have been killed off as a management concept, let alone a discipline. *The Multichannel Challenge* is a most welcome contribution to this. It illustrates the need for and value of an integrated and customer-led approach, not one focussed on administering the various channels we happen to have. It is over fifty years since the late Peter Drucker made the simple point that the purpose of every commercial enterprise is to create a customer (he later added 'at a profit'). The point is not the channel or channels, it is how the customer feels about the product, the service and the people selling it. Channels, all of them, are just one part of the system.

So please don't read the title of this book the wrong way. It is certainly a challenge to design channels that are fit for purpose and to manage multiple channels for consistency. But the purpose is to get and keep the customer. To meet this challenge the focus has to be on this real purpose-ironically not on 'channel management'. Or at least, not as it is commonly practised. To manage channels as a discrete activity can only deliver sub-optimal results for the enterprise as a whole. Worse still, as the authors demonstrate, to manage each channel individually inevitably puts channel efficiency measures before the real purpose, usually creating additional cost elsewhere in the organisation. The concept of a 'channel owner' is downright dangerous.

I suppose you could call Marks & Spencer's first Sixpenny Bazaar stall a 'channel'. But Mr M's and Mr S's focus was on the customer's perception of value, trustworthiness and convenience. The stall itself was part of the means to this end. Today for all businesses the number of channels has increased and customers' expectations are higher. What has not changed is that customers still seek value, trustworthiness and convenience. It is just that some businesses manage their channels in a way that makes it hard for the customer to form a consistent impression from all the faces of the business. Inconsistency does not inspire confidence.

When we started First Direct our competitors told us that it would not work: "people want to know their bank manager, a faceless voice at the telephone just won't do". Pleasingly, we were still being told that a few years later when we had taken over a million customers from them. Some still perceive First Direct as a 'channel proposition' which it is not. To have the channel as your management priority would be to miss the point. The truth at First Direct was much more simple. People do not want to know their bank manager, but they emphatically do want to be known by their bank. And they want to know that their bank cares about their relationship. As one customer elegantly put it to me: "Looking back, I can hardly believe that I was paying £35 a month for a 'Personal

Account Executive' who provided a service inferior to yours. I cannot commend any individual by name, as I speak to a different person every time I call, but you truly succeed in giving the impression that I have a very personal relationship with First Direct, which of course sounds utterly daft." Confidence in the result and ease of purchase can be as powerful as value in attracting and retaining customers.

What a shame that in the early 1990s many companies started to manage channels separately, or even individually. And as cost centres of all things. Customer contact is and has always been an opportunity, not a cost. Hugh Wilson, Rod Street and Lindsay Bruce have to be correct with their call to start from the overall experience the customer gets and to integrate channels so the customer can be in control of how she or he buys.

For the customers to feel in control is a good thing, if you want to keep them. And the commercial reasons are overwhelming, not counter-intuitive. Measurement of the effectiveness of the process as customers hop between the various ways of dealing with us returns very different and more representative results than the measurement of an individual channel. Analysis of the process will reveal far more opportunities for improvement than just looking at one part of it. Starting with the customer and their aspirations will achieve lower costs and greater efficiency as the authors illustrate. Working on one channel, or even all channels, separately from the rest of the organisation cannot possibly be as effective as considering the whole. One does not need to be a student of W Edwards Deming to see the sense of this. There are two options: be like a market or be an organisation. Markets can allocate resources and weed out poor performance with ruthless efficiency. Businesses are sometimes described as organisations for good reason: they organise in order to gain the benefits of co-operation around a shared strategy and shared purpose for collective benefit. To operate a business in a way that impedes this is plainly nonsensical. The Cranfield/IBM team succeeds in illustrating this with practical advice on the better alternative.

Then there is the most important thing about channels, the thing you would think no one could ever overlook, yet remarkably in my experience some organisations still do. We all gain our most powerful opinion of a business from our direct experience of its people. We all do this and we all know it. Yet there are still businesses that manage their front-line people to be ignorant of the rest of the customer's experience and drive employees by short-term transaction targets. To my eyes this is not management, it is a gross abdication of management responsibility. Worse, it wastes what is the business's most potent asset. Front-line people have the power to create, or destroy, trust and confidence in the business. The authors illustrate this well.

It is pleasing to see Wilson, Street & Bruce's codification of tools and methods that can help managers to implement this common-sense approach to customer development for the organisation as a whole. The result will be more custom, lower costs and happier people. Within three years of adding the internet channel to the First Direct service it accounted for two-thirds of all customer-instigated contact. This was because we put integration of the overall customer experience first when we built it. And costs were down and sales were up. Customer satisfaction was already high but it rose too, particularly with the now less-used telephone service. This was no paradox. Customers chose the telephone if they wanted an explanation or had a problem. The potency of highly competent and thoroughly well informed front-line people increased in such circumstances. And yes, the occasions on which customers chose to buy an additional product as a result of talking through their needs in this 'expensive' channel increased alongside new internet sales. The effect on profits was very pleasing indeed. A win-win all round, because all the pieces were in place, all organised to operate in concert with each other in a way that allowed the customer to stay in control.

A one-off? Not only have these influential marketers given many case studies that show the value of this approach but also their analysis and tools can encourage similar solutions to emerge. Some managers talk as if customer experience, market reach and cost-efficiency are in competition with each other for resources. The insight that allows all three to be improved simultaneously is to think of channels not as alternatives but as parts of a system, members of a team, that can be honed to roles that mutually support the customer's ease of doing business with us. Customers are only too delighted to use a low-cost channel when it's right for the job, but there are other times – such as when they have a complaint – when we would be mad not to roll out the cavalry of warm human contact. The authors' tools can help managers to unlock their creativity to put this jigsaw together properly.

So I commend this holistic approach. Start from the customer's needs, for confidence and convenience not just for the actual product or service, then plan the customer's experience around that. Never forget the key ingredient: people in the organisation with the knowledge, the confidence and the will to make it work. After all, each person a customer deals with can build or ruin an organisation's reputation. So don't manage each of them as a stand-alone channel either.

Alan Hughes
Cropthorne
January 2008

Note: Alan is the former Chief Executive of First Direct and General Manager in charge of marketing, products and service at HSBC and Midland Bank.

■ ■ Introduction ■ ■

For most of us there can barely be a week that goes by without participation in one of the most commonplace activities of modern living ... a call to a contact centre (sometimes abroad, sometimes at home). These features of modern life remain somewhat like traffic lights – very popular, in terms of the time and frequency with which we use them, and very unpopular, in terms of gossip, experience and comment.

They are events in our lives that many people love to hate; where the bad experiences stay with us so much longer than the good ones that they easily pass into the background to become another of the irritants that we have to live with.

The call centre is a feature of our convenience driven, 24/7 service-oriented environment. Even now, several years after the peak of the dot-com boom, call centres are only just starting to be rivalled by other forms of consumer communication for business interactions – like the web, SMS and chat. They established their pre-eminence as the default channel in both business-to-business and business-to-consumer markets in the 1990s. Fuelled by better support systems, information access and increasing telecommunications bandwidth, they have become an essential sales and service delivery point in modern life. And it's clear their irritating mix of music, menus and wait times has quickly been rivalled by equivalents in each of the newer channels – broken links, dropped calls, slow-loading pages or pop-up ads. As the web increasingly becomes the new base channel we may yet see these become the dominant irritants of modern life.

However, in the light of the transformation of our channel use in just 20 years, it is surprising that so little thought is being given to the strategy and shaping of them. As consultants in this area we see few businesses with a well-founded strategy, or an analytic review of the composite performance of channels. It is equally rare to hear a clear strategy articulated and explained by a business leader. More often than not it seems that, as managers, we end up with a strategy inherited from the often disparate set of initiatives that have taken place in the organisation over the last decade. Channels are too often the business equivalent of islands of automation, created and then left isolated.

However, as many businesses are realising, this is not a stable or sustainable position. As communication technology develops and consumer fragmentation advances, the failure to set a clear path for channels leads to a legacy of tremendous variety, complexity and cost ... and insufficient value.

This is the rationale behind this book. We see this area of business as one that deserves much more attention and thought, and where that attention will be repaid readily.

Channels are the lifeblood of organisations, as well as consumers, and their contribution to customer experience, operating costs, and ultimately market success and failure, is immense. Channels create challenges, and we see the need for thinking in this area to catch up with the real world. This book is a contribution to that thinking.

It is not all our own thinking; it is based on over 5 years of work within a research forum in the School of Management at Cranfield University; the consulting experience of IBM's Global Business Services; and the many participants and contributors to the forum. It draws on the authors' experiences with many businesses who have participated in this venture and on consulting projects.

It endeavours to synthesise and structure the learning from all this experience and provide practical and proven tools for the improvement of multichannel operations – for both customer and business benefit.

We hope that readers will find it useful, stimulating and, above all, practical.

■ So what is multichannel?

We use the term to define the use of multiple channels, in an integrated fashion, to provide access to an organisation for the customer.

Searching for 'multichannel' on the Internet brings forth a varied selection of articles relating to television, communications and other media-related items. Even in business circles, many people think of multichannel as something that relates just to contact centres and the use of SMS and the web alongside the telephone.

This is not what we mean. When we use the term throughout this book, we are describing *all* the multiple different routes by which customers and businesses interact with each other. These include on- and off-line channels, and many distinctly older methods such as outlets or field staff.

We also use the term for customer contact through all the steps of a lifecycle between organisation and customer – from when the potential customer first discovers the service, all the way through purchase and usage until he or she finally stops using the service. In this way we are covering all customer contact functions – marketing, sales and service.

This perspective is different from that of many other analysts, who consider only parts of this lifecycle and constrain their viewpoint by function or scope. Our perspective is shaped by that of customers who, even though they recognise the steps in the cycle and the differences in the media, expect an organisation to operate in an integrated and consistent manner.

As increasingly empowered customers exercise their choice both in what they buy and in how they access services, they are increasingly using several channels to interact with an organisation in the course of an individual journey (e.g. to resolve a complaint, conduct a purchase, secure product support, use a particular service), and through the course of an extended period on different journeys they make extensive use of these. If customers see value in this approach, we see value in the study of it and in trying to provide perspectives, concepts and tools that help businesses to address the topic more effectively.

■ The structure of the book

> The best place to begin the creative process is at the end. What is the final result that you want?
>
> Robert Fritz

The book offers the reader several different paths. It is possible to walk through the process of innovating with a multichannel strategy from start to finish. Alternatively, readers can start from where they currently find themselves facing a challenge and dip straight in to the chapters discussing the key questions that they are confronting.

With this in mind, the book is organised into three parts.

Part 1: The case for multichannel

Part 1 provides the context for the book and an introduction to the key questions that frame multichannel strategy. It also provides something of an overview for the rest of the book and for the tools and concepts that we will introduce as we go through.

Chapter 1 – The importance of channels

Chapter 1 introduces our subject. In addition to describing the 'what' of the scope of the book, it provides the rationale for the difference between this book and others that the reader may pick up on channels. It describes how the challenges most businesses face today relate to the multichannel customer, and the need to operate and innovate across integrated multiple channels. This is a topic that we do not feel has been well handled in the literature.

Chapter 2 – Making multichannel a source of competitive advantage

Chapter 2 provides an overview of the structure we have used to examine the 'how' of innovating across multiple channels.

The book is organised as a set of tools, concepts and experiences that address the key questions managers face in the organisations that we have dealt with. This wheel of questions forms a natural progression that serves as a useful vehicle for 'walking through' multichannel strategy. These questions are the pillars around which we have structured the lessons and concepts that we have uncovered through the research forum, consulting, and other organisations' experiences. They should help the reader to use the book in one of two ways:

1. As a means of navigating through a multichannel innovation from start to finish. Here the questions provide a step-by-step approach and the considerations at each stage. In the process, they also provide tools and concepts that can help support innovation.
2. As a way of delving into the book just at the point of immediate concern or interest. The chapters in Parts 2 and 3 are organised by these questions and enable the reader to pick off just the concepts and topics of immediate interest in their own journey through multichannel innovation.

Chapter 3 – Multichannel diagnostic

This chapter provides a diagnostic that will help explore the need for change. This is designed to help readers who find, as they read, that there is still a level of uncertainty about the need to innovate in this area of the organisation.

From the authors' viewpoint, those who struggle with the idea of needing to innovate are probably not paying attention to the needs and desires of their customers! There can be few areas in business where innovation is not needed, and the fast-changing area of channels seems to us to be especially important. The real challenge is how to innovate and, in the context of all business priorities, whether this is something close enough to the top of the agenda to warrant investment now.

The diagnostic is most useful, therefore, in understanding where and how to innovate and in shaping other aspects of the initial goal-setting process that needs to frame a reason to change. It takes an 'outside-in' view of the channel position, and identifies where the organisation is taking pain. This is invaluable. For any change to happen, there has to be dissatisfaction with the current state of affairs (either because of a better future opportunity or a present problem). And to embark on a major multichannel innovation, given the disruption and investment needed, there needs to be a compelling reason to act. For readers who seek that, the diagnostic makes a good starting point.

Part 2: Developing multichannel strategy

Part 2 explores the strategy generation phase of change. Some might see this as the fun bit of innovation – the time for ideas, analysis and creativity. In our experience, however, one of the distinguishing features of a multichannel challenge is that it presents many competing faces and is often difficult to structure and address effectively both conceptually and in sequencing for action.

Our approach is a pragmatic one. It is not that the tools and steps cannot be used for a grand strategy but that, in our experience, managers typically find one of many other issues to be the most pressing and enter the journey through that door. As a result, we break down the steps in this process in the way we have found most readily accessible for

managers – with the inherent limitations and benefits of this – by following the questions called out in Part 1.

Chapter 4 – Defining the right channel combinations to offer

This chapter examines how to decide what channels to offer the market;
more specifically, what channel combinations to offer for each product
and each customer group, and how these channels will work together in
customer journeys.

The chapter highlights the need for a sound market analysis as the
base for the channel definition, and describes the core elements of this. It
then moves on to provide one or two key tools that we have found helpful in addressing this challenge, and some examples of leading organisations – as diverse as a car company and an orchestra – who have worked
with us to create new channel chains for their market.

This chapter provides an insight into the research and work that needs
to be done to design a multichannel approach and really create something that is new and advantageous.

Chapter 5 – Integrating the multichannel proposition

This chapter takes the creative and potentially divergent possibilities
that are explored in the previous chapter and addresses the third of the
major questions that we set out in Chapter 2: how do you draw up an
integrated strategy for channels?

There are two integration challenges: the first is the mechanical consolidation and integration of the various channel chains across customer
groups and products, while the second is the integration of the customer
experience across these multiple channels. Both represent significant
efforts in diverse and large organisations, and we provide some examples
of major businesses that have stepped up to the challenges and are reap-
ing impressive business benefits from doing so.

We also introduce a number of tools and frameworks from our work
that managers have found helpful in identifying and resolving the integration task.

Chapter 6 – Building the case for change

It is one thing to have a clear vision of the intended channel strategy, and
how in the future the organisation's channels can best combine to meet
customer needs and save costs – the topic of the previous two chapters. It
is quite another to persuade the Board to invest in this vision. This chapter deals with how to construct the case for change and investment.

We describe how to prioritise the multiple projects that are typically
needed to get from the organisation's current channel model to the
intended future one. Each project is considered in terms of the benefit
it will give to customers – using a tool we term the *channel curve* – and
the benefit it will give to the company due to cost reduction or other
factors. We combine these analyses into a prioritisation matrix, which we

illustrate with a large financial services company which has successfully applied it.

Finally, we look at the investment case itself.

Part 3: Making multichannel work in practice

Part 3 addresses the next step in the process – putting a new multichannel model in place and making sure that it works. This requires some restructuring and new organisation to ensure that systems and processes are able and likely to deliver the customer value required. This process of organisational change will naturally require measurement of the effectiveness of the new structure and organisation. The new strategic model may also require a 'shift' of some customers across different channels, or for them to be steered through new channel chains. These are the points we cover in Part 3.

Chapter 7 – Organising for successful change

In Chapter 7, we deal with the question of organising for successful change. In doing so, we look at organisational structure – what is the best structure to deliver successfully in a multichannel environment? We then look at the broader question of change management, but particularly from the perspective of multichannel change – what are the aspects of change management that are especially pertinent when dealing with multichannel change, and what tools can we recommend to help?

Chapter 8 – Tracking and measuring effectiveness

In Chapter 8, we look at tracking and measurement. Always a difficult task, our experience is that this becomes altogether more difficult in a multichannel environment, where customers have a tendency to channel-hop and channel effectiveness is hard to track as sales efforts in one channel often contribute to a resultant sale in a different channel. In this chapter we look at how to identify what needs to be measured, understanding and taking account of channel crossover effects. We discuss how to gather the necessary data in practice (one of the questions we are most frequently asked), and how to pull together the data into meaningful information that can inform management teams and future iterations of the multichannel strategy.

Chapter 9 – Encouraging customers to use channels effectively

In Chapter 9, we look at the question of customer migration. An evolving multichannel strategy usually demands some movement of customers if it is to provide the return that makes investment worthwhile. In this chapter, we look at what makes customers migrate from one channel to a new channel and how to help make that change happen more quickly. We also look at how remuneration and incentives affect customer channel migration, and ways to encourage customers to move to new channels by rewarding or discouraging different behaviours amongst employees and customers.

PART I

The case for
multichannel

CHAPTER 1

The importance of channels

Strategy without tactics is the slowest route to victory. Tactics without strategy is the noise before defeat

Sun Tzu

■ Another book on channels?

Yes, indeed; but with good reason.

Channels are still one of the least well exploited areas of organisational effectiveness, underestimated in their significance by many organisations. Indeed, it is only in recent years that sectors such as the government, retail and construction have started to pay attention to the opportunities for advantage presented by them.

Even then the importance of a *multichannel* strategy is underestimated, and the development of management tools and approaches to make effective decisions is still in its infancy. Yet the need to develop and apply these is not diminishing but growing in the face of marketplace changes that affect most categories across developed economies.

The Voice

For one of the authors, a reminder of the importance of a multichannel strategy is provided every day after getting out of bed … by the shower!

The shower in question is periodically prone to seizing up and offering little more than a cold, icy dribble of water. This is not a great start to the day! A combination of local water composition and use seem to be the trigger. However, it has proved to be an easier problem to resolve than the multichannel service delivery that inevitably seems to flow from the company that supplied the shower.

An initial telephone call to the shower manufacturer's helpline – a convenient and popular channel for most service requests (and only found because the installation booklet was left in the house by the previous owner and Google provided up-to-date contact details) – was answered cheerily by a voice that seemed not in the least bit surprised to receive a call.

The Voice then proceeded to ask lots of difficult questions that, given the shower owner was in the office rather than the bathroom, seemed a little difficult to answer: 'What shower model is it?'; 'Is it a pumped unit?'; 'when was it installed?'. These are the sort of challenges that are difficult to cope with before a couple of coffees, and the kind that invariably prompt a desire to phone a friend (often the friendly father-in-law who knows all about these sort of things!).

No sooner had we finished these mental gymnastics – often on the following day, after the necessary research had been conducted – than The Voice would conclude the call by explaining that she would arrange for an engineer to call and send an appointment card in the post.

It only took one experience of this to recognise the weakness in the design of this multichannel process. The card arrived the following morning, naming a time and date that was totally inconvenient. A further call to The Voice was needed, and she seemed to think this was no problem and said she would reorganise it. Another card came the following day with another impossible date. It required three calls to secure a convenient time, and a wait of nearly 10 days for the shower to become operational again.

The process illustrates how multichannel customer experiences are ill-thought through. The engineer and his schedule were of paramount importance in the life of the enterprise – his timetable was optimised to enable him to cover the geography easily (and maintain his utilisation), and his boss was clearly senior to the customer service head that looked after The Voice.

It took a couple of years and several bouts with The Voice before it became obvious that there had to be a better way to resolve this challenge … buy the necessary tools to fix the shower!

Three channels – phone, post and face-to-face delivery – were coordinated in this one service interaction, but insufficient thought and priority had gone into the design to ensure a process that would work for either organisation or customer, and would optimise customer experience and profitability.

The outcome? Excessive costs (multiple calls to the contact centre and, despite their endeavours, suboptimal utilisation of the engineer), lost revenue (no more call-outs and spare parts) and a lost customer (we have made a note not to buy another shower from this group). In short, a wasted opportunity all round.

There has to be a better way, and this book should help readers to construct that for their own organisations.

Here are four reasons why what we all learned in business school about channels is no longer enough.

Channel decisions need to be taken strategically

Channels have always had the power to transform markets. They are the fundamental drivers of consumer access to business, and their composition has a profound impact across both the revenue and cost base of the enterprise.

This is most readily demonstrated when we see rapid change in the structure of channels, such as happened with the advent of the railways – a physical channel whose arrival transformed business back in the mid-nineteenth century.

In 1850, the USA had 9,000 miles of railways – the largest network in the world. However, over the course of the next 10 years an additional 21,000 miles were laid across the country, creating a network bigger than the rest of the world combined. The railway breached many natural barriers – rivers and mountain ranges – crossed the continent, and brought fast communications alongside it with the telegraph.

The impact of this new channel and its close cousin the telegraph were enormous:

- All transport costs fell sharply (even on the roads and canals, where prices were reduced in order to survive).
- Traffic on the rail network grew quickly, despite its premium price, making those towns at the rail junctions very prosperous, and withering those it bypassed. As a result, places like Chicago grew more than threefold in the 1850s.
- Transportation times were decimated: New York to Chicago took 2 days to travel rather than 20; shipment times from Cincinnati to New York fell from 50 days to 5.

The impact on markets was massive! Price differentials, reflecting the imperfections in marketplace access and information, fell sharply. For example, the difference in wholesale flour prices between New York and Cincinnati fell from $2.48 to 28 cents. Information, in the form of newspapers, mushroomed as the instant information from the telegraph and rapid train transport increased circulation twice as quickly as population growth.

New industries were born from the changes. Textiles, footwear and firearms all grew rapidly on the back of the improved communications and access to wider markets. In many ways the growth helped lay the foundations for the strength of the US economy for the next 150 years, and enabled the scaling up of an industrial approach to business. All this came about from the changes initiated by a key channel that enabled much easier and lower costs of interaction.

In many respects, there has been a similar scale of impact from some of the changes in channels that we have seen over the past 10 years (although this is hotly debated by analysts). The significance of the Internet as it has taken hold has been no less profound, even if many of the dotcom start-ups have gone the same way as many of the rail companies did in the USA after their decade of growth.

Andy Grove (ex-Intel Chairman) is famously quoted as having said that, 'in the future, all companies will be internet companies'. This is certainly coming to pass as more and more businesses realise that this means of communication is having a major impact on consumer and business behaviour, providing ubiquitous information (where did you last look when you did not know something, or wanted to research a product?), opening up new digital channels (to your bookshop, bank or auction house and many other businesses) and creating an increasingly digital society that encompasses not just trading and communication but also information and social networks.

A look through the famous names in the business world quickly reveals many that are actively exploiting this new channel – Amazon, Cisco, Tesco, IBM, Capital One, First Direct. Companies compete as much with their innovative channel strategies as on innovative products or services, and, while many of the dotcoms have fared poorly, more and more web-inclusive, multichannel businesses have started to capitalise on the changes in the way that businesses and consumers want to interact.

Even in well-established channels, the innovative use of channels treated as an integral part of the business proposition has made fortunes. Tesco is well-versed in using its channel strategy to defend and attack markets. One of its many initiatives has been the use of its Clubcard, launched in 1995 and now established with 80 percent of its shoppers, alongside the development of Tesco.com to successfully push back Wal-Mart's advance through Asda in the UK. It already has an online business which was worth over £1bn in sales by 2006, boasting 220,000 weekly deliveries across the UK and 750,000 regular customers.

Starbucks' meteoric rise to pre-eminence in the global coffee market as a specialist roaster and brand was driven by its differential channel strategy: a clear picture of the experience that the company wanted to give the consumer in store. Similarly, First Direct (a subsidiary of HSBC), launched 17 years ago as the UK's first telephone bank) made its mark through its channel strategy and has continued to innovate in this area since – recruiting 75 percent of its customers through electronic channels, using text messaging ahead of other retail banks, and taking its customers through a truly multichannel experience with web, email, phone, text, paper, kiosks and outlets integrated to provide the most recommended service of any provider year-in and year-out for over 10 years.

It is no different in the business-to-business space, where companies like BT in the UK have transformed their approach to major customers through the use of a multichannel approach, and delivered benefits to customers and shareholders alike (see Chapter 5).

Yet despite the significance of channel decisions, many organisations still treat them tactically. They often look at their channels as being fixed elements in their strategy, dictated by their current situation and market position. Rarely do other elements of the classical marketing mix – like price or product/service – end up being treated similarly. These are almost always reviewed carefully at an operational board level before changes are made; there is multifunctional involvement in agreeing the decisions; and the consequences of actions are pored over and performance reviewed carefully thereafter. It is not so with channels. The consideration of them is rarely called out at such a senior level, they are not reviewed regularly, and key decisions are often taken within one functional silo or another.

It is this lack of top management focus that leads to strange customer experiences such as that described above regarding the shower. It also leads to other customers' experience of channel gaps. These gaps emerge between sales and service channels; between the web channel and the customer-care centre; or even between the direct mail that drops through the door which treats the recipient as an anonymous prospect and offers a deal that is better than the one they already have (although not the direct selling bit!), as a loyal customer with the same company.

Channel decisions are strategic, and their consequences can be hugely significant. Engage in dialogue with any consumer products supplier, and very quickly they will share the challenges of dealing with the new international behemoths – Wal-Mart, Tesco, Carrefour or Metro – whose aggressive negotiating position and increasing market power have systematically eroded the suppliers' share of value-add over the past 20 years. The strategic impact of these retailers on suppliers' growth, position, required strategy and profitability has been enormous.

The opportunity to break out of the box has been there, but has not been taken. Food service operations, convenience, impulse and vending channels, strategic engagement with the leading retailers on category and supply management, franchise and downstream distribution acquisition have all provided opportunities that few suppliers have really engaged with. The result is that, for many, they have been increasingly boxed into a slower growth path, at a greater distance from the consumer and with lower margins. Few have executed their strategic decisions in the channel area in as timely and effective a way as a Pepsi or a P&G, to build additional or alternate routes to market for consumer engagement, research and selling. This is not to say that the opportunities are not still there. Who knows where the 2005 purchase of Body Shop by L'Oréal might take that leading consumer goods giant? Or where developments in food-purchase patterns might take suppliers?

Too often, strategic moves are made by industry outsiders – Dell, Direct Line, Starbucks, Amazon, Expedia – rather than those enmeshed in the market. Their impact is often only appreciated after the decisions have evolved and a conventional channel approach has been undermined by an innovative outsider.

Dell's approach to both business-to-business and business-to-consumer channels permeates its business model, and has historically enabled it not only to offer product at lower cost in comparison with competitors whose business model is wrapped up with resellers, but also to offer fresher, more tailored specifications that have provided greater customer appeal and minimised discounts and end-of-line markdowns.

Many top managers do not appreciate the importance of the decisions that they make each year in the channel arena, and consequently delegate these decisions to too low a level in the business or rarely re-examine assumptions they have made at a strategic review point. Decisions on channels should be on a par with those regarding geographic reach, product portfolio, outsourcing or HR policy. Too often, decisions on channel selection and integration, sales and service partners, sales and service goals and investments are taken at a junior level inside one of the functions. And then they are reviewed infrequently – more in crisis than forethought.

Those who doubt this should check when their channel strategy was last discussed at board level. Channels are a vital decision area for organisations, with big ticket cost and revenue impacts.

Channel choices have increased rapidly

A second reason for the need for new approaches to channel strategy is that their importance is increasing as more and more channels become available and in new and different forms. All the way through the customer lifecycle, there are more interaction options open to organisations and their customers.

The number of types of media available over the past 20 years has grown enormously. All these are 'new to the world', mass-market channels:

● web
● email
● mobile voice
● mobile data
● text (both SMS and MMS)
● kiosks and multifunction ATMs
● interactive voice technologies (both recognising voice and using synthetic voice).

There are still more technologies to come in the next few years that will revolutionise these, and the established channels of face-to-face and standard voice. Increasing bandwidth, common messaging standards and better network capability for the mobile customer will all contribute to this. This revolutionary pace of change affects every industry, even those with physical products at their heart. It presents a mind-boggling array of choices and complexity.

The increasing range of choice is accompanied by new opportunities to access channels without owning them. Third-party contact centres, web channels, and field forces for sales or support are all on offer and can be combined with increased sharing of information between parties in the channel. This creates opportunities for both 'white label' services and the provision of complete, integrated channels for 'rental'. In many industries, the use of third-party logistics providers and outsourced call centres can mean that huge parts of the customer lifecycle are merely rented by the brand owner. Such opportunities have enabled many companies to avail themselves of competent channels that they could never have hoped to create themselves – sometimes many thousands of miles away, on the end of a helpline or website.

Conventional treatment of the subject of channels ignores these opportunities, treating ownership as a key distinction and labelling 'direct' or 'indirect' as a fundamental break in design rather than another factor that needs to be considered in the definition of policy. It also frequently fails to address the complexity of dealing with the whole lifecycle. The discussion often centres on the selling and physical distribution of product rather than on its support and servicing. Yet these aspects can be fundamental to the economics of the channel, and a differentiator in the eyes of the customer – consider mobile telephony, machine tools, cars or office equipment.

Customer behaviour is under rapid change

Channels are made even more important by the rapidly changing behaviour of both businesses and consumers in the face of new channel options. Customers flow to new channel combinations like water through a stream bed, seeking out more convenient and appealing options, and leaving costs stranded for those businesses that have over-committed to particular channel combinations.

Just as in the food sector the growth of large-space superstores has undermined the viability of local high street stores in many towns, the rise in the importance of the Internet in travel, books, music, personal computing and brown goods has rapidly damaged the economics of even established players and forced them to reappraise their strategies – whether high-street retailers, out-of-town hypermarkets, or wholesalers and their product suppliers.

In banking and insurance, many consumers – and often the upscale, most valuable ones – have migrated quickly to more convenient telephone and net-based channels, even whilst still availing themselves of the comfort of the branch or outlet when needing support or making a complaint.

Consumers are increasingly intolerant of not having control and of being forced to choose company-determined routes for service or support. This intolerance is fuelling the changes in channel combinations offered. As the average consumer becomes much more expert in making choices, the speed of this movement and the extent of pressure will only increase.

Consumers who are unreasonably channelled or frustrated in their efforts to find what they want have started to fight back. The customer as terrorist is likely to be a growing phenomenon, with customers deliberately venting their anger when forced to access a company through an unattractive channel, or to wait too long for support. This already costs companies money – in overlong contact times, vulnerable customers and multiple contacts, or in difficult account negotiations and payment schedules etc. in the business-to-business arena. This problem will get worse.

The web will be a great force for this. Already, there are many consumer support and champion sites that help consumers to tackle typical annoyances and frustrations, assess the organisation's service record or make comparisons regarding alternative sources of supply.

In addition to these, there are the sites that frustrated individuals have set up in response to poor service from individual companies, and more general sites for consumers (see, for example, www.saynoto0870.com). These will have an impact, especially as networking on the web continues to grow. It will not be long before the presence of websites (such as www.gethuman.com) that provide information to consumers on how to speak to a person and not a touch-tone driven menu force policy changes in enterprises' channel policies and operation.

Choice is about combinations, not solo channels

Combinations are the real issue
Most discussions about channels presume that the choice to be made is that of one channel over another. Most analyses look to the primacy of

one selected channel. For instance, people tend to think of examples like the Dell direct model, IBM's account management model or Amazon's web-based model.

However, of critical importance is the reality that most businesses do not operate a single-channel approach, or even one using multiple but separate channels. By far the majority of organisations need to operate with intertwined, multiple channels. The challenges they face are about optimising a much more subtle set of decisions if they are to compete successfully with this multichannel strategy.

This reality presents a quite different set of questions to be addressed than those posed by conventional approaches to the topic. Indeed, most organisations we have worked with find these questions much more pressing than the others – even before they have managed to answer the last set suggested by channel strategists. Such questions might include:

- How should we match channel combinations to our market strategy? What framework should we use to define and evaluate the options?
- Should different channel combinations be offered to different segments? If so, for which parts of the customer lifecycle (marketing, selling, support), and how many?
- How do we best to manage the natural inflation of the cost base that offering multiple channels seems to generate? What tactics and approaches can we use to offer better value and not just higher costs?
- What methods should we use to manage the complexity of multichannel operations? Do we organise around a channel as an entity, or multiple channels, or do we leave them as part of the wider business and treat them as a function? What roles best manage service delivery to customers?
- How do we decide where channels need to be integrated (an often costly process) and where they can remain separate?
- How should we measure the performance of channels that are integrated? How should we measure and reward their managers?

These are all significant and real challenges for those engaged in multichannel planning and operations, but they are all issues that are rarely well handled and supported by the literature. Yet these are questions attached to significant value for both shareholder and customer. The financial and market impacts can be considerable. Take a retail bank, automotive company, insurance business or telecoms business. Each will tend to have web-, contact centre and outlet-based operations. These questions represent some of the most significant items in their overall cost base. They represent some of the most potent ways to win, to increase the value of and retain customers. They also comprise some of the thorniest issues in the day-to-day manager's agenda, draining energy, time and focus.

In conditions where there are so many choices and the potential financial impact (costs, revenue and margin) is so significant, it is vital to define a clear and effective strategy for multichannel operations.

■ The significance of your multichannel strategy

As we have observed, for too many organisations multichannel operations are simply a fact of business life – little attention is paid to the
overall strategy for designing and operating them. Yet it is possible to
create a strategy for this environment, and our experience over the
past few years is that shaping these important building blocks of modern business is vital for organisations and their customers, as it impacts
many of the most important drivers of value for both parties.

The correct strategy is key driver of revenue

The customer is the ultimate source of all revenue in every business.
Whilst it is obvious that without any channel to the market there can be
no revenue, the correct multichannel choices make a substantial impact
on marketplace success.

Ease of access is critical for customers. Retailers who dominate the
right sites in towns and cities have known this for years. Location, location, location has been a mantra. Being positioned where the customer is
going to be is vital for success. In a multichannel world, the same holds
true for not just retailers but for many other sectors as well.

Whatever the target customer, the right management of distribution is
critical. Research last year from Akamai found that 75 percent of shoppers would abandon websites that took longer than 4 seconds to load
(and, to add insult to injury, a third of these would form a negative perception of the company from this and share that with their friends).

Even now, 75 percent of online shopping carts are abandoned before
the sale is completed (source: Shop.org, referenced in Practical eCom-
merce 05/01/07) for a multitude of reasons, many of which might be
readily addressed by effective telephone support at point of purchase.
The same goes for financial products or automotive parts (when, for
example, potential buyers cannot decide which oil really is best for their
engine, or whether or not they will be able to wire up that car stereo).

This does not just apply to business units that engage customers
directly. The challenge of effective multichannel operations extends far
into the enterprise, to business units within these. For instance, in many
large organisations it is perfectly possible for subsidiary parts of the
enterprise to have very limited market access, even when the enterprise
is well endowed with channels to market. We have seen this in financial
institutions, business services and technology companies. Specialist units
with high-value offerings and skills that are relevant only to a small sub-
segment of the institution's customer base, or strategically significant but
low ticket-size services that are of wide relevance but further down on
the immediate agenda for channel managers, can all find themselves in
this position.

We have heard this story several times in the Customer Management Forum at Cranfield. In one case, the unit of a large banking institution that focused on servicing high net worth individuals found it very difficult to access its target customers effectively through the extensive retail network in all its forms. This was not so much a matter of policy as a matter of priority and resource, but the inability to leverage this fundamental corporate asset – the channels to market – held back growth in the unit.

A similar challenge exists in many large enterprises – when a failure to 'join all the dots up' across resource, skills, policy and goals leads to revenue generation being undermined.

Conversely, a well-functioning strategy generates revenue. This can be easily experienced as a customer. For instance, imagine a customer who goes into an REI store and buys a roof box for the car but then finds that all the necessary fittings to fix the roof box to the particular make and model of car are not in stock. In store, the customer is able to turn to a kiosk and simply order the missing parts for home delivery – a small detail that saves an additional trip to the store and ensures a complete sale for REI.

It can be seen mathematically that easy and prominent access pays dividends with a time-starved customer. In work that we have done with a drinks supplier modelling the quantitative impact of various marketing initiatives, the most powerful driver of volume was invariably the distribution drives that secured wider and more prominent presence in store. On-shelf availability is an immense driver of sales and revenues, but even now joining the pieces up to provide a smooth flow of goods through a retailer is quite a challenge, and not all have yet got effective measures in place for real availability.

It can also be observed in the movement in market share. The effective interplay between retail promotion and point of sale, a well-engineered web presence and effective telephone support has been one of the drivers of the increasing share taken by supermarkets in the UK in financial services for insurance and savings products.

One white-label insurance supplier working in partnership with a leading UK supermarket chain radically increased not just overall sales but also web-completed sales (by over threefold) by using much more direct language and pictures at point of sale in the stores in a way that matched up with the website journeys; by experimenting with different options on leaflets in store (alternative branding approaches, bin positions etc); and by catching potential customers' attention at the right time in their shopping and then putting them in control to complete their purchase late at night on the web.

Perhaps most tangibly and obviously, it can also be seen when companies use their natural lifecycle contacts with the customer to sell additional products to them or encourage them to upgrade their service. A well-designed multichannel strategy provides many opportunities for up-selling and cross-selling when the customer is most likely to want to purchase, and also for retaining otherwise lost customers. The result is a quantifiable uplift in short term revenues that even the most cynical financial controller cannot deny.

There are many examples of this. Capital One, the US credit card business, has become so successful at this that even 7 years ago it was able to sell on 1 in 11 *inbound* calls (i.e. when the customer called the company for some specific service) at low incremental cost. Similarly, in the UK, O2, the mobile telephony company owned by Telefonica of Spain, uses a real-time decision-aid called Vision in its dialogue with certain segments of customers to help its service agents to provide appropriate enhancements and cross-sales when customers call in with service queries. The incremental revenues are readily demonstrated against control cells, and help enable O2 to decide how agents can add real value on service queries as well as offering additional revenues.

A well-executed multichannel strategy determines customer salience, convenience and availability. It drives significant improvements in revenue and market share when structured and executed well.

Strategy determines a large share of operating costs

Many commentators have remarked on the way that, over the last decade, organisations have outsourced parts of their value chain to access better skills, lower costs, faster innovation and key technologies with other organisations.

In many industries the supply chain is now a Russian doll of tiered suppliers, each playing their role in the value-add that builds to the final product. Each contributes key aspects of the product or service, both on an operational basis and in the cycle of innovation, and increasingly this is being seen as a source and driver for innovation. Indeed, it was highlighted as one of the key areas that CEOs are using to generate innovation and growth in a global study published in 2006 by IBM's Institute of Business Value.

The impact on each participant in the chain, however, has been that an increasing proportion of its own controllable cost base is now consumed with the cost of managing the interface with its customers and prospects – a good proportion of which is the cost of access through distributors and sales-force, web-channel and service operations.

Think about this in your own situation. What percentage of operating costs is consumed in this way? It is not uncommon for it to be over 25 percent.

In many industries, especially those where the 1990s helped to place the telephone at the heart of sales and support, channel costs can seem almost uncontrollable. There is a dynamic in industries as diverse as telecommunications, technology, financial services and government that is tending to push these costs up. Greater competition within categories, often from increasingly global and numerous competitors, demands innovation and increasingly sophisticated offerings. However, this increasing complexity and change in the offerings means that customers need more support through the purchase decision and in using the service. This pushes up contact frequency and time as customers call for more support and information – and contact costs companies money in agents and systems and support.

Across banking, telecommunications, consumer durables and even the automotive industries, these costs are now the single largest category of spend for many divisions. Multichannel demands investment and inevitably incurs overheads, but a well-engineered multichannel strategy can manage this dynamic.

Better strategies encourage customers to conduct more transactions via lower-cost channels, tailor support to key points in the lifecycle, eliminate wasteful interaction and engineer cheaper costs to serve. These strategies can benefit the bottom line in lower costs and higher margins. They can also bring superior customer appreciation if executed well.

Too many practitioners assume that a people-intensive, personal approach is always preferred by customers, and that anything that promotes self-service (or often web-based service) is going to provide a worse customer experience. This is simply wrong! The insurance company mentioned above found that most people preferred to complete their life cover on the web late at night – not with an agent or dialogue in store. The flexibility and control provided by the right experience was both better for the customer and cheaper for the company. The overwhelming move to self-service in retail stores of all types – food, electricals, home improvements, sports goods, furniture – reflects not just the economics that self-service can unlock, but also the attractiveness of the experience when designed well for the customer.

However, merely focusing on near-term revenues or costs, vital as they are, underplays the significance of the multichannel strategy now.

A critical avenue for knowing the customer better

In the past few years, those marketing and advertising executives responsible for spending large sums of money to communicate with the customer have begun receive a much more resistant response from an increasingly savvy customer (whether in the street or in the office). The slow tidal outflow of interest in advertising that was evident in many sectors in the last decade has now left many broadcast communication approaches beached like whales without water. The customer is simply not listening when companies are talking.

The result has been the rapid growth of interest in finding ways of becoming relevant to customers once again, by communicating with them both when they want to listen (often when they contact the company rather than just the other way round) and with what is relevant to them at that time, offering the most relevant piece for that situation, customer type and segment objective.

To do this strategically demands that companies adopt an information-centric approach to the customer. This requires that they collect more profile and behaviour data, organise it more accessibly and make much better use of it to create and sustain a dialogue.

In this type of war, multichannel strategy and management is one of the core capabilities, as the channel is the 'gateway' to the customer.

This kind of dialogue war is well evidenced in the superstore battle between Tesco and Asda (the Wal-Mart business) in the UK. Tesco's understanding of the individual customer collected through its loyalty card scheme, one of the most successful in the world, makes it very difficult for Asda's normally advantageous low-cost positioning to succeed.

Tesco's scale has enabled it to minimise the price differences between itself and Asda on the standard basket of known-value items (KVIs) in the price-sensitive shopper's basket. Its ability to then engage through the mail, at point of sale and even through Tesco.com enables it to go further:

- by specifically targeting just those shoppers in areas where Asda launches a recruitment initiative (e.g. a new or refurbished store) whose purchase behaviour indicates that they are sensitive to a price-based proposition with vouchers to retain them
- by winning back those whose behaviour indicates that that they are switching to the competitor, using offers known to appeal to them and thus making it 'not worth' switching, and
- by doing all of this directly, so that it costs a lot less than any Asda assault or defence and can be tailored to the exact needs of the individual.

Similar strategies are being followed at many other supermarket retailers. In the US, Safeway, the number two supermarket retailer, is using the data gathered from its sales and loyalty card to tailor experiences in different stores by locality (source: GMA Conference, 2006).

This kind of warfare for an increasingly digital customer demands insight into the customer that can only be gathered through a well-designed multichannel strategy – i.e. one that:

- carefully chooses what data to collect on each journey (maximising insight, but only when there is the consumer incentive to respond accurately)
- can operationalise segments at point of contact with the customer using the insight gained
- aligns channel choices to customer types and contact types, to find points at which more insight can be gained, better experiences delivered and vital behavioural information can be collected
- partners effectively, to share not just business but customers and insights to create additional opportunities for superior experiences
- has the necessary governance and technology to collate, clean and provision data effectively, often in real time

An effective multichannel strategy will be integral to the economic collection of data to give businesses the ability to understand their consumers at a micro-level. This could become one the most important capabilities of successful competitors in future markets.

Channels are becoming the key communication vehicle for the brand – usurping mass media

Effective multichannel operations can also help to address the rapidly increasing difficulty of relevant brand communications to today's customers. The challenge of this goes hand in hand with that of increasing customer insight.

There are real difficulties in reaching customers with brand messages. Not only are customers not listening; they are also becoming much more expensive to talk to. This is well illustrated by one of the significant television events of this decade – the end of the 10-year run of the sitcom *Friends*. It was estimated that when the final episode of Friends was shown in 2004, it attracted 50 million American viewers and advertisers paid $2 million for a 30-second slot in the middle of the show. However, compare this with a similar iconic event – the final episode of M*A*S*H in 1983. Here, it cost an inflation-adjusted $850,000 for a 30-second slot to reach 80 million people. The implied cost increase between these two events, just 20 years apart, suggests that conventional television advertising is up to four times as expensive in real terms as it used to be (Ayres, 2004). For most brands, this is an unsustainable inflationary increase.

As customers ignore an estimated 3,000–5,000 (or more) increasingly expensive messages broadcast to them each day (Smith, 2006), companies need better ways to communicate and to present their brand. For many, the prime alternative is their channel. At low incremental cost, and indeed with or without management intent, channels strongly shape how the consumer sees the brand.

When one of the authors recently purchased a laptop from the website of a leading electrical retailer, this was rapidly demonstrated. The core channel of the retailer is the sort of hangar-sized superstore that offers wide choice, but also demands extensive security to avoid shrinkage, and leads to a brand that is price-promoted in the local newspapers. Generally, therefore, it is a brand positioned in the low-touch category. Conversely, the bank through whose card the web transaction was conducted makes great play of its customer-focused policies at branches, in contact centre staff and in approach.

However, the web transaction rapidly – and more effectively than broadcast media – swapped the two brand images. The web purchase was rejected on security grounds by the bank (without calling the customer, whose mobile phone number it has for this express purpose), thereby leading to the order being rejected and potentially lost. The call to the bank led to one of those conversations about procedure and policy which is generally lost on the consumer (who thought that the purpose of the card was this type of payment). However, the call to the retailer was answered by an agent who was very apologetic (despite it not being the retailer's fault), managed to recover the deleted order and reinstated it in very good humour to meet the original order timescales – thus instantly repositioning the brand as consumer-sensitive.

The significance of this kind of opportunity for both branding and cross-selling was well captured by Elana Anderson and John Ragsdale of Forrester Research when they argued for the importance of marketing needing to start taking on a clear role for the contact-centre channel (Anderson and Ragsdale, 2004).

The most frequent messages a customer receives from a business are not those in mainstream media (when they are not listening) but those they encounter when carrying out everyday transactions with an organisation (researching product, understanding service terms, engaging in sales meetings, receiving goods, making calls to a contact centre, or wandering through a website or company literature or email). These are increasingly the powerful moulders of company image.

Think of the process of resolving a query, and the impact that has on customer perception. It leaves a much stronger imprint than any background media message. Equally, the character of the company often shows through in the way the customer is handled – how much choice is given? How do staff treat customers? How seamless is it to move between channels? How bureaucratic is the process? How much attention is paid to the customer's immediate needs and preferences? All these things are the essence of branding. All these things are also the experience of the multi-channel operation and strategy.

In many categories, these experiences are more significant than both the products themselves and external media messages. Their frequency, significance, attention and emotional impact are much more powerful than anything else. Increasingly, brand images are strongly shaped by the way that the business handles customers when they interact, and expensive marketing campaigns can easily be undermined by poor customer experience.

■ References

Anderson, E. and Ragsdale, J. (2004). Why Marketing should Own the Contact Center. Forrester White Paper, April.

Ayres, C. (2004). Friends and advertisers are united for secret but last show. *The Times*, 28 April.

IBM Institute of Business Value (2006). *CEO Study: Expanding the Innovation Horizon*. IBM.

Smith, J.W., President of consulting firm Yankelovich (2006). Quoted in *USA Today*, 10 October.

CHAPTER 2

Making multichannel a source of competitive advantage

Competitive advantage grows fundamentally out of the value a firm is able to create for its buyers.

Michael Porter

This chapter examines how to take multichannel, a feature of modern business and government, and create from it an advantage for your organisation and the way that it interacts with customers. We could have taken many approaches to this, but have chosen to major on the most important areas of questioning that we have experienced in the research forum and with clients and to use these as a framework around which to think about where advantage might come from.

In this chapter, we discuss the issues and factors embedded into each question. In Parts 2 and 3 of the book, we will then go on to provide examples and tools that help managers to address these questions and create solutions for the organisation.

■ How to create advantage from multichannel

Today's marketer faces a bewildering mix of technology-enabled channels. Where once the route to market was a straightforward matter of industry practice or practical possibilities – 'we sell via distributors', 'we use agents who sell through retailers' or 'we employ a sales force that calls on customers' – managers now find themselves faced with multiple routes and the opportunity to compete as much on innovation in channel strategies as on innovation in products.

The upside is opportunity; the downside is potential disadvantage and yet another area of business that now requires more consideration to ensure success. Furthermore, channels raise a multitude of challenges and, as with any strategy, the starting point for success is to understand what questions need to be asked (even before providing the answer). What are the key goals to be set, and the structure for addressing them? This is not necessarily as easy to identify as many assume.

Through our research forum, it has become clear that often analysts and consultants looking in on those engaged in the competitive battle reach for the wrong set of initial questions – ones that do not represent the key challenges and opportunities facing many channel owners.

Equally, some managers, when grappling with the immediate challenges of their position, often reach for a question posed internally or to advisers that frames the issues in a limited or inappropriate way. Indeed, this has happened so often that it is worth highlighting some of the most frequent questions because of the incorrect assumptions they reveal about the way to address the business impacts (Table 2.1).

These questions often reveal a failure to grasp the nature of competing with a multichannel operation, and the tremendous costs and benefits that addressing the right questions effectively can unlock. The answers to these

Table 2.1 Inappropriate channel assumptions

Question	Revealed assumptions
What's the right channel for my product/business?	...assuming that there is a singular and sometimes universal best solution rather than a need to define a creative competitive position through proper analysis and design
How do I shift to low-cost channels?	...assuming that any value so created will flow to the bottom line of the organisation and that cost is the only criterion and channels are the only unit of division
How can I replicate the success that X has had through its channels?	...assuming that our business has the same market goals, position and opportunities as it does, and that a me-too approach is the best one
How do I reduce the cost of my direct sales/contact centre?	...assuming that the cost (rather than the value in terms of insight, reach and incremental sales) is the issue
How do I maintain my power with indirect channels?	...assuming that if we do not own a channel provider that is a weakness

will feed into many areas of the business, not just the channel operations, helping to match the right customers to the right channels and unlocking the value of opportunities to (for instance) gain or enrich insights into customers and ensure that these insights are deployed to modify the way that customers are handled and sold to, rather than just being locked away in some analytics department in the heart of the enterprise.

■ The big questions

In our work to date we have been searching out these 'big questions' – the ones that shape the strategy and reflect the major challenges; the ones that need to be grasped to create advantage from multichannel.

In the course of several years and countless discussions with companies, we have identified and refined seven questions, the answers to which lie at the root of an effectively realised multichannel strategy and determine the best way for an organisation to approach the channels through which it interacts with its customers. They represent the dimensions against which we see companies simultaneously creating value for themselves and their customers – the only long-term winning strategy for any business. They also represent the questions and discussions that practitioners have presented to us both in the forum and as consultants – issues

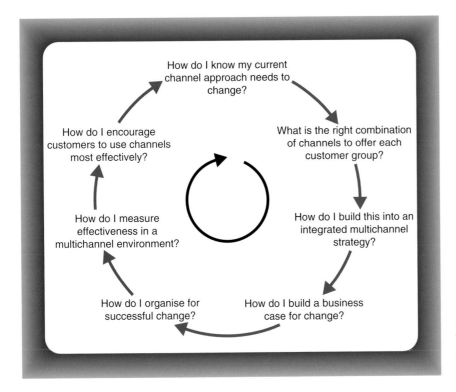

Figure 2.1
Wheel of innovation
for multichannel
strategy

which, when organisations really engage in the topic and assess their position and their management of customers, costs and capabilities, rise to the surface again and again. On these dimensions, they rise to the multichannel challenge and succeed.

In practice, these questions represent seven key points on a wheel of innovation for multichannel strategy (Figure 2.1). Moreover, each point on the cycle of innovation:

- represents a key point of leverage for creating and delivering an effective multichannel strategy
- summarises a step that we have seen organisations go through as they review and improve their strategy and its execution
- enables the subsequent question to be answered more robustly
- will, when answered, tend to lead to the next.

Clients and forum participants have raised and discussed these questions or analogous ones on many occasions, and so we have endeavoured to show where and how these fit together and to gather the tools and concepts of the book under these headings.

We hope that this will enable you to make best use of the various tools and insights that we have gathered and answer for yourself and your organisation the overall question: How do I gain advantage from my multichannel operations?

1 How do I know my current channel approach needs to change?

Not many firms have the opportunity to write their channel strategy on a blank sheet of paper. Most inherit a history with its current mix of products, customers and capabilities, and with all the day-to-day pressures and expectations that this creates. The strategy challenge is a different one, and they have to evaluate the opportunity open to them from their current market position.

It is perhaps therefore no surprise that it is easier to identify radical reinventions of channels where the perpetrators are new entrants, 'outsiders' to the industry – names like Dell, Amazon, eBay and Direct Line spring to mind. These mould-breakers entered the industry with sharply differentiated channel strategies, exploiting the reticence of incumbents to make a major shift in their own approaches. Ironically, in some cases they exploited the early learning that might have been provided by an incremental toe dipped into the water by one of the current players. However, it is they that have assaulted incumbents with an aggressive and category-breaking customer proposition that is well integrated with a channel positioning. It might have been disintermediation by phone or web, offering a beautifully aligned product and channel proposition, or exploiting the latent frictions and frustrations. Rarely, however, is such innovation the action of a well-established player.

This lethargy on the part of incumbents is a reflection of the value they have created through their current channel approach, and a failure to appreciate the level of exposure created by the many new opportunities provided by channel and customer developments.

Few are the names like Cisco, Tesco or REI whose aggressive adoption of new multichannel methods of interaction has strengthened their competitive position and enabled them to increase share in the face of accelerating competition.

Three strategic criteria for change

How do you decide that your business is exposed to risk in the multichannel arena? This is the first question most of our clients and forum members face when looking at the opportunity of multichannel marketing.

Changing your channel strategy and opening up new or more integrated channels (especially when, in reality, the old ones can rarely be abandoned) is an expensive pursuit, especially as increasingly it requires investment in the infrastructure and changes throughout the length of customer lifecycle (not just selling or marketing). For even a mid-sized business, changing the route to market and reorganising or re-ordering operations is almost always a major multimillion euro task with many risks – not one to be initiated without good reason. It is therefore very important to know when a change is needed.

We have found that the analysis can be best framed around three strategic criteria – cost, experience and access (Figure 2.2).

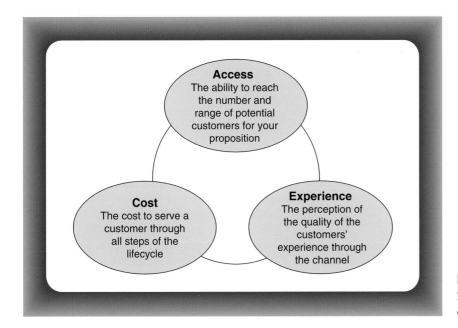

Figure 2.2
Strategic criteria for channel change

Cost: lowering the cost to serve Perhaps the most frequent cause of a coherent review of channel strategy (and too often the most defensive) is one made on the basis of cost. Companies often need to review their channel approach because they need to reduce the cost to serve customers. More often than not, the trigger for this is competition from new or renewed competitors.

Two examples paint this picture clearly. In the airline industry, the arrival and growth of low-cost carriers like Ryanair or Southwest have strongly challenged the traditional industry channel (and operating) structure of airlines who have handled the sales process through third-party agents. In efforts to get the overall consumer proposition back in line with the new competitors, airlines have had to revisit their approach. Its cost disadvantages – roughly a 10-point difference when combined with other aspects of the model – has forced many airlines to move to a radically lower-cost direct model and extend this through sales, check-in and marketing.

The seismic impact of this change in the past 5 years is similar to that felt in the PC industry when Dell's direct-to-consumer phone- and web-based model undermined the economics of traditional channel management through value-added resellers and retailers in the late 1990s.

However, these dramatic examples are not the only types of competitive cost pressure that signal the need for a change in channel strategy. The pressure on costs can be just as significant when it manifests itself through sustained pressure on profit and growth across the industry.

Both retail banking and the telecommunications service industries are good examples of this. As more complex products have been launched and the categories have started to consume a higher percentage of disposable income, so the number of contacts per customer has risen as consumers have sought to understand the most appropriate offer, access add-on services or query complex charges. This has driven up costs to serve at the same time as maturing of competition in the industry and expensive mobile licences have capped growth and margins. This squeeze on profit is producing pressure on industry players to look at how they best manage the challenge of the ever-expanding contact-centre and network costs needed to engage their retail customer base.

Many business-to-business firms face similar (and sometimes more complex) challenges as their customers use global markets to find the most competitive prices and yet still expect the traditional personal (expensive!) sales and service that they may have enjoyed for some time. It was for this reason that BT's Major Business Unit, dedicated to serving its largest customers, embarked on a major channel strategy shift. Traditional telephony revenues were flat or declining as costs fell throughout the industry. Growth was to be generated through increased sales of IT-related solutions such as routers and servers. However, margins are lower in IT versus telephony, and the channel 'norm' was different – indirect channels and self-service over the Internet. BT could not profitably compete in the new areas whilst retaining its channel structure and cost. The result was a complete redesign of the channel approach over the course of 5–10 years to address this challenge and secure the optimum position for growth.

The challenge facing any organisation on this topic is timing. There are often good reasons for retaining the current channel approach, but understanding the extent to which this exposes the business to excessive cost in the channel area is a judgement which needs to be made soon enough for any change to take place. Fighting to address channel innovation in the teeth of a competitive storm – with cash, profits and managers under the squeeze – is typically too late. This needs to be anticipated and actioned ahead of time.

Cost pressures often generate an immediate need to reappraise channel strategy. However, they are by no means the only reasons for change.

Experience: improving the customer experience In the past few years, an increasing number of organisations have started to re-examine their channel strategy in order to improve the customer experience. This trend has been growing in importance and frequency as executives have started to raise the priority of finding an effective growth engine for the revenue line of the business, and as sources of advantage from products have proved difficult to attain and sustain.

By 2005, many executives had begun to target improving the customer experience as the most significant business goal for revenue growth. Over 95 percent of North American companies rated improvement as very important or critical (Temkin *et al.*, 2005), and decision-makers were twice as likely to prioritise it over goals such as improving loyalty (IBM, 2006).

This kind of focus reflects the steady increase in the number of companies that recognise the vital significance of revenue growth as a driver of shareholder valuations and as a measure of consumer appreciation. Despite the cost pressures that many firms feel, customer experience is also a major trigger for re-evaluating channel strategy.

In some respects this has been most noticeable in the public sector, as managers there seek a win–win situation by improving customer experience and, at the same time, lowering costs. This is readily possible in many service environments, where the cost of not resolving service queries first time and the failure to action a customer journey without rework very quickly align the economics of better service and lower cost. Costs can often be reduced by a quarter at the same time as customers see a marked improvement in responsiveness, focus and quality.

This is part of what has been behind the UK government's drive to e-enable services and streamline service delivery in local and central government. Aside from the evident cost advantages to be gained from e-enabled services, especially those with effective through processing, the contrast between private net- and phone-based channels and the relatively restricted face-to-face or form-based model of the public sector repeatedly exposed the government to criticism regarding the quality of the experience.

A similar drive to enhance experience is one of the primary reasons that banks, automotive companies and utilities are pressing forward with their goal to integrate channels better and create a more timely and seamless service through outlets, telephone, the web and third parties.

It is even one of the primary drivers behind the move to modify pharmaceutical companies' almost exclusive historical channel focus through the sales representative. Physicians are increasingly blocking access and opting out of intrusive selling methods under pressure of time and aggravation with the selling 'arms race' that has driven the ratio of salesmen to physicians up over the last 10 years. The dissatisfaction and reducing productivity of an almost exclusively field-based approach is driving pharmaceutical companies to change their approach and find new ways that provide a better experience for physicians, as well as delivering improved sales.

Businesses recognise that customer experience links closely with customer retention and advocacy. These are powerful drivers of shareholder value, and act directly to improve growth prospects and close out competitive exposure. However, improving customer experience normally entails costs – new channels, revised staff selection and development, better integration, more training, improved systems and more flexible capacity.

The decision to invest is easy when an improved experience can be delivered at a lower cost per customer, but this is not always possible. Increasingly, companies are prepared to alter their strategy to ensure a good customer experience by increasing staff/customer ratios in store, linking web and telephone channels, providing kiosks in store or investing in multiple outlet formats to enable better reach.

Experience is the second of the key criteria to consider when assessing the need to change a channel strategy – not only to assess competitive exposure, but also because it offers a more powerful growth stimulant than simply cost base because of the innovative pressure it injects.

The clothing company Lands' End epitomises this attitude in its adoption of the web. As a successful mail-order retailer, the company quickly embraced the opportunities of the Internet to extend its great experience for customers to this new channel. It uses the Internet to extend and enhance its customer experience by providing complementary services – for example, one can design and dress up a virtual personal model to 'sample' clothing virtually. Nonetheless, Lands' End displays prominently its toll-free number, so that online customers can immediately access helpful call-centre staff. It offers real-time chat and personal assistance. Lands' End's investment in the online channel was not justified by reduced call-centre costs; it is there to provide a better customer experience.

In many of the engagements we have had as consultants, and indeed in much of the discussion in the research forum, the experience question is the critical trigger that prompts the channel rethink. A vitriolic major customer or defection in the business-to-business space, a catastrophic customer satisfaction rating or a new manager whose initial horror is evident at the way customers are being handled when she listens in to calls or reviews web traffic is often the starting point for a strategic review.

Access: reaching the right range of customers There is a third strategic reason for changing the channel strategy. This is to extend or sustain access to chosen customer segments – geographic, demographic or behavioural.

This is the foundational reason for channels, and yet it is very easy for the channel model to fall out of alignment with the shape of the marketplace and the needs of the business. When this happens, significant sections of the market can become inaccessible either practically or economically. The move out of town for many categories of shopping has stranded some high-street chains in locations where customers no longer visit, the change in household behaviour has greatly reduced the effectiveness of most door-to-door selling approaches, and the globalisation of many industries has often left local suppliers with many fewer buying points in their country to supply.

These moves normally take place over many years and pass almost unnoticed. This is particularly true in many business-to-business markets, where change in the structure of supply and customers is less analysed by external commentators. Relatively few businesses invest in a rigorous, regular review of their market position, and this exposes them to this risk. We have been engaged in many channel redesigns in industrial, technological or business service marketplaces which have been triggered by this sort of movement. When the headroom in the market moves to areas poorly served by the current channel approach, a review is urgently needed.

New technology only adds to this challenge. Through digital channels, companies can now offer almost ubiquitous access to sales, service and customer information. They can access segments hitherto unreachable or unprofitable to serve. If incumbents fail to use their channels to serve these segments, then new entrants do not.

The growth of telephone and then web channel for sales and service in insurance, banking and utilities has created a whole new range of competitors for incumbents. Direct Line and First Direct in the UK created a new class of competitor, while in the US incumbents like Geico entered the 24/7 telephone channel in 1980 and grew steadily from there, while new entrants like E-Loan (which launched in 1997) brought in simple web-based financial services and have established a strong reputation for the security, simplicity and customer-centredness of their approach. These companies typify the way digital channels can unlock access to certain customer groups and lock out those competitors who do not adapt their channel strategies fast enough.

Historically, there has been a great deal of protection for incumbents if they controlled key assets like retail sites, networks or mass media. Increasingly, these are neither as effective as barriers nor as powerful in reaching the customer, and this presents more frequent and serious challenges to established channel approaches.

BT's Major Business Unit's recent channel innovation reduced its costs and, critically, also allowed BT to increase account penetration. For example, a BT Account Director might negotiate the right to sell leased lines (typically low-value items) to each branch of a national financial services company. Whilst the deal is negotiated with the customer's head office, it is sold branch by branch via a desk-based telephone channel. Previously, the Account Director would have had to organise field sales-people to call on each branch – an uneconomical solution. With the new structure, improved access meant increased sales.

Many estate agents offer online services to improve customer access to their databases of properties and, more importantly, improve access to updates in property details. Previously, potential buyers would need to call agents regularly and receive updates regarding properties, changes in prices or competing bids by post. Now they can be notified online or via SMS messages. Indeed, the incumbent who does not respond to this with a competitive and integrated web channel finds itself at a serious disadvantage in gaining access to the right number of potential buyers and sellers.

A structured review of your access to customer segments and the headroom for growth provide by your channel strategy is a vital consideration in deciding to innovate.

Additional considerations

Whilst the three criteria mentioned above are the foundational reasons for reviewing your channel approach, there are at least two additional areas that might trigger change, although often more incrementally or in support of one of the major drivers mentioned above.

Insight Across markets as a whole, customers now face an environment with overwhelming and excessive choice. They are offered, in many cases, almost unlimited variations on products and service through a combination of global suppliers and customised product. As an example of this in practice, one needs only visit a local supermarket and look at the laundry aisle. An almost unimaginable array of detergent formats, variants, brands and packs competes to perform a task that was considered mature even 30 years ago. The drive for innovation when combined with consumer fragmentation leads to a frightening array of choice!

As consumers have started to get used to this level of choice and the accompanying cacophony of marketing and sales messages, they are simply tuning out and becoming much less responsive to advertising and information that is not relevant to their immediate situation and desires.

This increasingly common environment provides another reason for modifying channel strategy, in order to move to a position where insight and information can be captured and shared to improve service, cross-selling and product development. This is even happening now in sectors where previously it would not have been thought viable.

Many consumer goods companies are starting to look at new routes to access the consumer, not necessarily for direct selling but for dialogue, research, information provision and building affinity. Some higher-profile examples of this include Proctor & Gamble's investment in the Tremor panel for connecting with teenagers. This 250,000-strong panel of 13- to 19-year-olds in the USA has enabled new customer dialogue and serves as a valuable direct insight and marketing link for the company. Others have different community and insight activities – for instance, Nestlé's Casa Buitoni pasta club, Club Nokia or Club Philips. Despite the cost of these, companies are increasingly making moves in this direction to create new channels for insight and marketing, blurring the distinctions between research, community, marketing and day-to-day operation.

These steps are valuable regardless of the current state of customer satisfaction. One of the challenges that customers pose for organisations is that when things are going well, they stop communicating with the supplier. This lack of communication in and of itself can often lead to the supplier losing touch with its customer base. This oscillating cycle was well described many years ago by the then Customer Relations Director of British Airways, who observed how, after totally renewing the brand and service experience in BA through the early 1990s, customer satisfaction sagged as expectations shifted again unnoticed. The provision of increasingly interactive channels for customer feedback can be a key reason to modify strategy, either by creating new channels or by restructuring existing ones to enable effective insight to be gathered.

Taking the high ground A final accelerator for the strategic criteria can be the need to take a pre-emptive market position in anticipation of new competition or a significant consumer shift. This forward-looking position can be a very powerful competitive strategy.

This has been well demonstrated by Tesco's entry first into web-based home-delivered shopping, and secondly into local convenience stores. The first and most determined of the UK supermarket chains to add the web channel to its mainstream large-space chain, Tesco has worked hard to establish this and avoid the potential erosion of its highest-value segment – the money-rich and time-poor family that makes extensive use of the channel. This pre-emptive channel positioning has given it a lead that its other UK competitors are still struggling to address, and positions Tesco well against any future shift in customer dynamics. Tesco repeated the creation of this positional advantage with its entry into the convenience stores channel as consumer dynamics shifted again in the early 2000s.

A similar strategic rationale lies behind the use of flagship retail outlets by companies like Apple, Nike, Sony or Panasonic, or many of the patient-oriented information websites of pharmaceutical companies. These channels play a vital role in enabling the brand to take the high ground with consumers, helping to educate target customers and enhancing interaction and insight between the brand and its consumers.

When businesses review their strategic position in a marketplace and observe changes in customer structure and needs, this provides a powerful rationale for a channel strategy shift for defensive and offensive reasons.

2 What is the right combination of channels to offer each customer group?

Inevitably, a sound rationale for change against your strategic criteria will focus any channel strategy and help the business engage with the challenge of providing a new range of channels to match each customer segment's needs much more tightly. Nonetheless, successful multichannel transformation requires several key issues to be addressed if the strategic advantage of change is to be unlocked. Not least amongst these will be specifying the range of channels to be considered.

Challenges include the following:

- How wide an overall choice of channels should be offered?
- How much differentiation should be targeted between different customer groups?
- Should channel coverage be controlled by the supplier or left to customer choice?
- How should different steps in the customer lifecycle be handled?

Narrow or wide

At the height of the dotcom boom there were many who felt that the web channel would sweep all before it, and that clicks inevitably competed head-on with bricks. As the bubble burst, those on the physical rather than virtual side of the divide started to claim victory and pronounce the web a dead medium.

It is, however, becoming increasingly clear that the web is anything but dead and that increasingly bricks and clicks are both needed for a successful channel strategy (a conclusion very close to the heart of why this book talks throughout of multichannel strategy). Nonetheless, the fundamental question of how wide to cast the channel net is near the top in any change, especially from a well-established, narrow model such as that historically used in pharmaceuticals, retail or many industrial companies.

The reason is simple: adding new channels is a costly exercise, especially where property or staff are involved, but even when a new online presence is sought – especially if integration is needed. In addition to the cost, a broadening of channels can often present a market risk, as it disturbs the existing channel participants and may cause them to act defensively. Twenty years ago it was the traditional wholesale channel that would react aggressively to the decision by suppliers to sell direct to the new large-space superstores (in food, DIY, furniture or other sectors). Now it is these new retailers who are wary of suppliers who might want to bypass them and go direct on the web and telephone. In most business-to-business markets, complex channel chains generally make the focus on price and terms rather than supply. However, sensitivity is mostly reserved for the sales relationship. Looking more widely at the question normally means that the organisational challenge is different – consolidation and integration, or the creation of lower cost-to-serve channels (like web, intelligent voice recognition (IVR) or telephone) to replace expensive face-to-face interactions.

It is rare that a narrow channel strategy is the preferred choice for a channel change. More often than not these are start-up or new-entrant approaches where the narrow channel offer is integral to the proposition or provides an easy underbelly to attack by a focus on just one or two segments of the market. Once established, the channel position often extends to allow other customer groups to be served. Dell changed its model to address corporate customers, adding extranets and account managers (and now retailers!); First Direct added the web and made more use of the HSBC branch and ATM network to enhance service.

In practice, most businesses, when they examine what customers currently do, will find that individual customers, in whatever segment they sit, use a mixture of channels, depending upon their priorities and needs. The challenge is to strike the right balance between providing and integrating channels to meet customer segment needs, and the cost of this provision both for build and ongoing management.

As a result, understanding the key needs of customers through their lifecycle is vital in putting the strategy together and defining the right set of channels to offer to each group.

Differentiation – treating different customers differently

One of the keys to unlocking the challenge of breadth is to understand the importance of beginning your multichannel strategy from the customer viewpoint, even when the trigger for innovation is to do with costs.

Everyone knows that customers are not all the same; they have different needs, and are of different value to the organisation. They also behave differently, and use channels in different ways. Despite this, all too often businesses start out on a multichannel strategy with no effective segmentation as a basis for the channel approach, and this makes any innovation difficult to focus.

It has always amazed us how strong the herd instinct is in industries, and how readily organisations assume that what is good for another is good for them. Such assumptions are frequently the real undoing of benchmarking exercises. As Seth Godin points out so graphically in his book *Purple Cow* (Godin, 2003), the challenge facing organisations operating in oversupplied, hypercompetitive markets is to be different, to stand out and capture customers through this difference. This observation has much merit in the channel arena.

Yet, looking across industries as diverse as retail banking, automotive companies, pharmaceuticals, food and drink or building products, one could be forgiven for assuming that little attention has been paid to crafting innovative multichannel strategies. The limited differences that exist generally reflect the paucity of attention that has been devoted to really understanding how customers engage different channels.

One of the first channel strategies we were engaged in, over 20 years ago, was for an automotive company. Despite its different brand profile, small volume share (making outlet density an issue), strong brand loyalty and upmarket customer base, its channel strategy was identical to that of the leading volume manufacturer. An external perspective could see clearly that advantage, in terms of experience and cost, could be gained by an alternative approach.

To date, almost all pharmaceutical companies have assumed that all primary-care physicians (in most countries in the world) are best served by a face-to-face dialogue with a sales representative, or invitations to symposia and events. It is only now, as physicians continue to restrict their access and start increasingly to use other methods of information-gathering, and more complex account structures emerge, that big pharma is beginning to change its customer interaction model.

It is only in the past couple of years that telecommunications companies have started to segment their customers beyond the business, small-office-home-office (SOHO) and consumer segmentations (and, within the latter, identifying the high-value customers). Even then, they have done little to really look at channel usage and segmentation to create operational changes that impact cost, access and differentiation.

Many business-to-business organisations rarely get beyond industry sector and company size as a basis for segmentation, and then they fail to ground these sufficiently to make effective operational segmentations. We have worked with chemical companies and software businesses that have differentiated channels neither by product category nor by customer type, instead preferring to adopt a standardised structure for each aspect of the customer lifecycle. This frequently means over-serving low-value customers and under-serving the vital high-value ones.

As we will explore further in Part 2, this type of segmentation is inadequate to set a multichannel strategy, and will rarely enable innovative and advantageous approaches to be adopted in response to the need to change.

Customers need to be treated differently and, just as each chooses a different product, each will also choose different channel combinations for different transactions. The smart business recognises this and builds its strategy around it.

Coverage and control

In addition to how many channels are to be offered, consideration also needs to be given to which channels will be offered to which customers, and whether this choice is to be made by the organisation or by its customers.

This can be a sensitive decision, not just for customers but also for channel participants. We worked with one sales team in Ireland for whom the concept of concentrating on designated retail outlets (trend-setting, innovative premises) presented a real challenge to previous ways of working, culture and metrics. Creating the conditions to enable it was critical to enabling an effective multichannel strategy.

Forcing customers down one channel, especially when they would prefer another, is at best ineffective and can even be counterproductive. As many studies and analysts have observed, the most effective way to ensure that a customer uses the channel combination that you would like is to design it in a way that makes is easy to use. Failure to do this can totally backfire. The more often customers complain or push against a channel choice, the higher the operational cost in handling them … and the worse the customer experience! If customers find other aspects of the proposition sufficiently attractive to continue to trade with the supplier, then a train of higher-cost, aggravated customers and demoralised channel staff will result.

However, the benefits of a customer-oriented, differentiated coverage model can be huge. In work done with Nextel in the USA several years ago by IBM, the redesign of the service channel to make better use of IVR menus and improvements in the management of the contact centres supporting customers enabled Nextel to reduce operating costs by 40 percent whilst improving customer perceived service – not a prize to be overlooked, especially in the hugely pressured telecommunications marketplace.

Conversely, where the execution of the strategy is poor, customers will inevitably choose their own route to the supplier. Poor IVR menu systems (with too many levels and choices, badly identified categories and unfriendly routing) or poor contact-centre capacity and workforce management leave far too many consumers hanging on the line. In these circumstances, it is no surprise that websites like *www.gethuman.com* spring up to help consumers find a way to speak to a person to solve their problem.

Too often, companies try to make decisions on behalf of their customers rather than letting the customer decide. This is particularly true of business-to-business organisations where, all too often, the company decides how it will sell and serve its customers without adequate consideration or consultation with the customers themselves. If service standards, costs and propositions can be identified sufficiently clearly, then why not let a customer choose – even when as a supplier you might have the power to force a choice?

Establishing a new coverage model, the strategy for how customers will be served, needs consideration of how much control will be exercised over the route to market and, critically, how that control will be exercised (by management decision, customer choice, price and service differentiation).

This was one of the key aspects of its business model that IBM radically re-engineered in the 1990s to address a mix of the strategic issues identified earlier. The benefits of this were enormous, and included a significant amount of empowerment to customers to choose so that, through seven different routes to market, decision-making was a mixture of customer choice, management objectives and economics.

Defining channel combinations to serve different customer segments is the first step to be taken once a decision to shift multichannel strategy has been made. Although often conducted superficially or on a poorly segmented customer set, it is a foundational step in creating an innovative and economically viable strategy. When carefully mapped out, it enables huge benefits to both revenue and costs. The revenue benefits might take some time to materialise, but savings of 15 to 20 percent in cost to serve, combined with improvements in service, are regularly realised in redesigns of sales and service channels in many different industries – and these cost savings are often redeployed to widen reach, improve service or sharpen pricing.

3 How do I build this into an integrated multichannel strategy?

We all have experience of the fissures in many multichannel operations. There's the direct mail from your current insurance company that assumes you are not a customer and offers you a better deal than the one they are offering you as an existing customer in their standard annual renewal letter. There's the better deal that you can secure with a mobile operator by addressing the contact-centre retention staff rather than the store staff (or *vice versa*, depending on your geography!). There's the fact that the account manager visiting you at work today does not seem to know about the query you registered with his business over the telephone last week.

For a multichannel strategy to work effectively it must be carefully linked together, putting the essential joins in place, matching corporate goals, brand values and customer needs. This vital step is another that operational managers often discover has not been thought through effectively enough. Experiences such as that with Recreation Equipment Inc. (REI) are few and far between. In addition to their 84 stores, their web operation offers over 40,000 items and has, for many years, offered customers the opportunity to order online and collect from a store of their choice – an option that around 40 percent of customers now choose.

Similarly, the company offers kiosks in store to enable information-gathering and infill purchases to be made when needed. However, as the difference between Circuit City's 24/24 pick-up guarantee (a $24 gift card if a customer's online order is not ready to collect within 24 minutes) and Wal-Mart's estimated 7-day lead time proves, such integration is neither easy nor cost-free, and makes tremendous demands on the business. This is not something to be developed without a clear business driver.

Working the cascade

The challenge in this question is much easier to pose than to answer, as we have discovered in discussions with forum members. Any linear description of the approach invariably falls short of reality as it becomes necessary to iterate between steps and trade-off different aspects of the problem. There is, however, a general cascading approach to developing an answer that helps unlock the way forward (Figure 2.3).

Setting goals for each customer group The start point is to set goals for each of the identified customer groups, not just in terms of the criteria for the channel strategy but also in terms of the business objectives with that group. This is an important distinction, because business goals might be different by group (not necessarily always seeking to maximise immediate short-term profit but potentially seeking to increase penetration, reduce risk exposure, promote multiple product holding or other goals). This segmentation should draw on the exhibited channel usage by different groups, and their different needs.

This can provide a remarkable degree of focus. In the case of one financial services company, it enabled a much clearer set of business goals and desired service characteristics to be set around customers' attitudes to risk and their desire for advice, and the location of the highest value targets for growth within this.

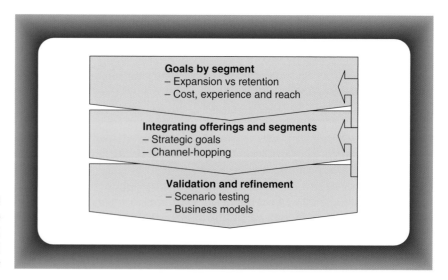

Figure 2.3
Creating the
integrated
multichannel
strategy

Similarly, the enterprise customer management (ECM) loop launched by GM (see Chapter 5) provides a great example of focused goal-setting. GM's initiative aimed to increase penetration through the characteristic lifecycle of car purchase and replacement, targeting those potential buyers who demonstrated an affinity with the GM brand. This goal drew together all aspects of the company's multichannel strategy (dealer, telephone, web, mail and magazine) to create a carefully structured programme that measurably increased brand preference and incremental sales.

Clear goals make it a lot easier to decide what is needed, and hence design a strategy. However, this requires real clarity in defining and selecting customer groups and setting goals for each that many organisations struggle to achieve because they do not effectively monitor channel usage by their customers.

Bringing the product offer and the segments together The main challenge that most companies face when they try to craft a strategy is finding the integrating elements that help to set boundaries. There are two aspects to this: first, integrating the nature of the transaction being conducted with the customer segment, and secondly, understanding the nature of the channel chain that needs to be created to deliver to each group effectively.

This can sometimes be quite challenging. In the automotive market, customers' needs at each stage of the lifecycle are different – especially for proximity. When researching cars, the benefit of a wide choice of vehicles far outweighs the need to be close to the customer. In servicing, the need is for convenience and therefore local operation; an integrated sales and service operation is therefore not necessarily the best structure to serve the customer most effectively, and the use of web and SMS to provide better customer interaction is different at each step of the lifecycle. Conversely, many industrial businesses intuitively segment by life-stage, providing a different mix of web, telephone and face-to-face support for pre-sales, sales, and service and support.

The failure to differentiate transaction types holds back many industries from really exploiting effective multichannel operation. Recognising that customers simply 'want what they want' when they interact with your organisation helps to free up thinking about channels, and is well worth a try.

Amazon created its 'where's my stuff?' button on the website in response to the web and telephone interactions that it tracked where customers simply wanted to know where their 'stuff' was, and used virtually that same wording when contacting Amazon. A similar need lies behind the now well-established tracking facilities on FedEx, DHL and other logistics operations websites.

Too often, businesses believe customers favour a human voice ahead of alternatives. Yet this is not always true. In the USA, Hertz's synthetic agent which allows gold-card customers to reserve a car is much preferred by these customers to human agents. Customers prefer its speed, assurance and low involvement – similar to the reasons why many customers like ATMs for simple banking transactions.

It is quite different, though, when the customer has a problem and the channel needs to cope with a significant delivery issue or complaint. At these points, people more often than not need to deal directly with other people.

When one of the authors ordered a Dell laptop that failed to turn up as expected and delivery seemed problematic, web-based information would not suffice. It needed an agent, with a name and a contact number, who could be relied on to find where the machine was and ensure delivery at a set time, much more reassurance, and contact confirming that the problem was being resolved.

Similarly, when ordering a relatively simple software upgrade or rolling out servers, IBM customers do not require (or want) a complex personal service. They simply want a low-cost and efficient service. However, when looking at a major consulting engagement, the same client will want to talk with potential suppliers and become confident of their capability and approach before making a decision.

Handling the channel-hopping customer To add further complexity to the issue, the same customer at different times will need to be served by different channels, sometimes in the same transaction. Many REI customers enter the store with information gleaned from the company's website to make a purchase that they could have made online. Yet they still complete their purchase at a kiosk or at the till. Similarly, the use by retailers of in-store giveaway catalogues to point people to their virtual online stores is a very powerful traffic generator, as several contributors to the research forum have attested.

Once upon a time, banking meant going to a bank. Then ATMs, cash-back (enabling your local store to provide cash when you buy something from them) and call centres appeared, but the branches didn't go away. The Internet, mobile commerce and interactive TV were then added to the ways in which you could access your account, but the branches still didn't go away. And, while text messages telling you that you're about to go overdrawn might be useful, no-one has yet suggested the pure play text-messaging bank! The management challenge of this range of choice is immense. Customers will often make use of many of these channels in one interaction with their bank – think of the channels you use when deciding on a mortgage, or looking at an investment.

In these situations, it becomes important to understand how customers are identified and how up-to-date a customer view is needed in each transaction to ensure good customer service and effective insight and revenue generation.

Some of the leaders in this space are the Canadian banks. In Canada, banks like the Royal Bank of Canada understand this challenge and, in addition to sophisticated segments that have been operationalised through core channels, they make sure, for instance, that their contact-centre agents are able to see what the customers can see on the web and even talk them through the web channel to complete a transaction if a customer gets stuck and uses the 'call me' button on the website.

We are still in the early days of managing the channel-hopping customer effectively, and few institutions can manage information-handling in anything but selected instances. However, this offers benefits to the business that does do it – and regardless, this kind of behaviour needs to be planned for in order to avoid leaving costly holes in the strategy through which customers fall.

Validating the strategy The validation of any strategy needs to consider carefully the impact on customers of the change envisaged. This helps to avoid gaps, and to ensure that customers' needs as well as your business goals are being met.

Validation is needed both at the inception and through the multichannel strategy change, and can be provided in many ways – for example, customer research, pilots, competitive observation, benchmarking in parallel industries, and iterative customer feedback.

Revisiting customer behaviour and needs and how well these are met by each channel helps to do this. It was this understanding that led Cisco to push as strongly as it did into online service and support. The success of Cisco's automated online approach to answering questions, diagnosis, solutions and assist, and the provision of commerce agents for configuring, pricing and ordering online, is down to the extent to which its technically very skilled buyers feel comfortable in using the web channel. Without this level of customer appeal it would not have been possible for Cisco to have raised customer satisfaction through the approach and to have successfully led 90 percent of its customers to draw on the web system for general marketing and enquiries and technical support.

In a very different setting, the UK Government's Driving and Vehicle Licensing Agency (DVLA) has similarly validated its multichannel strategy through extensive consumer research and testing both before and during its launch. The service provides an electronic vehicle licence by phone (IVR & agent) and Internet as an alternative to the face-to-face channel available through post offices. Although it provides an agent channel for complex enquiries and problem resolution, it routes straightforward licence renewals through the web and IVR. It uses its understanding and customer history to make triage easy. Integration with insurance companies and vehicle roadworthiness (MOT) checks, combined with flexible resourcing, enables the inevitable peaks at month end to be serviced effectively for both the agency and customers, providing very positive customer feedback and high reuse. This matches the conclusions drawn from pre-launch market research.

Another powerful tool in both design and validation is scenario analysis. These pen-portrait scenarios can be used creatively and analytically, and can help to shift the mindset inside the business markedly if they are well defined – something that is vital for the successful execution of the strategy.

One client we worked with in the hospitality sector found exactly this when it used these kind of pen portraits to differentiate sharply its approach and service to outlets. The outline of the character and needs of the key decision-maker in each Hotel Recreation and Catering businesses (HORECA) operation was called out on two dimensions. The first dimension was a business-like interaction to relationship-based interaction, and the second ran from a high to a low need for advice and support. When overlaid with examples, research and illustrations, the portraits helped account staff to see the value of the differentiated approach and segment the customer base. It also enabled a rich dialogue to be initiated over sub-segments and service standards that surprised channel managers in what was seen to be a very conservative industry.

We have seen these scenario portraits work in both business-to-business and business-to-consumer environments, and have found that they can provide a powerful antidote to the otherwise common focus on customer size and industry that seems to dominate business-to-business segmentations.

We will cover these approaches and tools in more detail in Chapter 5.

4 How do I build a business case for change?

The fourth step is one that needs to addressed even when there appear to be very good reasons for changing the multichannel strategy in the organisation. In the main, answering this question is essential for two reasons:

1. To ensure that the economics are sound and properly factored into shaping the decisions being made
2. To provide a valuable framework for managing to realise the benefits expected when the initiative is launched (you get what you manage for).

However, it has additional value. It prevents many (sometimes worthy, sometimes not) other changes being attached to a multichannel programme and potentially dragging focus off the core change. We have seen this in organisations where the channel innovation has 'strategic' importance and justification, and therefore gains the initial sponsorship and momentum to progress with fewer obstacles than other initiatives. However, as staff struggle to make sense of the initiative, other changes can come to be attached to the core multichannel change and pull it off course. We had experience of this in one consumer products business. There, as some of the other changes hit heavy water, the whole programme ground to a halt until key aspects of the channel change could be pulled out and executed.

At the very least, a business case will be needed by any self-respecting finance function trying to manage the limited resources of the business and seeking to confirm the value of any investment. Nonetheless, it amazes us how frequently a business case is not drawn up – or even a robust rationale created. One aspect of this could be seen in the channel innovation driven from customer relationship management (CRM). At the height of the CRM wave in 2000, Gartner estimated that as few as one in five implementations of customer management change actually had a proper business justification (Gartner, 2000), and yet the business justification would have provided exactly the kind of assurance needed: clarity concerning the objectives and budget for change, and strength through the governance of the change. These are three of the top five factors that differentiate successful from unsuccessful customer programmes (IBM, 2004).

Setting priorities

At this point in the multichannel review, there will no doubt be many exciting possibilities that could be pursued – creative ways to transform cost, experience or access. However, it becomes vital to define the key priorities in the face of limited time, budget and appetite for change – in opening up a new mobile channel to add to the experience; in integrating the existing bricks and clicks; in training staff or adapting metrics in the contact centre; or maybe simply in reducing or controlling the costs of the service channel. There are, even within a well-steered review, always many more options than energy.

In working with a company across several European markets that supported many businesses in the provision of communications equipment and systems, we ended up juggling some 14 different innovations to identify a near-term set of priorities that could be managed across three markets. From this, it became clear that only two of these could be pursued in the ensuing six months. Prioritisation was essential. In this client case, and with others, we found that the most effective initial means of prioritisation was not immediately to examine costs and revenues but to identify and rate priority to the customer and to the business, using a structured criteria based approach (described in more detail in Part 3). From this, 'win–wins' can be identified for the business that address both customer and supplier needs.

These 'win–wins' are a key part of any change, and are especially important if there are some less palatable innovations to be made. Both Cisco and First Direct found the growth of the Internet channel alongside human-assisted channels a lot easier because the organic growth of their businesses meant it was a service- and cost-winner for customers and a growth- and profit-winner for the companies, without the trauma of major lay-offs.

It is noteworthy that British Airways has managed to innovate through its Connect service much more easily since the low-cost carriers eroded the power of the established interests within both the organisation and the downstream channel, tipping the balance in favour of change. Similarly, greater use of IVR technology in Nextel to resolve customer needs became a lot easier when it became clear that it also led to more complex and interesting queries passing to agents, as simpler tasks were handled electronically.

Searching for these win–wins is a good starting point, and they can often be linked to more difficult-to-realise but vital channel shifts, to help ease programmes through.

Understanding the value to be unlocked

Beyond prioritisation a business justification needs to examine what benefits will accrue from the change, as well as the size and the drivers of such benefits. This is essential if channel innovation is to be managed effectively and the benefits captured through implementation.

This might appear straightforward in cases like that of Nextel, where the prospect of a 40 percent operational cost saving and the poor customer service provided a strong platform for innovation. However, prospective value and realised value are not the same, and most management teams will not proceed with change unless the case for it, and the explanation of the value levers that realise it, are tightly argued and well-evidenced, especially by customers.

Just such a detailed view became a powerful litmus test for the steering team of one global software company that we worked with, which was transforming its sales channel with a combination of new segmentations, skills and systems. In the phase 0 project work, the team identified exactly how the innovation would impact key business metrics. In turn it unlocked additional opportunity and improved customer interactions. These assessments were validated by managers across the business, and built on a strong competitive need that was also well shared.

However, creating this understanding can be much more complex than it first appears. Many innovations in and of themselves do not bring benefits: adopting a much more structured and rigorous service measurement process or installing a new multichannel management dashboard will not deliver assured benefits without other measures in place to exploit them, and a sceptical management team will query the logic.

A strong rationale built on well-understood and agreed principles is vital to secure buy-in and ensure that the contributing factors for creating success are put in place at the start of a programme of change.

Tools developed and tested within the forum have proved to be very powerful in crystallising this picture, and indeed also in helping to tease out the answer as to where to start the change process. In doing so they also help stakeholders establish a rationale, consensus about the value, the nature and sequencing of channel innovations. All of these are important, given the cross-functional nature of almost all multichannel change. These are explored in Chapter 6.

Building an assessment of the financial impact

The final piece of a robust answer to the business case is to draw up an assessment of the financial impact, embodying the priority, sequence and interdependencies involved in the innovation.

Given the scale of investment and potential benefit that many organisations make in this area, this is essential. Major changes can represent investments of millions of euros in letting staff go, putting in new IT systems and telephony systems, conducting training, acquiring property and providing for transition costs. Even decisions like that taken by JetBlue, the award-winning low-cost airline, to invest in prominent kiosk technology at check-in or televisions in the seatbacks of every aircraft represent multimillion dollar decisions that require an assessment to ensure payback and optimise the shape and form of the investment.

5 How do I organise for successful change?

Taking on innovation, even when it is going to create a better outcome, is not for the fainthearted. As Richard Nixon observed, 'Any change is resisted because bureaucrats have a vested interest in the chaos in which they exist'.'

The defenders of the *status quo* can be particularly strong when we come to any multichannel change, for three reasons:

1. Multichannel innovation tends to involve many if not all functional groups in a business – sales, marketing, service, systems, operations and HR – thus making consensus difficult. We observed this in 2006 in one of the retail banks seeking to create a more integrated channel approach. This decision, of necessity, engaged the heads of all product divisions, those in charge of the channel structure and the operational and systems functions – in effect, a full house of the senior management of the bank. It is not easy to gain alignment in this circumstance.
2. It connects directly and obviously with the customer and the revenue line – an area where planned change has always been viewed pessimistically in established organisations. This makes change highly charged, with the potential downsides being viewed carefully because they are seen to be significant and very fast acting.
3. Any major multichannel initiative typically has a significant upfront investment before benefits can be realised. Such a cash-flow exposure inevitably and sensibly demands careful senior management attention.

As a result, it requires careful handling in order to avoid adverse publicity and commercial damage rather than benefit. Memories of customer-visible problems last a long time – remember the Coke flavour change, the Hoover flights promotion and the Gerald Ratner comments about product quality? Major channel changes inevitably stir customer inertia and create comment – and, in our web-enabled society, this comment can be far-reaching and immediate.

As we write, First Direct Bank in the UK has just introduced a £10 monthly charge for its current-account customers (or at least those that do not qualify under certain criteria). This is a category first – reintroducing charges abandoned over 30 years ago – and is already on the pages of every newspaper and consumer website. (Although, given the rationale and care with which it has been done, it will be an interesting case to watch to see what consumer impact it has.)

Similar exposure and vitriolic criticism is the risk for any poorly executed channel innovation. Much of the web criticism of companies involves problems with overzealous sales staff, poorly provided customer service, or failures to deliver on service propositions. If a channel change is not well organised, it can easily result in such press.

In this book, we are not going to deal with the general points about good change management and project control. These are essential, but can be found in other publications. We are going to focus on the special aspects of the multichannel challenge and the key lessons to be gleaned from the experience of those companies that have embarked on concerted programmes of innovation.

The challenges of channel change

The challenges of managing channel innovation are unusual in that they engage both internal and external stakeholders, whereas most corporate initiatives engage largely the internal stakeholders. This demands a much higher order of care and focus.

One European paper supplier consolidated its customer sales and support operations across Europe. Previously, these had simply been local offices with account managers in the field and some sales administration support. They moved to a much more efficient model where, although field managers remained local, the sales administration was handled by a single European centre elsewhere. The successful channel innovation was only made possible by centrally-coordinated communications to customers that forewarned and helped them through the transition, and by specific efforts to uncover precisely what local terms and conditions customers were operating under and needed to be migrated from.

The size of this communications and procedural effort was initially completely underestimated by the company. It assumed that the written terms were those that individual customers thought that they were on, that the level of understanding about the change in their own team and the customer was much higher than it was, and that staff would be quick to communicate change in detail. Only during the detailed planning stage and pilot did the scale of the effort needed become clear.

Similarly, a drinks business that we worked with migrated to a new coverage model with much more telephone-based interaction. The business spent considerable effort making sure that the field managers, who had established relationships with customers, were entirely confident in and had met the telephone-based team to which contact was migrating, so that they felt able to talk the transition through with customers and had confidence to work effectively with the contact-centre teams.

Care is essential, as the statistics on customer-centred innovation indicate. Whilst the success rate is nowhere near as poor as some commentators have thought, it is evident that companies only achieve their expected benefits and results around half the time (IBM, 2004), and the success rate of initiatives that involve channel integration and optimisation are worse than average.

Four of the top five differentiators for successful programmes involve the *way* that the change is managed – see Figure 2.4. It is therefore worth

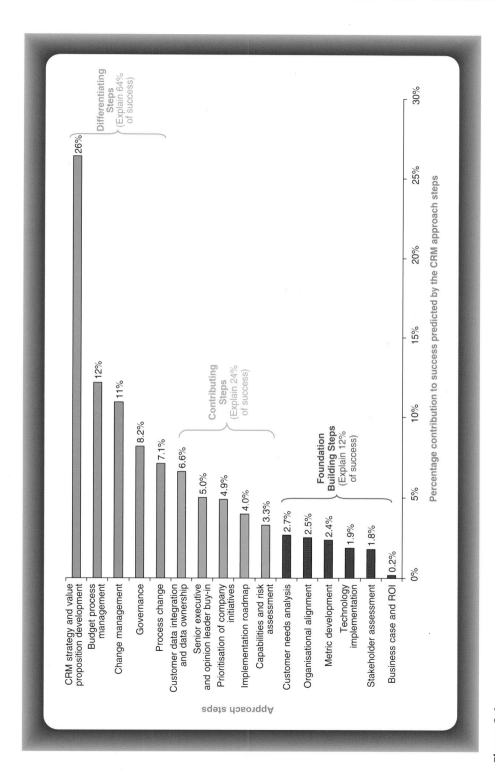

Figure 2.4
Global drivers of CRM success (IBM, 2004)

understanding how these key aspects can be managed more tightly to achieve success.

De-risking the change

Tackling the risks of change effectively is a rich mixture of personal, structural and organisational attributes. Critical amongst these is the ability to build the political momentum to secure agreement to the innovation in the first place, and then maintain the coalition of support through the programme's ups and downs.

A significant factor in this is the nature of the leader of the change. Picking the right person to lead on the change is essential, and it is often easy to see how likely an initiative is to succeed by looking at the leaders selected.

The most effective leaders bring the characteristics that Malcolm Gladwell ascribes to Paul Revere in his book, *The Tipping Point* (Gladwell, 2000). Paul Revere was the Boston silversmith who marshalled opposition to the British. As Gladwell explains,

> [Revere] wasn't just the man with the biggest Rolodex in colonial Boston. He was also actively engaged in gathering information about the British ... Paul Revere was a Connector. But he was also ... a Maven.

In other words, he brought both a great network and great insight. The key leaders of any multichannel change need to bring, collectively, these characteristics – in several people if not in one alone.

These characteristics come in many forms. Amongst the most effective change leaders we have worked with was a woman who had worked in her company for nearly 10 years and risen through the ranks of the customer services area to establish herself as one of the people on whom the Sales Director relied to make sure operations went smoothly. As one of the key participants in a radical set of innovations that altered customer segments, sales, logistics and service organisation and channels across the business, she was a passionate advocate of the change, with an excellent network inside the office and in the field and the ability to engage with people at all levels to explain its benefits. Combining her strong personal network and attention to detail, she helped to ensure a phenomenally smooth range of innovations in the multichannel operations of the business.

Personal skills are not enough, though, especially in large, international organisations attempting a significant programme of change that interacts with many business units, customers and functions. Here, a wide range of tools is needed. In addition to key individuals and effective communications, tools such as piloting, a clear 'road map' detailing waves of incremental change and a formal governance structure play key roles in enabling success. These tools will be described in more detail in Chapter 7.

It is a surprise to many that pilots are able to play a role in situations where it might appear that there is little ability to test and learn, or to reverse changes. However, innovative design and management can often enable this. One global pharmaceutical company prepared for changes in its sales channels through a series of 14 pilots scattered over the world, with a view to gathering together all the learning into a composite view for full-scale implementation.

Organising for successful change cannot compensate for poor design, but it can prevent a good design being wasted or stopped as a result of transition costs and obstacles. There are clear lessons to be learned from the special characteristics of channel change.

Although in answering this question we are moving from strategy into implementation, from the clean and clinical to the practical and untidy, there is still a lot of value to be gained from proper use of a number of the strategy and planning tools used earlier in the cycle. Perhaps unsurprisingly, those organisations that have a clear view of their goals and the nature and size of the benefits that they want from multichannel innovation find that their initiatives are more successful.

6 How do I measure effectiveness in a multichannel environment?

Metrics matter

People often remark that what gets measured is what gets done. However, in a multichannel organisation measurement is vital not only because of what gets measured but also because how it is measured, and therefore the amount of attention that gets paid to it. Metrics have always been one of the most contentious and challenging areas of discussion.

Choosing what to measure is one of the most powerful means organisations have of making their strategy happen. Tesco has famously used its 'steering wheel' to drive forward its business over the past 10 years. This balanced scorecard of metrics divides the business into four sections – customers, operations, staff and finances – using a 'traffic light' system to monitor performance, and is carried philosophically into the management culture of the business.

Effective metrics work powerfully, especially those that choose a limited and prominent set of key indicators to target and chart operations. However, poor measures have an equally powerful effect.

In one company we examined, the sales force was targeted on call rate (not an uncommon metric). The study found that one customer was visited 134 times in the course of a year – a monumental effort that delivered the princely revenue total of £94. Was this a poor choice of metric, or perhaps an absence of management? Was it a falsified record, or a case of poor judgement? Whatever way you look at it, this metric had failed the business.

Yet this case is just the visible tip of a very big iceberg when it comes to a multichannel environment. Metrics matter as much here as in a marketplace metrics, because metrics acts act as the signalling and coordinating glue in the system and, if they fail, can lead the organisation badly astray. In exactly the same way that prices signal information to participants in a marketplace, metrics signal performance and value in a multichannel environment … and they frequently make optimising performance difficult.

Key aspects for the metrics menu

There are many critical issues in the challenge of setting the right metrics. The intertwined issues that need to be resolved within any business cover many topics:

● Defining the critical aspects of multichannel performance to measure for each operational area. This is to avoid the sensation of drowning in data that can easily be created by the capability and ingenuity of the many new systems and the multiple sources of information that exist. The increasing capability of systems to produce data in real or near real time will only make this worse.

● Balancing the internal and external metrics to create a fuller picture of what is actually happening for all stakeholders in the system. These include customers, frontline staff, operational management and the strategic managers of the economics of the business.

● Deciding which metrics are to be linked to individuals' reward and recognition and how these will be used. There is always a difficult balance to be secured between ensuring an accurate picture of what is happening and incentivising individuals to perform more strongly. Many British customers will remember the bad publicity that surrounded the newly liberalised telephone number enquiry service with the 118118 number in 2003, after it emerged that agents were being so strongly driven by the call-duration metric that they were deliberately cutting customers off before giving them the right information.

● Managing the trade-offs between optimising pieces of the multichannel operation. This can happen within channels, such as when gathering additional data on customers (for research or more informed service); it inevitably raises average call time and therefore operational costs and capacity issues. When dealing with benefit payments or support services, governments need to trade off compliance issues, which are often better dealt with face-to-face, against the cost of delivery, which is almost always better dealt with remotely. Equally, trade-offs need to be made between channels. It was only after the separate web channels had started to enable customer live parcel tracking that the logistics companies began to appreciate how significant an impact it had on contact-centre volumes. Similarly, banks all over the world constantly reflect on the trade-off between providing efficient automated service points and promoting ATMs, and their desire to build contact with their customer base person-to-person in order to provide higher value (and more risk-laden) investment and savings services.

● Understanding the meaning of key performance indicators. There have been many consumer goods companies that have been challenged, critiqued and pressured by retailers on delivery metrics (full load, on time at distribution centres and stores), only to find that differences in reality and the system measured delivery reflect time cut-offs towards the end of the day and inefficiencies in the processing of delivery logs.

- Preventing unhealthy competition between channels. In large, multi-product, multichannel operations, this is one of the key challenges. Metrics both help and hinder because of the way that they try to promote accountability. The success of a business-to-consumer Internet channel cannot be assessed purely on the basis of sales made on the website. One department-store chain, when tracking customer behaviour, found that for every pound of revenue it takes on the web, three pounds are spent in the store after browsing online – so it works equally hard to help these customers through such facilities as store locators and information on the nearest store with a particular product in stock (McDonald, 2002). Similarly, it found the top driver of traffic to the site was brochures and flyers provided in store. In the US, around two-thirds of Internet purchasers sometimes browse in store and then buy online, and there are indications that this multi-channel behaviour is increasing rather than staying stable.

Resolving all these trade-offs properly is not possible. The best companies simply manage to get the right balance between them to provide clarity in the channels about how to behave to satisfy customers and business needs.

Examples of different approaches include IBM's balanced scorecards and careful measurement of contributions by each channel through the sales opportunity pipeline in order to assess more effectively the capacity, role and value of each player in its multiple channel model. This is a complex but data rich model for a large, integrated business. Others have taken a much simpler metric approach.

Uncorking the silos

Many people see siloed behaviour as something to be avoided. In practice, it seems to be a natural part of human behaviour. We inherently need to identify with someone, and we struggle to do that with numbers that are too large or very different. This can lead to fissures between the functions in an organisation every bit as wide as those between businesses – think buying and logistics in the average retailer, the sales team and marketing, customer service, and research and development. The gaps that we create in our businesses were brought home to us in work done many years ago under the Efficient Consumer Response (ECR) initiative in the grocery markets, where the attempts to build cooperation between retailers and suppliers demonstrated how big the internal as well as the external gaps to multifunctional working were!

With this in mind, in a multichannel organisation it is important to choose your ruts carefully, as the organisation will have to run in them for some time. Selecting these trade-offs carefully can make the difference between success and failure, smooth integration and frustration. Some of the most innovative organisations that we have seen in this space have made great use of metrics to help in not just the optimisation of ongoing performance but also in the execution of innovation in the channels area, and ensured that technical fissures or information holes have not undermined the strategy for engaging customers.

7 How do I encourage customers to use channels most effectively?

This question is phrased carefully. Customers' behaviour in the use of your channel configuration is the ultimate shaper of the value that is gained both by the company and by the customers themselves. Their behaviour will also help set the level of competitive risk that an organisation is exposed to. If your customers do not make best use of the strategy that you have designed, then the value that they receive in return for the price they have to pay may be too low. Assuming that you have answered the earlier questions carefully, this step is the one that seals the delivery of value.

Interestingly, the question can be asked in many ways – but the way we have phrased it is significant. The choice must reside with the customer. The company needs to see itself as orchestrator, facilitator and stimulus, but not as controller or commander. Rather too often we have found an inside-out approach being taken to the challenge, rather than an outside-in approach. This is not a recipe for success. The sustainable examples of successful multichannel businesses adopt a profit-focused outside-in approach, starting with the customer and working back to the business to create the value. Think of your favoured suppliers and the way that they approach their channels. They have an almost instinctively customer-focused approach, and this goes all the way through to the way that they address the behaviour of the customer.

In the words of Stew Leonard's famous inscription, carved into a three-ton rock at each of the Stew's supermarket entrances:

1. The customer is always right.
2. If the customer is ever wrong, re-read rule #1

A supply-side view manifests itself in the way the challenge is perceived in the business. The most frequent supply-side approach to this step betrays itself in a rather different question: 'how do we shift our customers to cheaper channels?' The two are not the same, and the difference is important. The latter assumes that the lowest-cost channel is the best route to engage customers. It also sometimes comes with a management mandate to move customers to cheaper channels (if necessary by force, it sometimes seems!). This looks at the issue in terms of a point problem rather than a holistic solution and, whilst it might be one desirable outcome, it is rarely the right ingoing approach. Indeed, it can create a major obstacle to the kind of corporate approach needed to encourage the optimum customer behaviour.

Often organisations leap from the cost of customer interaction straight to the desired outcome, without considering either the customer perspective or the organisation's needs. An example of failure to consider these important factors is to be found in the attempt by Abbey National (now Abbey, part of Banco Santander) many years ago to try to encourage customers to use ATMs (and so reduce costs and queues at the teller counter) by charging for counter transactions. Rather than incentivising a move (for everyone's benefit) to the ATMs, it chose a charge against teller usage. This annoyed customers, and created an image that the bank did not care and was penalising vulnerable groups (e.g. elderly customers) without due consideration for their needs. Overall, it badly mishandled the communications and underestimated the antipathy that many customers have for such unilateral action from a corporate organisation. The move stirred up so much customer criticism that it had to be abandoned.

The lesson provides a good base from which to approach this question and the rationale for the phraseology. The approaches adopted have to feel right for your customer base, and not risk alienating customers and commentators. Whichever of the many tools and approaches an organisation may adopt, it needs to start from the right perspective – the customer's.

Win–win, not win–lose

The goal is to find 'win–win' outcomes, where both the business and the customer think that they have gained from the choice of channel used. This is a mix of policy and practices: policy to avoid mismatched incentives and information, and practices to encourage the desired behaviour at the same time as respecting fully the rights of customers to make their own choice.

Some firms seem to excel at this. Many of the Canadian retail banks like the Bank of Canada or the Bank of Montreal provide great case studies in doing this effectively. Similarly, businesses like JetBlue also do the groundwork to make sure that they can find actions consistent with the brand and with greater operational effectiveness. Surprisingly simple actions can have a powerful effect. Moving the ticketing kiosks to prominent locations in the check-in terminal, flagging opportunities to use online/mobile channels on statements, regular correspondence and receipts, and using desktop pop-ups for support services all encourage customers to take the risk to change their behaviour, or prompt them to try something new. Do you remember the first time (assuming that you have done it!) that you used an ATM or self-service check-in at the airport, and how the encouragement of the customer-service agent helped to smooth the path?

All it sometimes takes is the imagination to think like the customer. Many years ago Servicemaster started to flag the 800 support number on the floors it cleaned, requiring the customer to call the number to find out how to clean it off. This simple idea enabled them to educate customers in the best way to clean the floor and prevent degradation of the surface.

First Direct has used its outstanding service reputation in the telephone channel to help drive up usage of their web- and SMS-based services, and, by retaining the commitment to talk with customers, they have helped to ensure that they concentrate on the easiest channel for customers (which, interestingly, is often the most efficient channel for the business). This customer confidence has helped to push their Internet channel into becoming their most popular channel for sales, comprising over 50 percent of sales transactions by 2005.

Businesses use many different tools to encourage optimum channel usage, and almost all of the best are informational, incentive or design-based. These treat the customer with respect and empower them. They naturally treat customer traffic like water – rapidly flowing to the easiest and most convenient route as long as no obstacles are put in its way. The corporate goal is to remove the obstacles.

Managing the flows

However, planning to stimulate and encourage channel usage is essential. Many online channel initiatives have quickly foundered because of the lack of traffic. Consideration needs to be given to:

- engineering where and how hand-offs between channels will be operated
- managing identity and security through multichannel journeys
- planning how customer information will be gathered
- considering how the channels will be optimised through time by making best use of tracking what exactly happens to customers in each channel.

The benefits of this can be impressive. Capital One, the US credit card company, has an impressive set of analytics that kick in every time someone calls it. The information system predicts who is calling (and learns if you use different telephones to call in) and why (based upon when you call and what triggers a contact). From this, the call can be routed in over 50 different ways. If the caller is a low-value customer who wants to cancel a card, he or she will be routed to an IVR which offers the opportunity to quickly and easily close the account. On the other hand, if the caller is a desired high-value customer that the system predicts is trying to close an account, he or she will be routed to one of their most skilled agents. As the call comes through to the agent, the system will present up to 25 different types of data for them on their PC screen, including possible offers to persuade the customer to stay with Capital One. Unsurprisingly, this level of planning and information helps to reduce churn and ease the normal angst of the touchtone menu. It also leads to a significant and measurable increase in cross-selling.

Mutual interest can sometimes be easily attained. Hertz gold-card customers, the most valuable group to the vehicle rental company, are now able to book cars through an automated agent which will talk with them to find out where and when they want to rent and which costs significantly less than a human agent. The ease and reliability of this approach has been a very significant win–win for Hertz, providing a perceived premium service at a low operational cost.

■ Conclusion

Facing up to the multichannel challenge is about working the cycle of steps identified in these seven questions. Addressing these points will help to ensure that both customer and organisation benefit, and thereby a sustainable increase in value can be achieved.

In Part 2 of the book we will uncover the tools and concepts that companies participating in the forum, and those with whom we have consulted, have found most useful in addressing the issues raised.

■ References

Gartner White Paper (2000). *The Economics of Customer Relationship Management*. Gartner.

Gladwell, M. (2000). *The Tipping Point*. Little Brown and Company.

Godin, S. (2003). *Purple Cow*. Portfolio.

IBM (2004). *CRM Works*. Institute for Business Value.

IBM (2006). *Advocacy in the Customer Focused Enterprise*. IBM.

McDonald, M.H.B. and Wilson, H. (2002). *The New Marketing*. Butterworth-Heinemann.

Temkin, B., Chatham, B. and Amato, M. (2005). *The Customer Experience Value Chain: An Enterprisewide Approach for Meeting Customer Needs*. Forrester Research.

CHAPTER 3

Multichannel diagnostic

When we got into office, the one thing that surprised me most was to find that things were just as bad as we'd been saying they were.

John F Kennedy

The diagnostic performs two roles at the very start of multichannel innovation.

First, it is an aid to those considering the need to innovate. It provides questions, a structure and the opportunity to focus on the need to address channels. It can lead the way into a critical foundation for successful change, by providing a forum and route to define the rationale for changing how the channels of the organisation are operating. As such, it provides one input into the management dialogue that needs to take place when considering whether this important enough to do *now*.

Secondly, it is a tool to help understand where and how to innovate and to shape other aspects of the initial goal-setting process that needs to frame a reason to change. In our experience as consultants, it is often a lot easier to gain agreement that change is necessary than it is to ensure that all have a clear direction for that change and its goals. The diagnostic, especially as part of a wider process, seeks to help do that.

The tool itself is nothing more complex than a series of questions. These are prompts that focus attention on the different dimensions that we have already described in the book to date. However, raising these questions and seeking answers, especially across functions, is often sufficient to get the ball rolling and begin the kind of cross-organisational communication that is essential for effective innovation.

It takes an 'outside-in' view of the channel position and identifies where the organisation is experiencing pain. This is invaluable both in terms of focus and as a trigger for action.

■ Use of the diagnostic

There are many ways that the diagnostic can be used. It can be employed by a single manager independently, with a small group, or in a larger workshop setting. Much of the value comes through the focus that it generates on the topics raised and the analysis that it provokes if a robust answer to the questions is to be provided.

For this reason, it is our experience that this type of diagnostic tool unlocks greatest value when it is used within a group setting, as a basis for framing a discussion, placing some structure around the debate and pressing for more analysis to verify the conclusions.

The aim of the questions is not to replace data analysis, but to help focus and shape the generation of hypotheses for analysis. Agreeing a point in a meeting is never a substitute for validating the conclusion with proper data – something that is too often overlooked in the goal-setting process.

The tool

The tool has four domains: an overview section, and then three sections covering the three key drivers of value: experience, access and cost.

Managers are invited to look at each of the domains and assess the risk that the organisation is running with its current approach on each of eight dimensions. Particularly in a group setting, the aim is to secure a consensus or conclusion across the team on a six-point scale ranging from a very high exposure (rated 5) to a very low exposure (rated 0).

These scales can then be presented as web diagrams to other managers to highlight key areas of focus and an overall level of risk. From this, the assessment of the need to change can be more robustly decided and the primary goals for change can be set. This is typically done with further analysis of the hypotheses that are developed.

The tool needs to be used as a part of an overall effort to review the channel position, especially if a cross-organisational team is involved. A number of caveats therefore apply to its use:

1. It is not designed as 'change' tool in itself. By this, we mean that it will need support when used as part of a process with other tools to ensure that the right stakeholders for any change are engaged and that adherence to a rigorous assessment is followed. It will not, of itself, provide a means of addressing the quite normal and legitimate resistance of participants who will seek to defend their performance, area of responsibility or department in the face of critical analysis.
2. It does not provide a comprehensive, off-the-shelf review. The diagnostic is a high-level checklist of items. It will need to be used alongside the collection and analysis of data if it is to provide a good basis for a significant change initiative.
3. It starts from the assumption that the 'basics' (product-market strategy, segmentation and proposition definition) are in place. This is a big assumption and, whilst it is virtually never the case that organisations have all these items covered off completely, there needs to be a high degree of clarity around them to enable the channel diagnostic to be used effectively. If these are not well enough defined, an initial piece of work will be needed here before engaging on the diagnostic.
4. The diagnostic will need tailoring for use in specific organisations – both for its terminology and to ensure that it picks up the key aspects of the market situation and channel use in the business. This kind of tailoring is especially important when the diagnostic is used in a cross-organisational group setting. It is easy for people to be unnecessarily thrown off the subject by unfamiliar terms and language that needs definition, when a more usual set of words could be used.

Scope

The overall scope against which the diagnostic is applied needs to be carefully thought through to enable valid conclusions to be drawn from it.

It needs to be applied over an appropriate market definition, and scoped to address any significant differences in channel configuration and integration by geography or business unit.

In any global business, it is almost certain that a nested set of diagnostics will be needed to appraise the position adequately and capture the significant market differences that can exist in each country. For example, even in the market for mobile phones there are significant differences between the way that consumers use channels, and markets are configured by country. A globally applied diagnostic would not adequately recognise this as a trigger for innovation. Similar issues arise in different product-markets even within otherwise comparable businesses.

Similarly, the diagnostic can be used across the whole customer life-cycle, or to address specific steps in the customer lifecycle or sets of customer journeys. Indeed, these can represent stages in the scoping of the innovation and prioritisation of the pain points in which innovation is needed. Frequently, clients choose to start in particular geographies and at certain lifecycle stages in their innovation effort in order to create a manageable roadmap for innovation or to capture the most significant business value.

Tables 3.1–3.4 demonstrate the multichannel diagnostic in the overview, experience, access and cost domains.

Table 3.1 Multichannel diagnostic – overview domain

Questions	Risks: High exposure to low exposure 5 – 4 – 3 – 2 – 1 – 0 Comment	Rating
Is there is a clear and explicit multichannel management policy, compiled centrally and under coordinated governance?	Exposure is high if there is no coordinated and explicit policy, one that would be drafted in a structured review process and therefore also regularly reviewed, and signed off by senior management. This is rare without a senior owner.	
Are there overall investment levels (people, money, and infrastructure) matched to policy and regularly reviewed?	Either the defined policy is being implemented properly in funding terms or sufficient investment is available to ensure effective operations and critical resource needs are met.	
Is there a significant mismatch between business strategy and market goals, and the channel policy?	Alignment between the business proposition and the channel approach is vital for a strong customer proposition. Significant contradictions offer a real improvement opportunity.	
Are there significant market shifts that demand a channel reappraisal?	Major competitor action on channels, significant consumer behaviour changes or new entrants with substitute offers all provide potential drivers for increased risk.	
Are there significant shifts in market strategy that impact channels?	Internally there may be changes in the product-market goals and strategy that require channel innovation to succeed.	
Is it a long time since the organisation last reviewed the effectiveness of its channel approach?	A channel approach that has not been reviewed for several years will be exposed to significant environmental changes: technology, competitive, customer, legislative etc. that carry significant risks.	
Is the organisation insufficiently differentiating between customers in deciding how to treat them when they are in contact with the business?	A 'one size fits all' approach to the market may significantly sub-optimise profit capture and expose organisations to risk from niche competitors. It offers scope to enhance channel interaction and approach.	
Does the current channel approach generate sufficient insight for shaping the go-to-market strategy of the business?	The channels are a key source of insight and insufficient customer and market insight from them exposes a significant medium term risk.	

Table 3.2 Multichannel diagnostic – experience domain

Questions	Risks: High exposure to low exposure 5 – 4 – 3 – 2 – 1 – 0 Comment	Rating
Does the organisation present 'one face' to the customer across internal operations and with partners in the channel?	Lack of capability or friction between functions and channel partners that create fissures in the experience delivered to the customer create risks regarding customer penetration and retention and weaken brand image.	
Can the organisation operationalise its segmentation effectively, and provide different customer treatments based on needs and value?	Many segmentations cannot be operationalised in the channel, especially multichannel, and this reduces customer value and profitability.	
Is a consistent experience being delivered multichannel?	Consistency is important for projecting the right brand values and image, both through time and across channels. Inconsistencies pose a brand risk.	
How well defined and implemented is the incentive and measurement system that supports the target experience?	Without the drumbeat of regular metrics to which the business is aligned, it is difficult to make the target experience a reality. Teams may operate to different goals, leading to weak execution.	
Is there significant customer feedback that would suggest the need to innovate in multichannel?	Customer surveys, account feedback, customer satisfaction data and *ad hoc* research may all provide key indicators of risk areas that need to be addressed for effective relationship and journey management.	
How well supported are contact staff across functions with the information to provide an effective experience?	Significant gaps in the amount, accuracy and detail of information provided at point of customer contact and its timeliness and personalisation compromise the experience for customers, especially when the journey crosses channels.	
Is there an opportunity to really gain advantage from a differentiated experience?	A significant and difficult to replicate opportunity might exist in this area – does it? If so, what channel capability would be needed to deliver it?	
Do customer traffic flows across channels match the desired profiles?	Customer experience often determines the flow of traffic between and across channels. If this is not in line with desired goals, it may indicate a significant issue.	

Table 3.3 Multichannel diagnostic – access domain

Questions	Risks: High exposure to low exposure 5 – 4 – 3 – 2 – 1 – 0 Comment	Rating
Are there any target customer segments that are difficult to reach effectively with the current channel approach?	There are risks that the channel approach does not enable access to current and target customer groups, as measured by both reach and penetration.	
Are there current customer groups that are under-penetrated by existing channel approaches (especially major accounts)?	Poor wallet share in key customer groups often results from weaknesses in the channel engagement and approach, not just in the sales area but also across the lifecycle and across channel.	
Are there significant opportunities for growth in the market served by the current channel approach?	There is a risk that the current approach addresses the existing market effectively but does not leave enough headroom for growth and so closes out a valuable shareholder value driver.	
Is effective use being made of the web to access new customer segments?	These offer low operational costs and an extended market presence. Their absence may indicate an opportunity, both in multichannel journeys and in extending reach.	
Does the current channel approach reach the growing product/market spaces?	Understanding the growing/declining parts of the market and the support that the current channel approach gives to accessing the growing sections may unlock considerable value and new segmentations.	
Is effective use being made of third-party channel partners to access specific customer groups or product/market spaces?	Consideration of channel partners to unlock geographies, segments or new product opportunities might represent a real opportunity for value creation through channel innovation.	
Is there unfulfilled customer demand for service? This could be evident in feedback, customer friction or enquiries.	This identifies aspects of the customer lifecycle that are being badly handled, or specific customer groups that are not well served by the current approach.	
Does the existing channel approach provide a good platform for new market propositions?	The extent to which the channel approach will support future solutions, products, services and segments is important for identifying risks to growth and strategic fit.	

Table 3.4 Multichannel diagnostic – cost domain

Questions	Risks: High exposure to low exposure 5 – 4 – 3 – 2 – 1 – 0 Comment	Rating
Is your cost to serve key customer groups high relative to competition?	High cost is not necessarily an issue, but it is vital that relative channel cost is clear. Cost can be high without issue if it offers additional customer value. If not, it offers a real opportunity for business model innovation.	
Is cost negatively impacting either market share trends or relative profitability?	Weakness in the relative value offered will be evident in reduced market share or price challenges that are impacting profitability.	
What is the trend in the operational costs in the channel area?	Trend costs need to be under control and have a sustainable trajectory. Cost drivers should be clear and controllable.	
Is there any customer segment which cannot be addressed economically because of unit cost?	Business definitions which rule out customers or product sets and reflect a need to sustain high prices can often represent an opportunity that can be unlocked with an amended channel approach.	
Would you describe any types of channel cost as unmanageable or unpredictable?	Control of channel traffic and costs is important. Significant cost areas that are effectively out of control present a risk.	
What competitive exposure is there to significantly lower-cost channels?	Exposure to the low-cost channels – especially where this is in adjacent market spaces (even if not developed) – may provide a strategic threat, if not an immediate threat, to market share.	
Have any competitors made significant reductions in their channel costs?	Is there any evidence of any strategic shifts in channel approach being made by others?	
What use of channel integration is being made to reduce cost to serve within customer journeys?	Weakly segmented coverage models, little channel integration and poor multichannel use almost always constrains the ability to manage cost to serve effectively.	

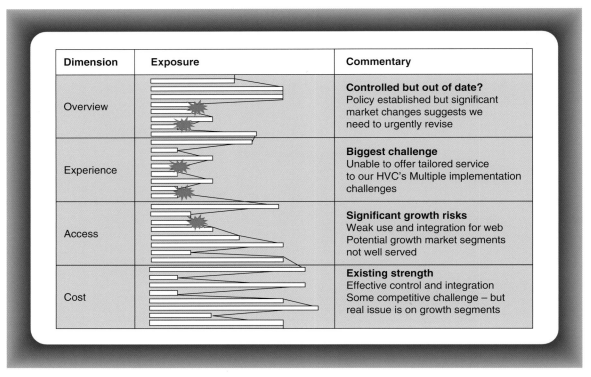

Figure 3.1
Summary exposure chart (illustrative example)

The ratings and associated comments from the use of the diagnostic offer a great way to engage people in the need for channel innovation. They assist in building up a coherent story for the case for change – and indeed in setting down hypotheses that might be validated by analysis to build a robust basis and direction for multichannel change.

In terms of presentation, we have found that feeding back the results in the form of web diagrams or exposure charts, with associated comments and conclusions, offers the most impactful way of using output and suggesting appropriate next steps.

An illustrative example of a summary exposure chart used to compile and feedback the results of the diagnostic is shown in Figure 3.1, while an illustrative example of output from the overview domain in the form of a web diagram is shown in Figure 3.2.

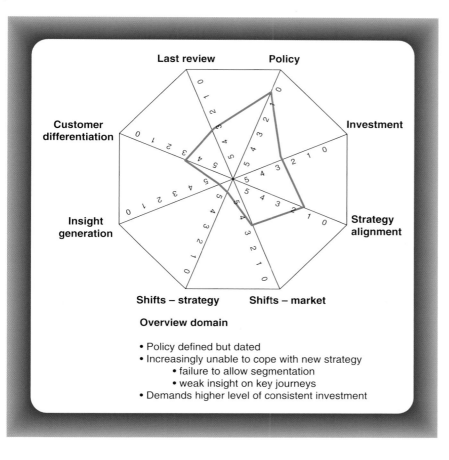

Last review   Policy

Investment

Customer differentiation

Strategy alignment

Insight generation

Shifts – strategy   Shifts – market

Overview domain

- Policy defined but dated
- Increasingly unable to cope with new strategy
  - failure to allow segmentation
  - weak insight on key journeys
- Demands higher level of consistent investment

Figure 3.2
Output from overview domain (illustrative example)

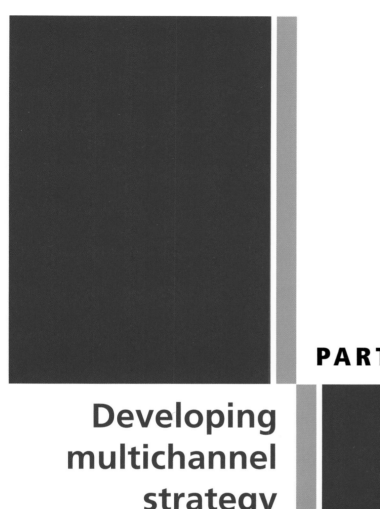

PART 2

Developing multichannel strategy

CHAPTER 4

Defining the right channel combinations to offer

It takes a certain kind of mind to see beauty in a hamburger bun.

Ray Kroc

By this point, it will be clear that multichannel strategy is vitally important and that it needs to be developed at a senior level. In Part 2, we describe a detailed process for developing a multichannel strategy, which has been developed through several iterations with members of the Cranfield Customer Management Forum as well as in IBM and Cranfield consulting engagements. Figure 4.1 provides an overview of this process.

Step 1, 'Identify the need for change', was the subject of Chapters 2 and 3. This chapter and the following two chapters address the next three steps in the process, steps 2 to 4, which develop the multichannel strategy and the associated business case. Step 5 on implementation is covered by the Part 3 of the book."

The purpose of this chapter, then, is to decide what channel combinations to offer for each product and each customer group, and how these channels will work together in customer journeys. To help answer this challenge we use a key tool, channel chain analysis, which forms the second part of this chapter.

Multichannel strategy cannot operate in a vacuum. It needs to build on broader work on marketing strategy that needs to be in place before channel chain analysis adds real value. We assume, in particular, that readers will have a clear understanding of the organisation's mission, including which markets it serves, and what its distinctive competences are within those markets.

We also assume that the market structure is well understood, that the market can be segmented, and that these segments can be prioritised. We will first discuss why these issues are important in forming multichannel strategy.

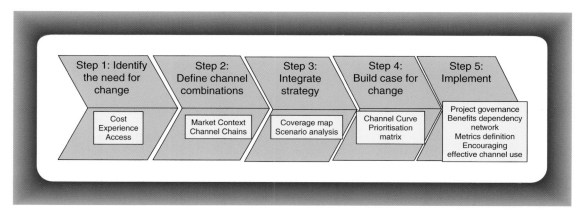

Figure 4.1
The multichannel strategy process

■ Understanding market context

Segment far enough along the market map

Market maps show the full extent of where an organisation sits in the market and how the enterprise is connected to its end customers. The map may be redrawn as a result of the multichannel strategy process, but the first step is to understand the current market map. In particular, we need to look far enough along the map towards the end customer when segmenting the market, as we may decide in the channel chain analysis which follows that the indirect channels we are currently selling through will be replaced or complemented by other routes to market. The first web boom was driven by a large swathe of businesses trying to disintermediate existing participants, and even now, without a proper base of analysis in this area, it is possible to have missed whole segments of the market that might otherwise be profitably addressed.

The end customer is often the consumer, but may equally be businesses in the case of IT suppliers, telecommunications companies and so on. For channel strategy purposes, segmentation needs be done at the furthest point in the map towards the end customer where a significant proportion of the buying decision is taken. Generally, this means segmenting at the level of the end customer. This is illustrated in Figure 4.2 for an insurance company. The map shows its route to market for a particular country in mainland Europe. Below the map is a table showing who influences the buying decision, according to estimates by the company on the basis of market research.

In this example, all types of customer are most heavily influenced in their buying decision by the distributor, which may be a broker, agent, bank or direct sales representative. Whether the customer is a consumer or a corporate client, though, the distributor has a much easier job recommending a particular insurer if the end customer has heard of it and has a positive image of it. So, a proportion of the decision – ranging from 10 percent for consumers to 25 percent for businesses – is thought to be made by the customer as a result of other influences – advertising, the Internet and so on.

In this situation, segmentation at the level of distributors is certainly relevant for many purposes. However, for forming channel strategy the end customer needed also to be segmented, to evaluate whether its needs could better be served by a different route to market. We will return to this example later.

Make sure there is enough accessible market

Another reason for looking far enough along the market map is to compare the routes to market currently being used with the overall market use, to ensure that there is enough accessible market to be able to achieve the company's objectives. This is illustrated by the market map of an office equipment manufacturer, shown in Figure 4.3.

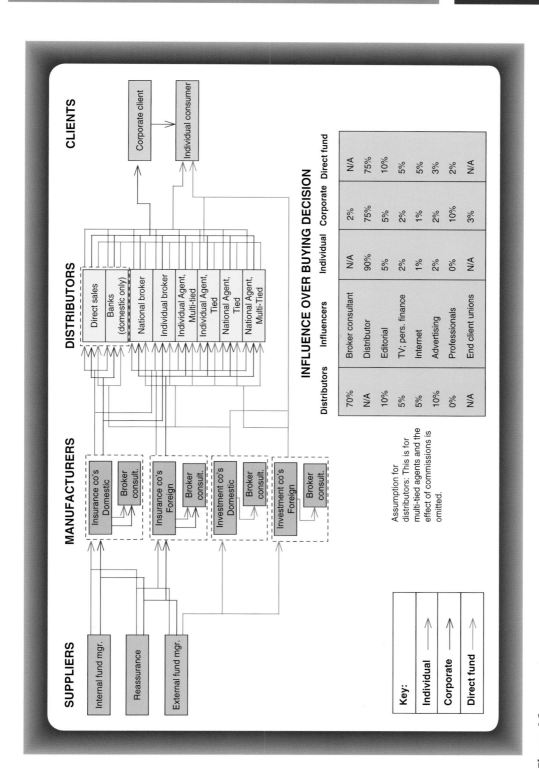

INFLUENCE OVER BUYING DECISION

Distributors	Influencers	Individual	Corporate	Direct fund
70%	Broker consultant	N/A	2%	N/A
N/A	Distributor	90%	75%	75%
10%	Editorial	5%	5%	10%
5%	TV; pers. finance	2%	2%	5%
5%	Internet	1%	1%	5%
10%	Advertising	2%	2%	3%
0%	Professionals	0%	10%	2%
N/A	End client unions	N/A	3%	N/A

Assumption for distributors: This is for multi-tied agents and the effect of commissions is omitted.

Figure 4.2
Market map – insurance company

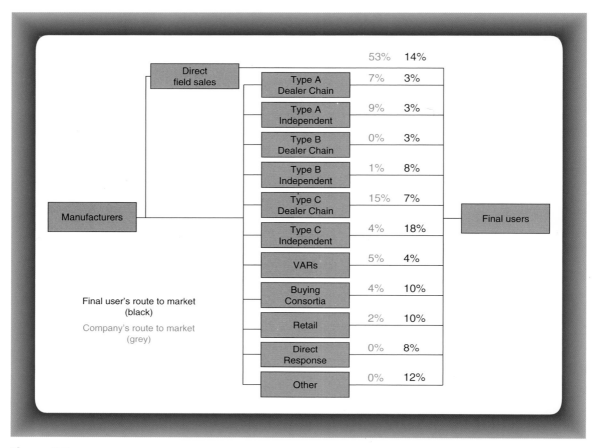

Figure 4.3
Market map – office equipment manufacturer (Source: McDonald and Dunbar, 2004)

The company had a bias towards its direct sales force, with 53 percent of its sales coming from this channel. In the market as a whole, though, only 14 percent of sales were made through direct sales forces. The company was under-represented in several other categories of intermediary, including the fast-growing retail sector, and there were several routes to market, totalling 23 percent of the market, in which the company did not compete at all.

Clearly, in cases such as this it is not sufficient just to focus on the intermediary as the customer, important though such relationships are, but to segment the end customer and develop a multichannel strategy appropriate for each segment.

Different segments suit different channel combinations

Having decided who our customers are, we then need to segment them. The best form of segmentation for forming multichannel strategy is one

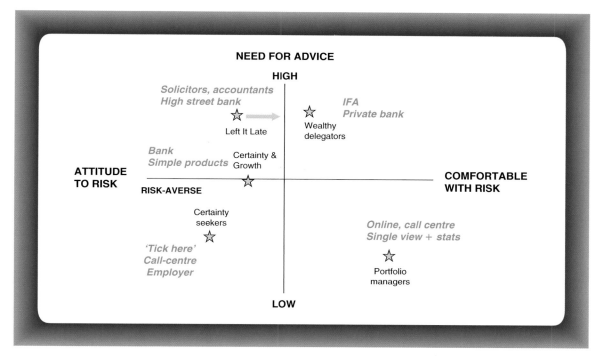

Figure 4.4
Segmentation of market for annuities

based on different customer needs or buying criteria, as opposed to segmenting purely on industry sector or size of company (which is common in many business-to-business companies), or indeed segmenting on such sociodemographics as class and wealth in consumer markets. Once needs-based segments are understood in detail, it may rapidly become intuitively clear which channels or channel combinations will best suit each segment. This was the case for another insurance company considering its market for annuity products, which segmented as shown in Figure 4.4.

The market for annuities is dominated by individuals at the moment of retirement, who have built up a pension pot and wish to convert some or all of it to an annuity which pays a guaranteed amount each year until they die. Consumers vary in their attitudes towards such financial decisions, on two key dimensions shown in the figure: their need for advice, ranging from highly independent decision-takers to those who prefer to outsource their financial decisions; and their attitude to risk, ranging from those who are very comfortable with risky investments such as shares to those who are risk-averse.

The largest segment is of 'certainty seekers', who wish to convert their pension pot to a guaranteed income with the least possible trouble. Members of this segment typically take out an annuity with their pension provider. A slightly less risk-averse segment is that seeking 'certainty and growth', representing people who are prepared to take some risk in order to achieve a greater return – for example, by investing part of their pension pot in a stock-market based product. 'Wealthy delegators' have a sufficiently large fund that they feel able to take more risk with its investment, and prefer to delegate the fine decisions to an adviser. 'Portfolio managers' may have similar funds but vary in their attitudes from wealthy delegators, preferring to manage their own fund portfolio. Finally, the 'left it late' segment has little or no pension provision.

Clearly, the segments vary not just in what product propositions they want but also in what channel to market will best suit them. 'Certainty seekers' can be efficiently served through a simple 'tick here' form, perhaps backed up by a call centre to answer any questions, so as to keep the process as simple and reassuring as possible. 'Wealthy delegators' need to be reached primarily via advice-providing intermediaries such as independent financial advisers. Members of the 'left it late' segment are likely to turn to their bank, and perhaps also their accountant or solicitor. 'Portfolio managers', by contrast, want hard information rather than personal reassurance, and so the Internet, backed up by skilled telephone-based advisers, may combine a low cost of service with immediacy and a sense of control for the customer.

In this case, the most actionable insight for the insurer concerned the growing 'certainty and growth' segment. The company decided that, while these customers were unlikely to use an independent financial adviser, they needed some face-to-face contact for help in selecting the right product and to provide reassurance. Thus, distribution via a bank seemed the best option. This led the company to develop a special product variant which was suitable for this channel, and to it working with a high street bank to distribute it.

Another example of needs-based segmentation, a large IT company, is shown in Figure 4.5. Its customers vary as to whether they are seeking 'relief' or 'reward', as well as whether their focus is on business or technical issues. Again, some implications for channel strategy can be drawn fairly easily from the segmentation by a knowledgeable team of managers. A 'save my career' customer will need plenty of face-to-face reassurance from an account manager. A 'save my budgets' customer may be perfectly prepared to buy at a distance in order to reduce the cost of sale and thus the price, as well as researching the best possible price by shopping around or holding reverse auctions. A 'radical thinker' may wish to be offered white papers and seminars with industry opinion leaders. A 'technical idealist' may want to see the company's technical staff, but as little as possible of the besuited account managers.

By simply asking ourselves what the right channel strategy is for each segment, then, we may improve on an undifferentiated channel strategy which treats all customers equally. However, two further refinements are often needed. First, the right approach may vary according to the priority the organisation attaches to each segment, and the overall objectives for that segment. Secondly, that approach will often require a combination of channels rather than a single channel. The export consultancy we discuss next illustrates both of these points.

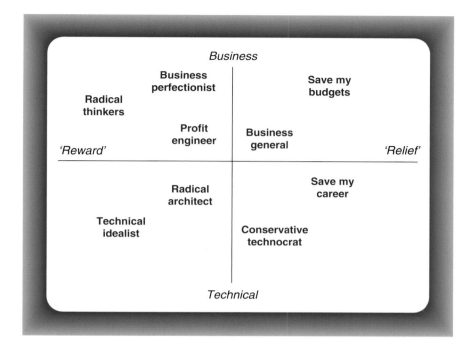

Business

Business
perfectionist

Save my
budgets

Radical
thinkers

Profit
engineer

Business
general

'Reward'

'Relief'

Radical
architect

Save my
career

Technical
idealist

Conservative
technocrat

Technical

Figure 4.5
Perceptual map – IT
company
Source: Robert
Shaw (personal
communication)

Segment targeting will affect channel strategy

Multichannel strategy is about creating win–wins which satisfy the customer and the organisation. How much we can afford to invest in acquiring and retaining members of a segment will depend on the attractiveness
of that segment. An ideal precursor to the development of multichannel
strategy, therefore, is to have some kind of segment prioritisation model,
such as the well known Directional Policy Matrix.

This is illustrated by the case of an export consultancy that gives
advice on exporting to small and medium-sized enterprises (SMEs). It
had so far served these SMEs through a single channel: face-to-face consultants operating out of a network of local offices, who would guide the
SME manager through the development of an export plan. However, this
approach did not suit all its target segments. A perceptual map showing
how its market divides into segments is shown in Figure 4.6, while the
relative prioritisation of the three principal areas on this perceptual map
is shown in the Directional Policy Matrix of Figure 4.7.

SME managers vary in their exporting experience, and also in their
independence and attitude toward receiving help. The two segments that
have been grouped as 'aspirants' on the perceptual map have little or no
exporting experience, and are eager to get help with forming an export
strategy. 'Reluctants' are also inexperienced exporters but, by contrast,
are fearful of the complexities and risks they associate with exporting,
creating deep-seated barriers to progressing beyond the fulfilment of the
few leads which happen to 'walk in the door' in response to the website, for example. 'Confidents' export as a matter of course, and are only

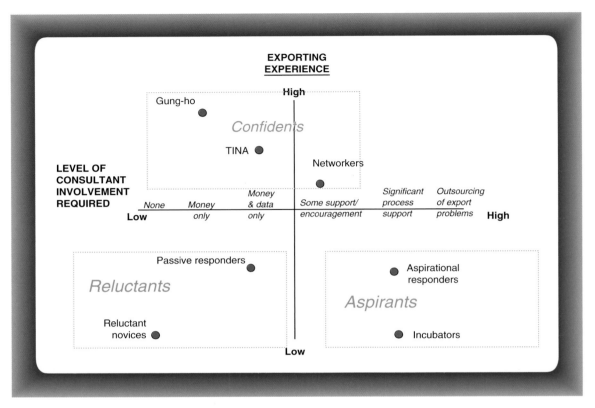

Figure 4.6
Export consultancy – perceptual map

likely to turn to the consultancy for help on specifics – such as identifying a distributor in a new country.

The 'aspirants' were reasonably well served by the organisation's traditional channel strategy. The last thing the 'confidents' wanted, though, was to phone a local office and have an appointment made 2 weeks hence when a consultant happened to be free. Instead, they needed some kind of approach giving quick answers to the specific queries which they had at a given moment. The face-to-face model was equally inappropriate for the 'reluctants', who only approached the organisation for help with fulfilling a specific order that happened to come their way, such as 'how to get money out of Saudi Arabia' or 'the customs paperwork for China'.

Which of these needs should the consultancy be concentrating on fulfilling? To help answer this question, a Directional Policy Matrix was developed, shown in Figure 4.7. This tool compares segments by their attractiveness to the company on the vertical axis, versus how strong the company is in fulfilling customer needs on the horizontal axis (with high strength to the left).

The 'aspirants' were both highly attractive and well served by the company, and little change was required. The 'confidents' were also an

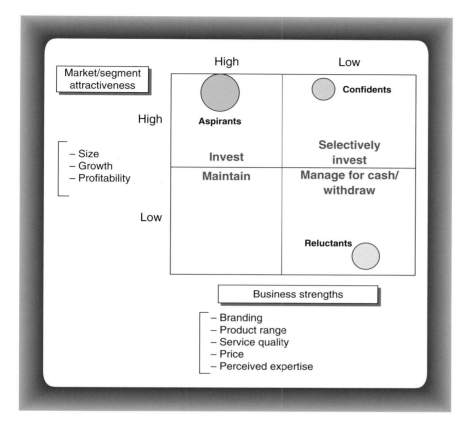

Figure 4.7
Export consultancy –
Directional Policy
Matrix

attractive market, but the consultancy's business strengths were low, largely due to the inappropriate channel model. The organisation did not want to ignore the 'reluctants' entirely, but it was clear that, due to the difficulty in persuading these managers of the potential of exporting, this was a less attractive segment. The challenge in this segment, then, was to form an effective channel strategy of sufficiently low cost to justify continuing to serve the segment.

Deciding how to square this particular circle required some creative thinking on the part of the consultancy's management team, regarding how to construct channel combinations that satisfied these different segments at reasonable cost. For this purpose they used channel chain analysis, a tool that, in our experience, managers find very helpful in defining an appropriate multichannel strategy.

■ Channel chain analysis

This simple but effective tool helps to work out how channels will best combine by drawing what we call a channel chain diagram. In this diagram, the stages of the buying cycle are drawn down the left. (The details might vary for each case.) Then, against each stage, the channels used to accomplish it are listed. The channel used for one stage will often affect which channel is likely to be used at the next stage, so the relevant boxes are joined with a line, hence creating one or more 'channel chains'. Figure 4.8 shows an example drawn from a major department store chain, with three such channel chains.

The company's first attempt at e-commerce in 2001 is shown in the channel chain on the left. The idea was to recruit customers through banner advertisements, who would then buy on the website and be posted their goods. However, the economics just didn't add up. Only 0.3 percent of people viewing a banner ad clicked through to the company's website – a figure which would have been around 2 percent a few years before in 1997, repeating the pattern of reducing media effectiveness we discussed in Chapter 1. And only 1 percent of those who clicked on the ad actually bought something. As a result, it was costing £1600 to recruit each customer to make an initial purchase of, say, a £25 kettle!

Now, in terms of competitive strategy for the department store, this was paradoxically good news. That pure-play channel chain was the only business model open to its dotcom rivals, who were therefore unable to sustain their business model. The department store, though, was able to start experimenting with other 'bricks and clicks' channel chains, such as that illustrated in the middle of Figure 4.8. It handed out leaflets in shopping centres, with an incentive for the first purchase online. It emailed its loyalty-card holders, and teamed up with complementary retailers such as grocers to email theirs. And it encouraged customers who looked at products online to go into the store and complete the purchase – the channel chain on the right of the figure, popular for goods such as beds, which customers want to bounce on before buying. Many

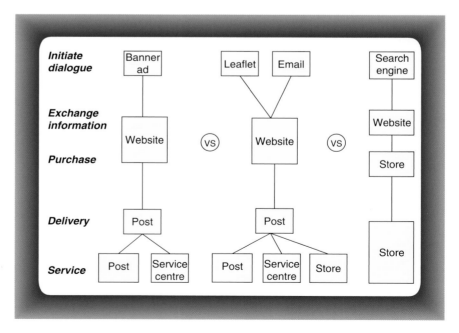

Figure 4.8
Channel chains – a
department store

people might see this approach as a strategy of 'hustle' rather than bold plays, but, through continuous measurement and incremental innovation within these three basic models, the store's dotcom division rapidly reached profitability, well ahead of its major rivals, and it created a sustainable and defensible business model.

The best channel chain will vary by product, and also by segment. The export consultancy we discussed in the previous section is a good example. Taking into account the relative priority of different segments, the management team developed the channel chains shown in Figure 4.9.

The 'aspirants' were reasonably well served by the organisation's traditional channel strategy of face-to-face consultations with advisers who guide the entrepreneur through an export planning process. For the 'confidents', though, a 'buffet' approach was developed, dominated by the remote channels of a call centre and the Internet, which provides quick access to the answer they need to their immediate query.

The same remote 'buffet' met the desire of the 'reluctants' for specific information on fulfilling an order which happened to 'walk in the door', but needed to be supplemented by a cost-effective communications campaign to address the segment's attitudinal barriers to being more proactive about exporting, using such techniques as seminars and white papers. The aim here was to convert some members of this segment to become 'aspirants' and, in due course, 'confidents'. Communications mechanisms such as seminars which serve multiple customers at once

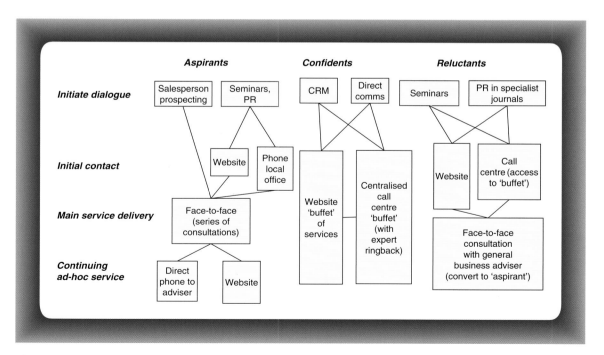

Figure 4.9
Channel chains – export consultancy

were chosen as being sufficiently cost-effective to be justifiable, given this segment's low position on the Directional Policy Matrix which we discussed earlier. At the very least, with this approach the organisation would avoid continuing to waste precious resources by sending a consultant for an expensive face-to-face meeting with a client who was unlikely to proceed.

Understanding current channel chains

Before we can design future channel chains, though, we need to understand how our customers are currently using the channels we make available to them. This can be done in many ways, but one of the most useful starting points is to draw up a table of channels against phases of the purchase process, as illustrated in Figure 4.10. The proportion of each phase – such as the purchase itself – that is conducted using each channel is estimated as a percentage. For example, this business school (loosely based on Cranfield School of Management, with illustrative figures) estimated that 85 percent of the time the customers first got the idea of going on a short course for managers from a mailing. Although exact figures may be available on which channels are used to place the order itself, filling in the other columns will generally require making some estimates and, often, the conduct of some additional research.

Next, proposed figures can be added (in italics in the figure). While not set in stone at this stage, these can be used to explore initial ideas on optimising

		Purchase phase				
Channel/medium		Initiate dialogue	Exchange information	Negotiate & tailor	Commit	Exchange value
	Face to Face		5% / *5%*	10% / *10%*		95% / *90%*
	Mail	85% / *60%*	60% / *40%*	20% / *10%*	20% / *10%*	
	Tele	5% / *5%*	10% / *10%*	40% / *20%*	80% / *70%*	
	Web	5% / *15%*	20% / *40%*	0% / *25%*	0% / *20%*	5% / *10%*
	Email	5% / *20%*	5% / *10%*	30% / *35%*		

Illustrative figures only

■ %age of current business using the medium to perform that task in the sales cycle

▪ Future target

Figure 4.10
Channel phase table – a business school

the mix of channels, in order to save costs, give more value to the customer, or both. For example, where a lower-cost channel can be used to perform a task at no disadvantage to the customer, its percentage can be increased. In the case of the business school, some of the proposed changes were:

- *Initiate dialogue.* Mailing course brochures was an expensive and imprecise way of telling the business school's existing customers about courses they might be interested in. The limited experience so far suggested that many customers would be just as happy to be sent carefully tailored emails, and just as responsive. It was believed that recommender facilities on the website might prove an even better way to steer the customer in the direction of the courses they need.
- *Negotiate/tailor.* For tailored courses run for particular companies, an element of face-to-face discussion was likely to continue to be desirable. However, it was thought that perhaps it would help customers to feel in control of the negotiation if they could experimentally assemble a possible course from standardised modules using a configuration facility on the website.
- *Exchange value.* The means by which the course is delivered was also being reviewed. There was scope for efficient distance learning of standard components of theory, such as accounting basics, but the business school envisaged that, for its particular target market, most of the course delivery would continue to be face-to-face, where the scope for teamwork, networking and a rich discussion of practical issues was greatest.

Drawing up a channel phase table is a useful starting point, but it suffers from two drawbacks. The first is that it lumps customers together, and does not tell us about the very different behaviour of different segments. The second is that it does not give us any information on transitions between channels – where customers go next after leaving a channel. This is crucial if we are to ensure that the customer is seamlessly handed over from one channel to the next; moreover, if we wish to steer the customer to a different channel, this is the point at which we will need to intervene.

The first problem can be fixed using cluster analysis of channel usage data collected by market research. Figure 4.11 shows an example of concert-goers booking tickets for the London Symphony Orchestra (LSO) at the Barbican Centre in London. The chart shows how much the respondents use the five available channels: phone, face-to-face at the venue, on the LSO's website, on the Barbican's website, or by post. In each case, respondents were asked how frequently they used the channel first to collect information, and secondly to book, on a five-point scale.

There were four clusters of channel behaviour. The 'low-use traditionals' mainly decided on their concert-going by poring over brochures from the orchestra and booking by telephone. 'Regular use traditionals' were similar, but attended concerts more frequently. 'Barbican loyals' mainly used the venue's website for both information and purchasing of LSO concert tickets, as they also attended other events at the Barbican venue. 'LSO web loyals' were also heavy web users, but mainly used the LSO website, complemented by the orchestra's mailings.

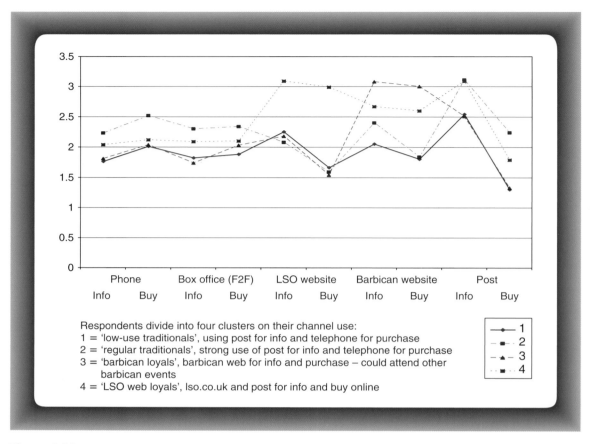

Figure 4.11
Cluster analysis of channel use – London Symphony Orchestra

This analysis surprised the marketing director in showing how many customers looked at the LSO website, even though only the 'LSO web loyals' went on to purchase on it. She had a strong interest in increasing online purchase rates; this channel was not only low cost compared with post and telephone, it also offered a much more responsive vehicle for selling unused seats as well as building closer relationships through regular contact. She therefore focused her attention on communicating the benefits of the online booking facility – such as the ability to select seats visually – to all segments, as well as making sure that the user-interface design steered browsers towards booking readily.

A channel chain presentation of how different segments behave is, though, even more transparent in showing how customers move from one channel to the next. A luxury hotel chain used this approach in its market research into how its guests found and booked their rooms. Three of the seven resulting channel chains are shown in Figure 4.12.

Around 10 percent of customers were still 'conventionals', initiating their search for a hotel room with a printed guide, and going on to phone

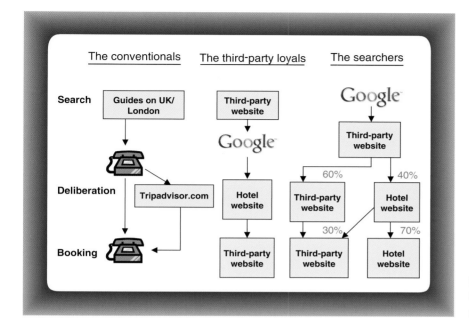

Figure 4.12
Current channel
chains – hotel chain

the hotel. Some of these 'conventionals' were beginning to complement their search with information from a website such as Tripadvisor.com, which contains consumer reports on their own hotel stays.

A larger proportion of customers were 'third-party loyals', who put their trust in one of the online intermediaries or third parties (such as Expedia.com) due to successful previous experiences. The marketing director was intrigued to note that many of these were looking at the hotel website for further information, but then returning to the third-party site to book. This was expensive behaviour for the hotel chain, which had to pay between 10 percent and 25 percent of the room rate to the intermediary. As it was based on a pre-existing relationship with the intermediary, though, it was difficult behaviour to change.

More immediately actionable, however, was the third channel chain for the 'searchers'. These customers would start by typing a search term such as 'luxury hotel London' into Google or another search engine. Expedia and its peers were masters at search-engine optimisation, and would buy paid search entries just to make sure, so the customer would probably end up on one of these intermediary sites. Again, a good proportion (about 40 percent) of this segment would seek some further information from the hotel's own website. Having a lower loyalty to the intermediary, though, this time some of the customers would 'stick' on the hotel's site and book there, rather than returning to the intermediary. Nevertheless, in total 70 percent of this segment would book through the intermediary. Even if this booking was with the hotel chain rather than a competitor, this represented an expensive sale.

Fortunately, the research included questions on why customers were making their channel choices and, crucially, why they made these channel switches from one channel to another. To the marketing director's surprise, the main reason for returning to a third-party site from the hotel chain's site, even for these customers at the very top end of the market, was price. Consumers wrongly believed that the price would be better on the third-party site. With this insight, the marketing director was able to convey some simple messages on the home page to explain that the hotel always offered its best prices directly. Simple search-engine optimisation also meant that a fair number of these 'searchers' now came straight to the hotel's website, too.

So, an understanding of channel chains led the marketing director to some simple changes at virtually zero cost. By the time she repeated her market research a year later, it was clear that these changes had diverted many customers to buying directly, at considerably lower cost.

A thorough understanding of your customers' current channel chains, then, is essential if these channel chains are to be redesigned to provide added value to the customer, lower costs, or both.

Combining direct and indirect channels

This hotel example shows that channel chains may include indirect channels such as agents, distributors and retailers, as well as the company's own direct channels. Just as these direct channels (such as the web, call centres and the sales force) often complement each other rather than working as alternatives, so indirect channels do not necessarily 'own' the whole customer relationship; rather, they may be complemented by the company's direct channels in an integrated channel chain.

An innovative programme, termed 'Dialogue', at General Motors Europe provides a good example of the step-change improvements in customer acquisition and retention costs that can result from such creative new channel chains. It is worth describing this programme in some detail (Figure 4.13).

GM's Dialogue programme

The traditional channel chain used for consumer car sales is on the left of the figure. The Original Equipment Manufacturers (OEMs), such as General Motors, have traditionally had little one-to-one contact with the motorist, direct consumer sales instead being supported through a network of independent dealers. The manufacturer's communications role has historically been one-way. Advertising and product information is communicated to consumers through broadcast media and, to a lesser extent, more targeted channels such as direct mail. The aim is to create awareness of the brand and drive traffic to the dealerships. This model is analogous to that in most consumer packaged goods.

However, this communication approach allows no direct feedback from consumers as to whether they are 'in the market' to buy or not, resulting in large amounts of wasted money and effort, especially with infrequent purchase decisions. There is also little opportunity to distinguish between individual potential customers on the basis of model preferences, purchase intentions, and so on.

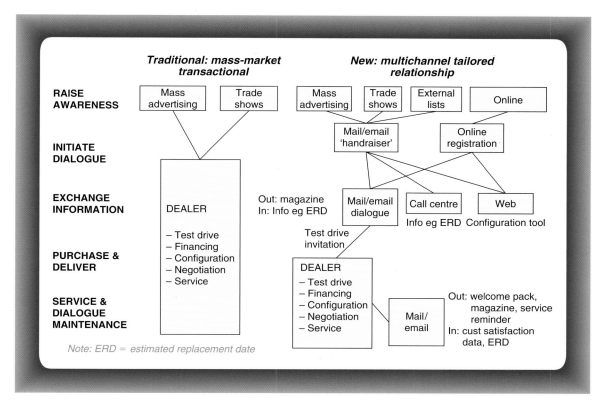

Figure 4.13
Channel chains – General Motors Europe

For the motor industry, the Internet has opened up real possibilities to move to a two-way communication model. The web offers an inexpensive channel through which consumers could respond to and interact with OEMs, and perhaps even purchase a vehicle online. The prospect of OEMs selling directly via the Internet inevitably sets alarm bells ringing among dealers, though, and has forced OEMs to think carefully before upsetting the distribution channel they have been so dependent upon.

The niche for direct online sales is now beginning to be significant, but GM's Dialogue programme, trialled on the new Vectra launches in 2002 to 2003 in seven countries in mainland Europe, sought instead to explore the hybrid solution shown on the right of Figure 4.13. The idea was to use the Internet to create relationships with customers, which might yield valuable information about their purchase intentions and enable higher-quality leads to be introduced to dealers during the time window when they were preparing to buy their next vehicle.

Cars are an infrequent purchase, but there is a high incidence of repeat purchase. This suggests there is a compelling case for maintaining contact with existing customers during the years between them buying cars.

In tandem with the arrival of the Internet, other developments in hardware and software created the possibility of fully integrating communications with consumers across a range of channels, both online and offline. Advances in database technology meant that it was much easier to 'clean' data held on individual customers so that names could be readily and accurately matched between purchase order systems, acquired lists, those responding to promotions, and so on. CRM software could then enable a complete view of the consumer across channels, enabling a true two-way relationship to be established.

The new channel chain In GM's new channel chain, the initial expression of interest could come via any one of a number of sources. In some markets, mailing lists were built through purchasing registration data; where this was not possible, lists were purchased through brokers such as Claritas, who offer the possibility of filtering for those who intend to buy a car in the next 12 months. People who responded to these mailings were termed 'Responders'. A second group, 'Handraisers', consisted of those who initiated the contact by registering on a website, calling a freephone number or taking a card from a dealership or at a motor show.

In a simple example of giving some channel choice to the consumer, these potential customers were then asked to nominate whether they preferred to receive communications by post or email. Much of the outgoing communication that followed – for example, newsletters and test-drive offers – could be sent electronically to those that requested it, although some other pieces, notably the Welcome Pack (provided on car purchase) and the prior to test-drive offer (called the Kitchen Table Pack) were delivered only in hard copy.

A further use of the online channel was the development of microsites for each model launch, as an interaction and information hub. The potential of these microsites was felt to be so high that targeted mailouts were sent to post-preferring prospective customers as well as those preferring email, to drive traffic to the sites, which was also boosted through point-of-sale material and so on. The microsites were linked to the main website for Opel, the brand under which the Vectra is sold in most of Europe, providing an opportunity for prospective customers to register.

In certain aspects of the Dialogue programme, then – for example, launch advertising – GM continued to depend largely upon one-way, high-volume channels such as TV and print media. However, in the subsequent phases interactive channels were essential to elicit the key information, such as the motorist's estimated replacement date (ERD), that would determine where customers were in the buying process and what products they might be interested in. Subsequent pieces of communication could still be mass produced – for example, a newsletter designed to keep prospects informed and interested – but they would only actually be *sent* to consumers according to their own individual calendar, which was determined by the ERD. A re-qualification process gave prospective customers the opportunity to re-affirm their purchase intentions in order to keep this vital data up to date, such as the 'Check/Update your details' prompt in the email newsletter (Figure 4.14). A high proportion

Figure 4.14
Inviting interaction –
GM's email
newsletter

of consumers, feeling they were engaged in a relevant conversation, took the trouble to update these details.

A key objective of GM's Dialogue was to supply dealers with well-qualified 'hot' leads at the point of readiness for a test drive, rather than the poor-quality leads generated by non-interactive and non-relationship based marketing campaigns. Ultimately, the programme aimed to better integrate GM's marketing with the work of this indirect sales channel.

This example is discussed further in Chapter 8, when we look at how to track and measure the effectiveness of channel chains. GM made successful use of piloting and control groups to measure the effect of the Dialogue programme on sales, and found that the additional cars sold as a result of the programme were equivalent to incremental revenue of over 300 million Euros and additional profit of over 50 million Euros.

An alternative presentation

The channel chain, then, is a concept that helps managers to understand and illustrate how customers flow from channel to channel in the course of a purchase. The diagram presentation we have used above is one way to illustrate channel chains. Another way is to lay out the same channel chain information in a tabular form. A travel company used the table shown in Figure 4.15 to design the right channel combination for its Sunworshippers segment, which is described in Figure 4.16. A glance at this figure compared with Figure 4.17 shows that the predicted channel usage of this segment is very different from that of the John and Mary Lively segment (Figure 4.18). This tabular layout is essentially similar to the channel phase diagram we discussed earlier (in Figure 4.10), except that we are analysing the main usage by segment rather than summarising the overall usage in percentages. The advantage of this tabular version is that channel chains can become quite complex when several channels are involved. The disadvantage is that it does not represent how the channels used by the customer at one stage might affect the channels they are likely to use at the next – recall, for example, the 'aspirants' from Figure 4.9.

Choice of presentation method is largely a matter of preference. Because it clearly illustrates the potential impact of one channel choice on future channel choices, we tend to prefer the presentation with which we began (Figure 4.8). If the channel chain is in danger of becoming too cluttered, a hybrid presentation also works well. Figure 4.19 provides an example of channel chain analysis in a field sales context.

Figure 4.15
Alternative
presentation of
channel chains – The
Sunworshippers

Constructing channel chains:
Infinite Innovation Inc.

Figure 4.19 illustrates the current channel chain for an IT services company's sales of complex applications to large customers. There are a number of shortcomings with this current channel chain from the point of view of the company, which we shall call Infinite Innovation Inc. The limited field sales resource is stretched by taking full responsibility at all stages of the customer engagement cycle. Whilst customers appreciate this simple and personal service, sales people do not have sufficient time to focus on developing big opportunities. During the early stages of a customer engagement, the channels operate largely in separate silos and respond to enquiries that come to them instead of operating to a set of business rules that determine where the opportunity is best handled.

Figure 4.20 illustrates the result of the creative process that generated a framework for team-based selling: integrating a number of channels to align the appropriate channel with the different tasks. Valuable field resources are focused upon the tasks for which they are uniquely and best suited: generating compelling sales proposals and closing the sale. Integrating the Internet- and desk-based channels into the process under the leadership of the field sales force qualifies out poor leads quickly and therefore allows the company to pursue more sales leads. The team-based

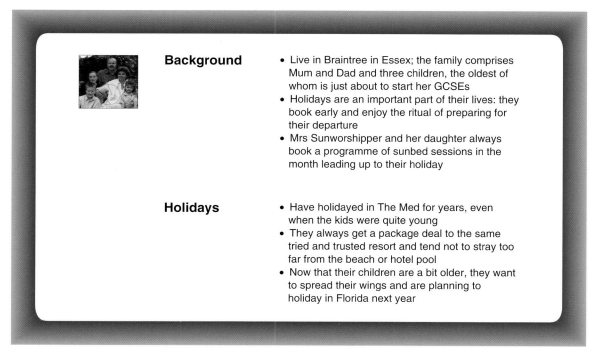

Background
- Live in Braintree in Essex; the family comprises Mum and Dad and three children, the oldest of whom is just about to start her GCSEs
- Holidays are an important part of their lives: they book early and enjoy the ritual of preparing for their departure
- Mrs Sunworshipper and her daughter always book a programme of sunbed sessions in the month leading up to their holiday

Holidays
- Have holidayed in The Med for years, even when the kids were quite young
- They always get a package deal to the same tried and trusted resort and tend not to stray too far from the beach or hotel pool
- Now that their children are a bit older, they want to spread their wings and are planning to holiday in Florida next year

Figure 4.16
Travel purchase – The Sunworshippers

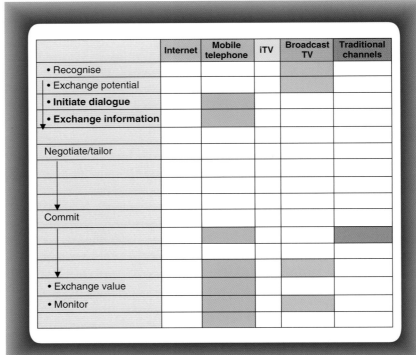

	Internet	Mobile telephone	iTV	Broadcast TV	Traditional channels
• Recognise				▓	
• Exchange potential				▓	
• **Initiate dialogue**		▓			
• **Exchange information**		▓			
Negotiate/tailor					
Commit					
		▓			▓
		▓		▓	
• Exchange value		▓			
• Monitor		▓		▓	

Figure 4.17
Alternative presentation of channel chains – John and Mary Lively

Background

- Live in Luton; childhood sweethearts, John and Mary have been seeing each other seriously for three years
- They were planning to buy a house together but put their plans on hold to ensure that they could take a holiday this summer
- John DJs part-time in a local nightclub and would happily leave his job as a mobile phone salesman to pursue a DJ-ing career in a European beach resort

Holidays

- Feel like The Med doesn't have anything else to offer them and are keen to travel further afield: Mary likes the sound of Tunisia
- Tend to book a holiday on the basis of the facilities available, and are always keen to get involved in water sports and other beach activities
- Wouldn't dream of holidaying anywhere that doesn't have thriving nightlife

Figure 4.18
Travel purchase – John and Mary Lively

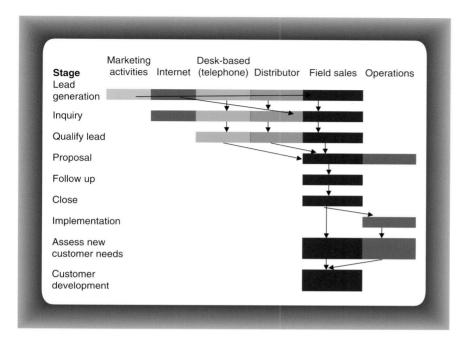

Figure 4.19
Current channel chain – Infinite Innovation Inc.

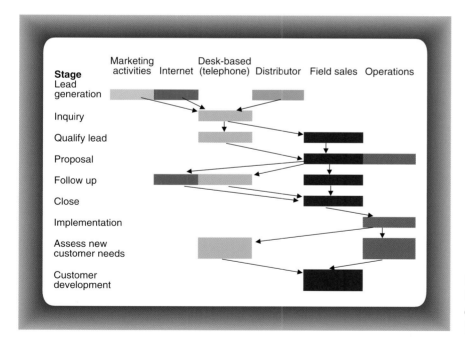

Figure 4.20
Future channel chain – Infinite Innovation Inc.

selling approach provides better response to customer queries throughout the selling engagement, and reduces the cost of sale to the company. So the alternate channel chain increases the number of sales opportunities, reduces the cost of sale and increases the sales success rate.

The channel chain tool has a number of benefits, not least in the overall design process of a new strategy. First, it helps managers to take a 360-degree view of interactions with customers, including all touchpoints within the strategy. Many organisations take a narrow view – separating sales from service or support, for example – and in so doing miss the customer experience and economic benefits of offering a much more 'joined-up' approach along the customer journey.

Secondly, it encourages an approach which tackles the problem in incremental steps – something that is very useful when turning to the implementation process. Channel chains will help to sequence and delineate steps, perhaps with several different variants of the current channel chain along the way to a future model.

Channel chains also help, in change management terms, to encourage managers to see the interdependencies between channels and to illuminate the need for close cooperation and mutually reinforcing metrics.

We have seen, however, that the right channel chain will vary both by customer group and by product, presenting the challenge of pulling together the work in each segment or product combination into an integrated strategy which has a reasonably small set of channel chains across the organisation. We have also touched on another integration problem – that of integrating the customer experience across the multiple channels that may be contained in the same channel chain. These integration challenges are the subject of Chapter 5.

■ Reference

McDonald, M. and Dunbar, I. (2004). *Market Segmentaion*. Butterworth-Heinemann.

CHAPTER 5

Integrating the multichannel proposition

The question is, then, do we try to make things easy on ourselves or do we try to make things easy on our customers, whoever they may be?

Niccolo Machiavelli

In Chapter 4, we discussed how channel chain analysis can be used to answer the second of the big questions we discussed in Chapter 2: 'What is the right combination of channels to offer each customer group?' This chapter addresses the next question: 'How do I build this into an integrated multichannel strategy?'

There are two integration challenges. The first is that the future channel chains we have designed will vary both across customer groups and across products. Pulling these together without ending up with an over-complex strategy is a real problem in an organisation with multiple product lines and multiple markets. We will discuss how coverage maps can help with this problem.

The second challenge is that of integrating the customer experience across the multiple channels in a channel chain. No global citizen today needs telling how important it is for this to happen properly, as we all suffer when it doesn't. Just as this book was about to be sent to the publisher, one of the authors bought a big basket of goods online from Boots, a large UK-based pharmacy chain. She shopped online because her nearby store with a specialist baby section doesn't have trolleys with baby seats! At least, she thought, she would earn plenty of loyalty points … But the confirmation email said:

> You can collect your points by inserting your card into a card point instore. Points are available for collection 5 days after your order has been dispatched and will remain available for collection for 12 months.

Surely, she reacted in understandable frustration, they don't expect me to pack my baby into a car and go into the store just to collect my loyalty points when they've got my loyalty card details already? Her flabbergasted response will be familiar to all of us who have come across channels that don't work effectively together.

In the second part of this chapter, we will look at how to avoid creating this kind of disastrous customer experience. We will describe how scenario analysis can be used to design smooth transitions between channels, and how market research can help to pinpoint and resolve any lack of consistency in the customer experience.

■ Integrating across products and segments: the coverage map

In Chapter 2, we discussed how 'What's the right channel for this product?' is the wrong question, as it assumes that channels operate independently. In Chapter 4 we saw that it is also wrong to assume that customers buy in a similar manner to each other, so, to be precise, a more correct question would be: 'What's the right channel chain for this product/segment combination?' This is a complicated question even to ask, let alone answer, and the heart sinks at the prospect of developing channel chains for every product sold to every customer group.

Fortunately, the coverage map tool provides a graphical means for simplifying this problem, and turns out to be surprisingly useful in practice.

In its simplest version, shown in Figure 5.1 for a business-to-business telecoms firm, the tool summarises how different channels are used by different customer groups and for different parts of the product range. The vertical axis plots customer groups, ranging from low value to high value. This is based on the observation that we are more likely to be able to afford the use of high-cost channels for valuable clients.

The horizontal axis lists the company's products or services in order of the complexity of sale. Hence a simple product with few options, which requires little explanation to the customer, will appear to the left, while a complex product requiring configuration and consultancy and involving price negotiation will be to the right.

This reflects the observation that channels vary in their ability to handle complexity, and customers are well aware of this. An IT company's key accounts or an insurer's high net worth individuals may rightly demand face-to-face meetings with account managers or financial advisers to discuss complex, high-risk decisions, but equally they are generally more than happy to use low-cost channels such as call centres and the Internet for routine, lower-value transactions.

A good coverage map will have several features. The simplest is that it will have good coverage: there will be a channel for each area of the

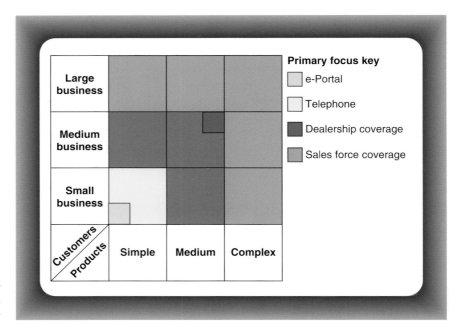

Figure 5.1
Coverage map –
business-to-business
telecoms provider

map – or at least each area which represents a target segment for the company – and channels will not be competing for the same space on the map. A good map will also use high-cost, high-bandwidth channels, such as the field sales force or face-to-face meetings with a financial adviser, only where they are needed – typically in the top right-hand corner of the map, where the customer value justifies the cost and the sales complexity necessitates it. Low-cost channels such as the Internet will typically dominate the bottom left-hand corner and, in many cases, the whole of the left-hand side of the map.

When companies first draw the map to illustrate their current channel model, it often demonstrates the lack of conscious management attention to the design of the channel strategy, by revealing one or more of the following faults:

- overlaps, where product/customer combinations are unintentionally served in multiple ways
- holes, where there is insufficient coverage of target customers or parts of the product range
- a resource balance directed to existing rather than potential business
- irrational use of expensive channels, with little differentiation between the channels used to serve each area of the map.

The company in Figure 5.1, while not wholly dysfunctional, illustrates some of these faults. In particular, there appears to be an unnecessarily heavy use of the sales force. It would be worth checking out whether the high-value customers were happy to conduct simpler transactions remotely instead, and whether the sales force really pays its way for the lowest-value customers or whether this business should be delegated to dealers. Moreover, although the web and dealership channels seem sensibly positioned on the diagram, they are in an immature state. The size of their boxes reflects the proportion of business coming through this channel – so, for example, only about 10 percent of simple products purchased by small businesses are bought over the web. The telephone channel is also underused; its success with simple products for small businesses could be extended upwards on the diagram to medium-sized businesses, as well as towards the right to medium complexity products.

You may have noticed, however, that this example makes a major simplification. We have described the tool as if each area of the map – that is, each product/segment combination – has one and only one channel serving it. Indeed, that is the way in which the coverage map has generally been described and used in the past. We saw in Chapter 4, though, that frequently several channels are needed in the same channel chain to serve a particular product/segment combination. Thus the tool is far more powerful if each shaded or coloured area on the map is thought of as a channel chain rather than a single channel, even if, for shorthand, the area is labelled by the 'leading' channel in the channel chain – typically, that where the order is actually taken. This point will become clearer in the following examples.

By developing a current coverage map and brainstorming a future one, major opportunities for improving cost, reach and customer experience often emerge. Before we give a worked example of how to construct the map, we will describe two detailed case studies of its use. We begin with a highly successful project we mentioned briefly in Chapter 2, within the BT division which has been widely credited with turning around the fortunes of the UK's former monopoly telecoms provider.

BT Global Services goes multichannel

In 2000, BT's Major Customers, a £5 billion turnover division of BT serving the UK's top 1,000 companies (now part of BT Global Services), faced some major challenges in its route to market. All sales were booked by the field sales force – from a £5,000 leased line to a £100 million outsourcing contract. Despite a sales force numbering 2,000 people, BT was unable to serve the market adequately as it compensated for the decline in traditional fixed line telecommunications with growth in ICT products and outsourcing services. Some of these ICT products attracted much lower margins than BT's traditional business, suggesting a lower-cost route to market. Conversely, outsourcing contracts required intensive consultancy-led selling. Undifferentiated handling by a single field sales force was no longer sustainable.

To put it another way, the coverage map was entirely populated by one channel – the field sales force – despite the product range displaying a much increased variation in sales complexity. BT began to hypothesise a new coverage map, a simplified version of which is shown in Figure 5.2.

The field sales force would be needed more than ever for the highly complex deals, such as outsourcing with high-value customers, but BT suspected that a large area in the middle of the chart could be handled

Figure 5.2
Coverage map – BT
Major Customers
Division

effectively by the new channel of Desk-Based Account Managers (DBAMs) – fully professional account managers, but working entirely from the office. These staff would spend a higher proportion of the day in contact with customers, which, combined with savings on supporting staff on the road, would lower costs considerably. It was hoped that customers would also benefit from being able to contact a member of the account team at their convenience. At the bottom left-hand corner of the chart, simpler transactions with lower-value customers would be carried out either online or via partners.

A successful pilot with 12 DBAMs found that sales and marketing costs did indeed reduce dramatically, from 25 percent of revenue to 17 percent, adding 8 percent of revenue straight to the bottom line. It also actually found increased customer satisfaction, as customers preferred the highly available DBAMs for their simpler needs. As a result, BT had, by 2005, rolled out 400 DBAMs and reduced the field sales force accordingly. They had also introduced Desk-Based Technical Specialists to support them. BT estimated that as well as reducing costs – each field sales person costing 2.5 times as much as a DBAM on a fully allocated cost basis – this was generating over £100 million of additional annual revenue, as the field sales force was able to concentrate on high value opportunities.

The word 'led' against each area of the coverage map is significant, as the named channel is really the name of a channel chain in which the named channel is the likeliest to take the order itself. For example, the web is playing a significant role throughout the sales process in all areas of the map. Dedicated pages for large customers and web conferences help the customer to research BT's offerings, while business rules built into the web solution ensure that customer enquiries and orders are routed to the appropriate person for fulfilling. After-sales services allow customers to access basic service and billing information quickly and report faults. This takes pressure off the field and desk-based sales resources – for example, the well-supported web-based customer conferences save field sales over 500 person-days a year.

This closely integrated channel mix required careful attention to reward systems. To break channel silo habits and encourage cooperation early in the change process, BT experimented with what they called 'double bubble' – paying both desk and field resources for sales on which they cooperated. Within 6 months this was deemed too expensive, and a new system was developed that rewarded both field sales people and DBAMs for all sales over their annual targets without paying twice for each sale. The remit of each was clear – DBAMs were responsible for bringing in new business on their accounts, account managers were responsible for the entire account balance. It was in the account manager's interest to help the DBAMs sell aggressively to his or her account, and it was in the interest of the DBAM to help the account manager develop opportunities within the account that the desk could exploit.

BT has developed comprehensive business rules that allocate sales campaigns and leads appropriately, based on the logic of the coverage map. Each of the approximately 65 service and product areas sold by the division is scored on seven aspects of product complexity: product maturity, configurability and integration, commoditisation, pricing complexity, the length of time to complete the sale, the need for buyer education, and who in the client organisation buys. The scoring is agreed by the most senior people in the division and updated periodically. The score of each product determines which channel will normally sell the product. This preferred channel is embedded in the CRM system so leads are automatically allocated to the right channel, although this automatic allocation can then be overruled by the account teams if their account knowledge suggests it is wrong. Nevertheless, the DBAMs take forward more than 75 percent of enquiries that reach their desk, and win approximately 64 percent of these – an achievement that is well above BT's expectations. The DBAMs also perform a critical 'triage' function on leads generated from the web or from marketing campaigns, deciding which opportunities need to be referred to the field sales team for progressing, which need specialist input, and which ones they can action alone.

IBM rationalises its channel mix

The dotcom crash, along with a slowdown in the economy, saw a significant shift in the technology market at the turn of the millennium. 'Clients were no longer interested in technology for technology's sake,' said Kevin Bishop, Vice President of IBM.com for NE Europe. 'Instead they asked, "where's the benefit?" So it was time for us to re-evaluate our entire company structure, our whole way of working.' IBM saw that channels to market were no longer just a way of delivering sales; they had become integral to the product offering through the delivery of consultancy and service.

Analysis of customer buying behaviour provided a key insight: that the same company, even the same individual buyer, could behave differently when buying different products. Therefore, simple segmentation based on customer size and allocation of each customer to a single channel – then a common approach in the industry – was not enough to form the basis of an effective channel strategy. Instead, IBM created a coverage map, known internally as the 'nine cell blanket', which defined the various channel chains or routes to market that would be adopted for different product/customer combinations. The vertical axis considered client value; the horizontal axis considered client behaviour (see Figure 5.3).

The client behaviour axis, very close to the sales complexity axis we described in previous examples of the coverage map, divided client purchases into three groups: commoditized and simple transactions; technology platform and related services decisions; and integrated solution consulting engagements. A simple transaction could be buying additional desktop PCs or mainframe storage – in either case, the buyer would be expected to be broadly familiar with the product. The second type of transactions is typically carried out by technology experts, for example, network security products. The third category tends to be complex business

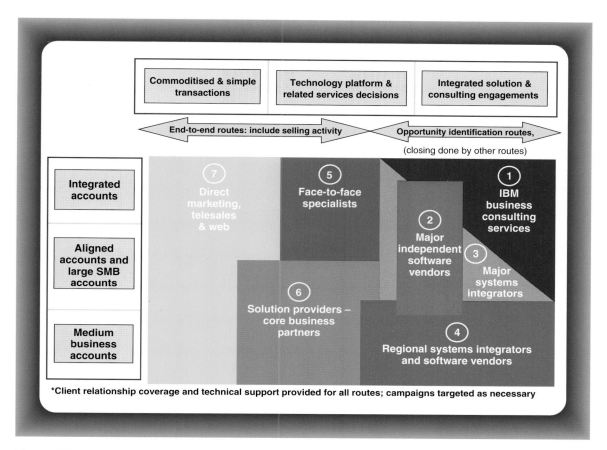

Figure 5.3
Coverage map – IBM

changes – for example, process re-engineering or applications hosting – in which the buyer groups would include both experts and non-experts.

The next step was to select a channel, or channel combination, for the different parts of this matrix. With a long list of distributors, internal client and support teams, telesales and web-based channels, the number of possible channel combinations was vast. Indeed, by the end of the 1990s, the complexity of different approaches in different areas of the business was baffling. IBM's solution was to identify seven 'preferred routes to market' (RTMs), or channel chains, which together could cater for the entire range of products and customers.

Routes to market (RTMs) were assigned a 'leading channel', but with several internal and third parties working together on the customer relationship. The channel chain in each RTM considers the value of the customer, ensuring that the transaction is economically viable. It also considers the nature of the transaction and the capability of different channels to add customer value both now and in the future.

Route 1, which addresses the most complex engagements, is led by Global Business Services, IBM's consulting arm, which includes the PricewaterhouseCoopers (PwC) Consulting operation acquired in 2002. At the other end of the spectrum, simple sales are directed to the Direct Teleweb route to market (route 7), even for major accounts. IBM's field sales force still has a vital role for large technology projects, as shown by route 5. The other routes are led by different categories of intermediary – independent software vendors, systems integrators and solution providers.

With the seven RTMs mapped over the 'nine cell blanket', clients were nominally assigned a route to market for a given product type. However, these are preferred, not prescribed, channels; ultimately, clients make the channel selection that best meets their specific requirements. The mapping is not permanently fixed, either, but dynamic and responsive to changes in the market.

To spell out how each route to market works, IBM used a standard six-stage customer lifecycle which applies to all products and services in its range, labelled relationship management, opportunity identification, opportunity ownership, fulfilment administration, implementation, and post-sale support. IBM then mapped which channels are used at which stage, how they should work together and how they hand on to the next stage (see the simplified template of Table 5.1). Thus, for each client type/product combination, who does what throughout the buying cycle is clearly defined.

This delineation of responsibility applies to both internal departments and external distributors and partners. In Route 1, for example, the resources are almost exclusively internal to IBM; the process diagram is used to delineate different roles within IBM and establish the hand-offs. In Route 6 (solution providers), it is mainly about providing the same demarcation between third-party resources; only when assistance is required are IBM resources called in. In each case, the form enables individuals – whether internal or third party – to know what part they play at what stage of the cycle. Note that the form is very similar to a channel chain diagram.

Table 5.1 Defining route to market responsibilities at IBM

	Relationship management	Opportunity identification	Opportunity ownership	Fulfilment administration	Implementation	Post sale support
Primary channel/team						
Secondary channel/team						
Deselected channels/teams						

The effects of this wholesale change to IBM's sales and marketing organisation were profound. One noticeable effect was in the generation of leads. Leads generated through the face-to-face channel dropped by 22 percent. However, a similar increase was seen in leads generated by other channels, mainly telesales and business partners. It appeared that, early in the buying process, customers prefer to seek information and make decisions themselves, either using the web or through intermediaries. This allowed IBM to shift a significant part of its face-to-face account managers to other responsibilities, such as providing support and service to existing customers. They also increased investment in web resources.

Perhaps most importantly, client satisfaction has increased, while the total cost of managing RTMs has been reduced by an estimated 50 percent, as the 'anarchy' that previously prevailed in use of channels has been curtailed and the seven RTMs are more readily manageable. At the same time, people satisfaction has also increased, both internally and among business partners, as people now understand what they have to do and where they add value.

Constructing the coverage map: Infinite Innovation Inc.

To show in detail how to construct a coverage map, we will return to the IT services provider Infinite Innovation Inc., which we used in the last chapter to illustrate channel chains – see 'Constructing channel chains: Infinite Innovation Inc.' on page 93.

In order to draw up the coverage map's horizontal axis, we need to arrange the organisation's products or services in order of sales complexity. Sometimes this can be done intuitively, but we have seen that some organisations, such as BT, find it best to draw up a number of criteria and score them in a table. We will explain this process for Infinite Innovation Inc.

The company provides three types of services: computer installation, configuration of sales and marketing software applications, and marketing consulting. Under each of these three service headings there are three to five more specific service offers. For example, the software configuration services comprise the installation of complex front-office solutions, databases, data-mining tools, sales-force automation systems and simple contact-management systems. The company has determined five factors which comprise sales complexity, and weighted each to arrive at the criteria in Table 5.2.

Against each of the services offered, the company has scored each of the complexity factors from 1 to 10 in order to create a weighted average score for each line of service (see Table 5.3).

The services are then listed along the top of the coverage map in order of increasing complexity (see Figure 5.4). The customer segments are listed down the side, with the highest-value group at the top. In this case, the three groups are large professional services companies, mid-sized retail financial services providers, and owner-managed businesses.

Table 5.2 Criteria for determining sales complexity – Infinite Innovation Inc.

Complexity Factor	Weighting
Order size – the bigger the order, the more complex	.15
Limited customer knowledge of the product or service – less customer knowledge creates more complexity	.25
Length of the sales cycle – long sales cycles increase complexity	.10
Difficulty configuring/installing – the more difficult to configure, the more complex the sale	.20
Training – the greater the requirement to train customers in the use of the application/equipment, the more complex	.20
After sales service – the more service required, the more complex the sale	.10

Table 5.3 Sales complexity scoring – Infinite Innovation Inc.

	Order size	Limited Customer Knowledge	Sales cycle	Configuration	Training	Service	Sales complexity score
Weighting	**0.15**	**0.25**	**0.1**	**0.2**	**0.2**	**0.1**	
Application Configuration							
Front office	10	7	7	7	7	4	7.15
Database	7	6	6	9	8	3	6.85
Data-mining tools	3	9	3	5	9	5	6.30
Sales-force automation	5	5	5	7	6	4	5.50
Contact management	2	2	2	2	2	2	2.00
Hardware deployment							
Desktop	8	2	2	3	3	3	3.40
Mobile phone	6	5	5	6	4	4	5.05
PDA	4	7	7	7	5	4	5.85
Laptop	7	3	2	3	3	4	3.60
Consulting Service							
DB management	5	5	7	8	6	7	6.20
Sales network	5	7	7	8	6	7	6.70
Customer strategy	3	10	7	6	N/A	N/A	7.30

Low sales complexity product-service → High sales complexity product-services

	Contact mgt application	Desktop deployment	Laptop deployment	Sales-force automation Appl.	PDA deployment	Database mgt	Data-mining tools	Sales network mgt	Database application	Front-office application	Consumer strategy
Large professional services	FS	FS	FS	FS	FS	T	T	D	D	FS	FS
Medium retail financial services	I	T	T	FS	D	I	T	I	FS	D	FS
Owner-managed businesses	T	D	D	FS	D	FS	I	I	T	FS	FS

I = Self-service over the Internet T = Desk-based account managers D = Third-party distribution partners FS = Field sales – account management

Figure 5.4
Current coverage map – Infinite Innovation Inc.

The middle of the matrix describes how the company sells each product or service to each customer, using a colour, shading or letter to indicate which areas of the map use which route to market. These are, in order of increasing cost: customer self-service on the net (I), desk-based sales conducted by telephone (T), distribution partners (D), and field-based account managers (FS). (Note: Distribution partners are often known in the IT industry as Value Added Resellers (VARs). They are often small to medium-sized IT services firms that provide specialist industry or application expertise.)

There are some obvious anomalies in the current coverage map:

● Expensive field account managers sell some very simple products; perhaps there is a culture that an account manager handles 100 percent of the customer's requirements.
● Distributors sell the company's complex database applications and sales networks to very large companies for historical reasons; does the company lack sales expertise in these areas? If there is a risk that distributors could intermediate the company and take control of key accounts, this may not be a wise policy.
● To owner-managed businesses, some of these complex services are sold via the Internet, which has a low success probability. Even smaller owner-managed businesses need some help to understand these services.

Figure 5.5 illustrates how the company drew up a future coverage map, assigning a 'lead' channel to better reflect differences in customer value and sales complexity. The redrawn coverage map focuses vital field sales resources on selling large, complex solutions to the highest-value customer group. Distributors sell large, complex solutions to smaller, lower-priority segments. Desk-based sales teams handle the middle ground: modest complexity across customer segments. Self-service over the Internet is reserved for simple products and services and for lower-priority customers, who are considered to buy largely on price and for whom a lower-cost sales model is needed in order to be competitive.

This exercise lays structure on the channel strategy, which can then be developed further to allow the channel chain to manage an opportunity through the sales and service cycle. With a lead channel for each opportunity, it can make available secondary channels to allow for individual customer preferences and to manage scarce resources optimally. Therefore, for each area of the map, a channel chain was drawn up identifying these secondary channels and their role in the process. We showed an example in Chapter 4 (Figure 4.19).

The coverage map is an equally useful tool in the business-to-consumer environment, where the consideration of sales complexity and customer value is just as relevant in taking coverage decisions, although the specific channels populating the map will obviously vary from sector to sector. Retailing operations, for example, can use the thinking to manage multiformat operations and target them to great effect to address different shopping modes and segments. This is well illustrated

Low sales complexity product-service ———→ High sales complexity product-services

	Contact mgt application	Desktop deployment	Laptop deployment	Sales-force automation appl.	PDA deployment	Database mgt	Data-mining tools	Sales network mgt	Database application	Front-office application	Consumer strategy
Large professional services	I	T	T	T	T	FS	FS	FS	FS	FS	FS
Medium retail financial services	I	T	T	T	T	D	D	D	FS	FS	FS
Owner-managed businesses	I	I	I	T	T	T	T	D	D	D	D

I = Self-service over the Internet	T = Desk-based account managers	D = Third-party distribution partners	FS = Field sales – account management

Figure 5.5

Future coverage map – Infinite Innovation Inc.

by Tesco, which operates four different formats: Tesco Express, a small-store format that sells fresh produce, wine and in-house baked goods; Tesco Metro (7,000–15,000 square feet); Tesco superstores (20,000–50,000 square feet), which also carry non-food items like DVDs and books; and Tesco 'Extra' stores (over 60,000 square feet), which have a much wider merchandise range including clothing, household goods, electronics, cosmetics and garden furniture. These stores are targeted to reach different geographic areas, and merchandise is then tailored to meet specific local requirements. The store formats are then overlaid with the Tesco.com offering in the UK to add the Internet channel, and supported by a communications programme that operates through direct mail and the web for its highly successful loyalty card.

Similarly, the multichannel approach of mobile telephony operators with stores, web, call-centre, mailing and (in time) device communications offers another example of the need and value of considering coverage.

However, in each of these cases the coverage map needs to be tailored to different ends, perhaps dealing with different steps of the customer lifecycle or considering geographic or other segment types. In each case, though, the coverage map approach can help to integrate the channel strategy into a coherent design.

■ Integrating across channels

We have discussed how to integrate the multichannel strategy across products and across customer groups. We will now turn to another integration issue: how to ensure that the customer experience is integrated across the various channels in a channel chain.

Scenario analysis

Once channel chains have been drawn up, particular attention is needed regarding how the customer makes a transition from one channel to the next, in order to ensure that the customer journey is seamless. For example, you may recall that the department store we discussed in Chapter 4 (see Figure 4.7) has a channel chain for products, like beds, which are frequently researched online but bought offline. The store made this transition easy by advertising a telephone number prominently on its website for customers to find the nearest store with a particular item in stock. This telephone number, along with a store locator, would also be automatically displayed in a message if a customer viewed an item which was currently out of stock on the website.

Drawing up detailed scenarios for common tasks that the customer might want to perform can help to with thinking through these handovers. Figure 5.6 shows an example.

	Name:	Peter Muller
	Job role:	MD of an IT company in Frankfurt.
	Background:	Herr Muller has been a standard current account customer for the last seven years and in that time his interest in investments and his financial sophistication have grown.
	Current portfolio:	Peter now has both a standard current account and flexible fund account. He holds cash, funds and securities in his accounts.
	Situation:	He has a good relationship with his broker, but also uses direct channels, especially the web, for convenience.
	Scenario:	Buying Alternative Investment Products (AIP)

Task	Channel	Experience	Implications
Initiate dialogue	Mail	Concise, signed personal note from broker, 2 weeks before annual review meeting, suggesting that Markus look into AIPs, with leaflet & web URL.	Integration of mail & face-to-face channels.
Exchange information	Web	Peter looks up his flexible fund account briefing on AIPs. He models impact on his investment portfolio using what-if facility.	Extensions to web-based portfolio management tool.
Negotiate/tailor	Face-to-face	Peter discusses options with his broker. Together they decide on appropriate level of risk.	Broker access to personal portfolios in meetings.
Etc....	Etc....	Etc....	Etc....

Figure 5.6
Scenario analysis

Here, a bank customer is considering the purchase of an additional product. At the top of the figure, the segment is brought to life by naming and describing a typical member of it. Then a table is drawn up, as shown, describing a walkthrough of the interactions between this named customer and the bank as he conducts the purchase. The walkthrough teases out ways in which the channels need to interact and support each other in order to deliver the ideal experience.

This process of 'walking through' scenarios, stepping into the shoes of the customer to make sure that the movement between the channels is smooth, can benefit from market research to *really* 'walk through' the customer journey as it is at the moment, in order to work out where the disconnects are and how better value can be created for the customer. This is illustrated in Figure 5.7, drawn from work in the travel industry looking at customers' highs and lows through their holiday experience. Travelling to the destination is often a stressful experience, battering much of the positive anticipation that has built up, to a point where some really dramatic positive experiences are needed at the start of the holiday itself if the mood is to swing up again rather than continue on a downward path. The journey back is another crucial time: even where this experience cannot be fully improved, the memory of the holiday itself can be reinvigorated by some warm communication soon afterwards.

Integration through technology

As the 'implications' column in Figure 5.6 shows, scenario analysis soon reveals many points at which data need to be shared between

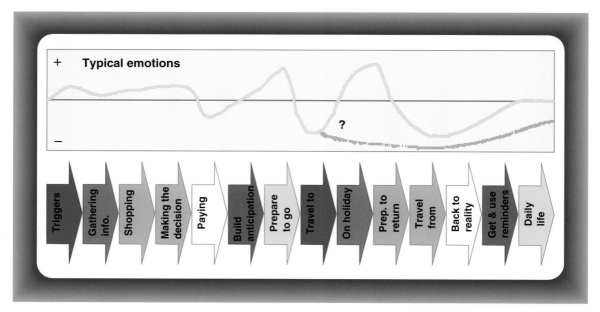

Figure 5.7
Scenario analysis and emotions – a travel company

different channels, if customers are to feel that they are dealing with an organisation where the right hand knows what the left hand is doing.

The most obvious solution is for the applications supporting the first channel to pass the specific information that is needed to the applications supporting the second channel. However, this soon results in a spaghetti-like set of connections between systems, with many performance issues and high costs of ownership. Even if it works, the end result is an inflexible system in which it is very hard to evolve channel chains over time, as is frequently needed.

A better solution, therefore, is to have a single central database for key information about the customer – at least, conceptually – with systems reading or writing to the database as required. This has been one of the major drivers of the substantial market for integrated master data and a stronger information architecture, and for the growth of broader, more integrated CRM application suites, Many organisations are working towards a unified view of the customer, so that all aspects of the customer interface can be coordinated.

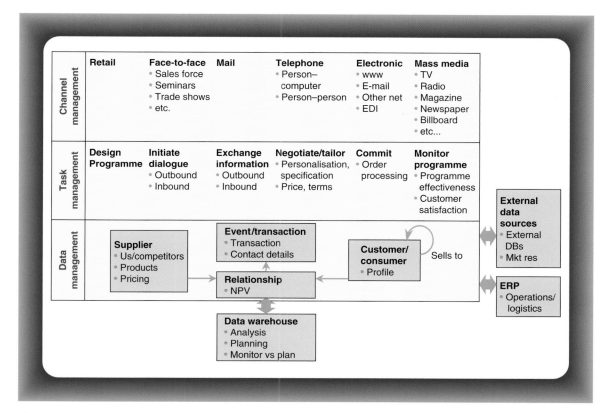

Figure 5.8
Towards a flexible CRM architecture

Task-independent data management

It is not sufficient, though, to have a single repository of customer data – difficult though that is to achieve for many long-standing organisations with complex legacy systems. The customer-facing systems also need to manage customer data independently of the task being performed. For example, if customers enter their name and address on a website, they do not wish to be asked the same information on the telephone. This requires all tasks to call on a single module which manages these customer data. We call this the principle of task-independent data management.

This point can clearly be seen in Figure 5.8. The 'task management' layer needs to be separate from the 'data management' layer, rather than systems for each task endeavouring to manage parts of the customer data – as is still often the case.

Channel-independent task management

Another point which is clearly illustrated by Figure 5.8 is the importance of channel-independent task management. The 'channel management' layer of managing different channels or media is often bundled in with particular tasks. A 'direct-mail system' will be *the* way in which the organisation generates leads; an 'order-processing system' will assume that orders come in to an order-processing clerk (rather than, say, being made by a website), and so on. Such architecture is inherently inflexible. An ideal architecture separates the issue of managing the medium from that of managing the task.

Extending the single customer view to indirect channels

It is widely accepted, then, that maintaining an integrated customer relationship is difficult, if not impossible, without an integrated customer database linked across channels as well as across products. Leading companies are extending this principle, though, to data held about the customer by intermediaries – indirect channels – as well as the company's own direct channels. The customer holds the supplier responsible for agents, distributors and retailers who provide frontline customer service, so it may be necessary to share customer contact information with them, or even to roll out the CRM system to them, too.

The logic for this is clear from our earlier discussion of channel chains. Lines on a channel chain connecting an indirect channel to a direct one will imply the customer passing between two organisations during the same purchase process. Thus, for exactly the same reason that integrated CRM systems are needed within the enterprise, there frequently needs to be data transfer between organisations to make this transition smooth.

The BT Major Customers case study we described earlier in this chapter is a good example. With a project entitled 'Managed Accounts Through Partners' (MATP), the Major Customers division reduced its number of partners to five, who collectively manage about 1,000 accounts on behalf of BT. These major distributors have access to BT's

CRM system, and record all their client details and activities on the same system. This allows BT and the partner to put together integrated marketing campaigns, as well as provide a seamless service.

General Motors' Dialogue programme, which we described in Chapter 4, is an example of the same principle of data sharing but with simpler technology. We saw how GM collected prospects' information through direct channels on such issues as when they intended to buy a new car and which models they were considering. Near to the time of intended purchase, they were therefore able to send local dealerships a list of genuinely interested prospects, along with this information. Information also needed to flow in the other direction if GM was to track the success of the programme.

Details of how this data sharing was achieved varied from country to country. In three cases – the Netherlands, Belgium and Italy – an online tool was deployed with dealers to distribute leads and collect feedback. In other countries, leads were simply faxed to dealers and, if necessary, dealers were chased regarding the end result by outgoing calls from GM's own call centres.

The role of market research

The development of an integrated IT infrastructure across channels is no small undertaking. We have seen that it is based on the principle that the customer views the organisation as a single entity and therefore expects a single, consistent response from each or any of the various individuals in many the different functional roles employed to deliver service, sales and support. Given the capital investment cost, though, hard-pressed directors might be tempted to ask: 'do customers really demand this consistency?'

Until now, the value of consistency across channels has been no more than a widely accepted premise. However, the case for the importance of consistency has just been strengthened by two pieces of research from the Cranfield Customer Management Forum.

The first involved a blue-chip organisation delivering products and services through a number of business-to-business channels. This research confirmed what CRM professionals have long suspected: consistency of information, impression and customer knowledge across different touch-points (or delivery channels) is critical. In fact, multichannel consistency ranked alongside product satisfaction in terms of its importance in driving customer satisfaction, trust and intention to repurchase (see Table 5.4). We were taken aback by quite how important multichannel consistency is – more so than website satisfaction, or call-centre satisfaction, or even sales-force satisfaction. It seems that, if the salesperson ploughs blithely on with a sales pitch without mentioning the complaint the customer made on the web yesterday, the customer is as unforgiving as if the product doesn't work.

As an important technical note to those involved in commissioning market research, the results in Table 5.4 were arrived at not by simply

Table 5.4 The importance of multichannel consistency in a large business-to-business firm

What parts of the experience matter most in driving …

Customer satisfaction	Trust	Intention to repurchase
1. **Multichannel consistency** 2. Value for money 3. Product satisfaction	1. Product satisfaction 2. **Multichannel consistency**	1. Product satisfaction 2. Value for money 3. **Multichannel consistency**

asking customers what drives their customer satisfaction, but by measuring customer satisfaction, separately asking about multichannel consistency, product satisfaction and so on, and then correlating the two using such techniques as multiple regression. This is a much more reliable way of assessing how customers actually behave.

In the second project, the same approach was applied in a business-to-consumer service organisation providing entertainment. Customers were asked the equivalent questions, and their answers again revealed the importance of channel consistency. Consistency of information, impression and customer knowledge was the only factor, apart from satisfaction with the basic entertainment service, that each time appeared amongst the top three drivers for satisfaction, trust and propensity to recommend.

Interesting it may be, but you might say this discovery is hardly going to rock the marketing world. Marketers have, after all, widely assumed the importance of consistency even without such research-based evidence. The challenge set by this research is not that marketers should *acknowledge* the importance of channel consistency, but that they should *measure* it – to make sure that they actually do something about it.

The billions that have been invested the world over in CRM software systems on the basis that the 'single customer view' will deliver an enhanced customer experience might suggest that organisations recognise the importance of channel consistency. Yet most companies continue to measure customer experience and satisfaction 'silo-fashion', with survey questions related only to certain channels. Better marketers benchmark their performance against competitors. The most innovative not only ask customers how well the company has performed, but also assess the importance of each aspect of experience through techniques such as multiple regression and structural equation modelling, to make sure time is not wasted fixing aspects of the experience that ultimately do not drive repurchasing and advocacy behaviour. However, even such relatively sophisticated techniques fail to measure multichannel consistency.

Table 5.5 Five killer questions to check multichannel consistency

In addition to your other customer satisfaction questions, ask your customers to assess their agreement with the following statements on a sliding scale

- I have a consistent impression from [company], regardless of the channel I use
- The information I get from [company] is consistent across all channels
- Rexgardless of the channel I use, people I deal with are informed about my past interactions with [company]
- I can choose among a range of channels while dealing with [company]
- Regardless of the sales channel I use to purchase from [company], I can use other channels to get information or help

So, how can you be sure that you are delivering a consistent customer experience across different touchpoints? As CRM system vendors will rightly point out, the software is necessary but not sufficient. Whilst the system may deliver a single view of the customer, it does not obviate the need for staff to be adequately trained, equipped and motivated to deliver an appropriate level of service. A bad-tempered, discouraged call-centre representative is unlikely to deliver good customer service, regardless of whether or not the CRM system has highlighted a cross-selling opportunity. Similarly, the fact that your CRM system identifies the different service-quality needs of customers will have little impact on your online sales performance if your website is unable to differentiate between and meet those service-level expectations.

If you want to know that your CRM investment is really paying off, you need to know that customers are receiving a consistent quality and value experience across all channels. This, as we have already discovered, is a core driver of customer loyalty and propensity to repurchase or recommend. Equally important, if you haven't yet got it right, is to uncover the source of the inconsistency. In doing so, you avoid being 'blinded' by your CRM system and blaming it when the failure lies in your own processes. Conversely, you also arm yourself with evidence to hold the CRM vendor to account if it is, indeed, the CRM system that has failed to deliver.

The solution is twofold. First, you need to include questions in your customer research that investigate whether the customer experience is consistent across your different channels. The five core questions used in our work with the two organisations we have described cover impression, information, choice and staff knowledge (see Table 5.5).

Secondly, when respondents are matched with their main channel chain, their responses can be broken down to identify where improvement is required. An example of this is shown in the graph in Figure 5.9. From these responses, it is evident that customers in this example who

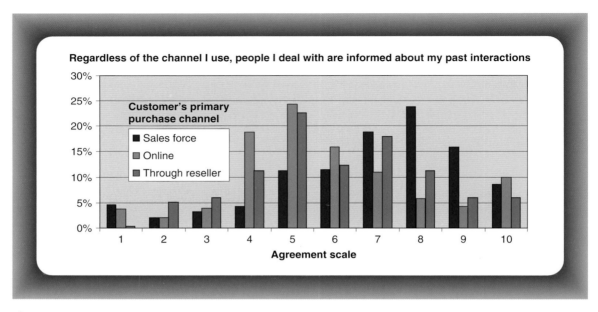

Figure 5.9
Differences in multichannel consistency across customer groups

buy mainly from the direct sales force perceive a greater level of consistency than those who most often buy online or through resellers. Further investigation will then reveal the source of this lack of consistency. It may be that the company's sales managers are particularly good at recording information in the CRM system; it might be a flaw in the online purchasing system or reseller extranet, where data is poorly recorded or utilised.

When it comes to customer satisfaction, companies are eager to deliver a good customer experience. Traditionally, marketers take a view from their customer insight and measure satisfaction against factors that they believe are important. However, even relatively sophisticated techniques fail to measure how consistent service delivery is across different customer touchpoints.

Consider the cost of investment in CRM software by organisations that fail to measure whether their CRM system actually delivers what it set out to achieve. Is your company one of them? Take a look at how your organisation measures customer satisfaction. Multichannel consistency is a crucial driver. With the amount that you invest in CRM, can you afford not to know whether it's working?

CHAPTER 6

Building the case for change

The world we have created is a product of our thinking; it cannot be changed without changing our thinking.

Albert Einstein

By this stage in the process, we have numerous ideas for improving our multichannel proposition. How will we prioritise these ideas, and build a business case for the investment needed? There are two pieces in the jigsaw that we need to fill in first:

1. What is the advantage to the customer of our proposed change? Although we have borne in mind segment characteristics when constructing channel chains, we have only assessed the customer's acceptance of our proposed channel chains intuitively. As this is crucial for estimating the impact of changes on revenue, it is best to do more detailed modelling of the customer perspective before proceeding to piloting. This is the purpose of the channel curve tool.
2. What is the impact on costs of the proposed change? Again we have assessed this only informally, in identifying the appropriate use of low-cost channels both on the coverage map and in individual channel chains. However, for complex projects, a more formal assessment will typically be needed.

We will then show how to combine this information into a prioritisation matrix, which has proved a powerful tool for board discussion, before discussing the development of a full financial business case for those ideas which have been prioritised.

■ The channel curve

Let us assume that, on the basis of our coverage map and channel chain work, we would like more customers to use a call centre or web channel in order to lower transaction costs. Clearly, we have to look at this issue from the customers' point of view: what is driving their current behaviour, and what would entice them to change? The channel curve analyses this, comparing how different channels (or different channel chains, as we will come on to shortly) rate in meeting the customers' buying criteria. This is illustrated in Figure 6.1 for a segment of the books market.

First, the main buying factors are listed along the bottom of the chart, with weights indicating their relative importance to the customer's buying decision (out of 100). These represent the key factors taken into account by the customer in deciding where to place business. In this example, these are: the cost of purchase (including mailing costs where appropriate); convenience, or the total time taken for the purchase; the ability to browse; and so on.

The ability of each channel to deliver against each factor is then rated on a 1 to 10 basis: the higher the score, the better this channel meets this buying factor.

Taking all the factors together, the Internet and physical stores have the best matches to the needs of this particular segment. In practice, different segments are best matched to different channels, which would show up

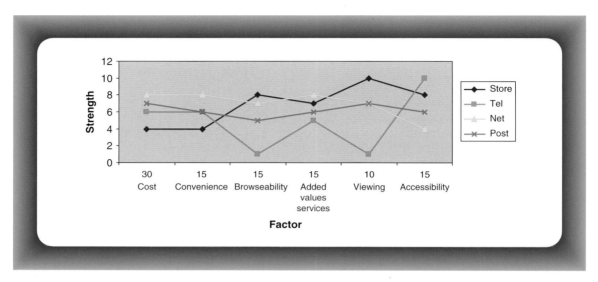

Figure 6.1
Channel curve – a books market segment

clearly if the channel curve were drawn for each segment, since each segment's buying criteria are, by definition, different from those of other segments. In practice, then, this particular manager would need to draw a similar chart for each major target segment.

If the channel phase table suggests that a particular phase of the purchasing process needs particular attention, the analysis can be focused on that phase. In this case the factors listed are those specific to that phase – those that determine which channel a customer would prefer to use for that phase of the relationship.

This example compares the inherent qualities of different channels, rather than specific competitors. If a particular channel is emerging as a candidate for improvement, though, it can be useful to benchmark the organisation's current offering through the channel against one or two major competitors, by adding a line for each competitor to the channel curve.

All this can be used to define a future proposition on the channel curve. This may simply be a question of adding a channel to the mix, or extending its capabilities to handle a wider part of the customer interaction. More often, it will involve improvements to an existing channel offer. In this case, two lines will be needed for the channel in question; one for the current situation and one for the envisaged future situation.

Collecting data for the channel curve
Where will the data come from to fill in the channel curve? Data warehouses, however sophisticated, rarely have this kind of information on customer needs. Broadly, there are two approaches:

1. Market research. This does not necessarily have to be formal: in business-to-business contexts, it can be just as effective to assemble a

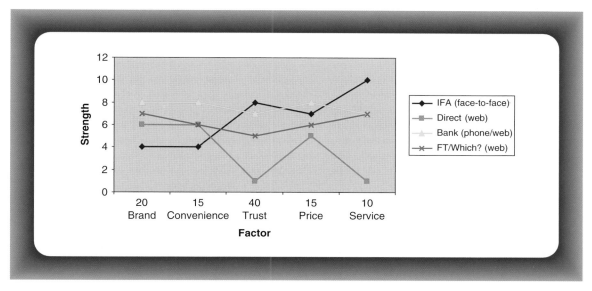

Figure 6.2
Channel curve – pensions

small team of customers, or customer representatives such as distributors or recently retired purchasing managers, and run a workshop
focused on filling in the channel curve from their perception.
2. Failing that, an internal workshop with a small group of those close
   to customers, drawn from multiple business functions, can typically
   make a fairly good estimate of customer needs.

A reality check of the results can be made by comparing the resulting channel curve with the percentages in the channel phase table. If the
channel curve suggests, say, that the call centre is ideal for placing orders
but very few customers are using it, then we have clearly got our data
wrong.

Comparing channel chains, not single channels
We chose the books example above as a simple illustration of the tool.
However, in doing so we made an important simplification: we compared individual channels that are competing against each other. More
often, as readers will know, channels work together to satisfy different
aspects of the customer needs. The example of the channel curve shown
in Figure 6.2 begins to reintroduce this complexity. This financial services
company was currently selling pensions through IFAs, but was con-
templating whether it should introduce any further routes to market –
direct on the web, selling on the web via a trusted intermediary such
as the *Financial Times* or *Which?*, or selling via integrated call centre and
Internet banks such as First Direct. This last option represents a call

centre/Internet channel combination rather than a single 'pure-play' channel. In this situation, such channel combinations can be compared on the channel curve along with any simpler 'pure-play' channel options.

In this particular case, it can be seen that the option of direct sales on the web falls down on the target segment's crucial buying criterion of trust. This reflected the conclusion from market research that while some customers were willing to do research of possible pension providers online, the great majority would then seek the approval of someone they trusted before they felt confident enough to buy such a high-involvement product. The company concluded that a website would be unlikely to deliver this trust – a conclusion which is so far consistent with the available evidence. As the chart suggests, though, they thought it possible that customers would trust a bank with high service standards, such as First Direct, sufficiently to have such a crucial conversation remotely, suggesting that some trials of this route to market might be worthwhile.

Constructing the channel curve: Infinite Innovation Inc.

For another illustration of how to construct the channel curve, we return to our example of Infinite Innovation Inc., whose current and future channel chains we described in Chapter 4 (Figures 4.18 and 4.19) and whose coverage map we showed in Chapter 5 (Figures 5.4 and 5.5). Figure 6.3 illustrates the channel curve for one of the target markets for

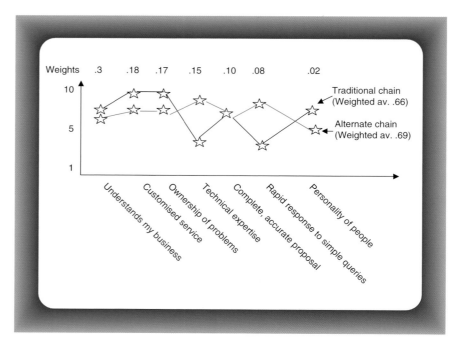

Figure 6.3
Channel curve

this IT vendor: large professional services firms. The new, mixed channel chain generates a slightly higher-weighted average customer utility score, but the difference is probably within the margin of error of the method. The extensive personal contact of the traditional channel chain generates small advantages for the more important customer criteria, but this is offset by a mixed chain's ability to respond very quickly to simple requests and greater access to technical resources 24/7 because field sales people do not have the deep technical know-how that is available via the desk and online channels.

The channel curve analysis reassures the company that the mixed channel chain is no less preferred than its traditional approach, and generates a list of key issues that the mixed chain must address – intimate knowledge of the customer's business, for example. These can be translated into key metrics against which to assess the new chain.

■ Calculating channel costs

The channel curve, then, helps us to assess a proposed future channel strategy in terms of what is in it for the customer – and hence what the likely impact on sales will be. The other main dimension we need to assess in constructing the business case is the impact on costs. This essential step is relatively easy to describe, though often a lot of work in practice.

The starting point is to analyse the costs of individual channels. Table 6.1 shows the results of an exercise to analyse costs per channel for a major airline for their four major channels: 'Trade' (the travel agents), direct sales online, and two categories of call centre. (The figures have been amended to protect confidentiality so should be regarded as

Table 6.1 Analysing channel costs – an airline

	Trade	e-Commerce	Call centre A	Call centre B
Fixed costs				
Staff & office	11.9	24.2	124.2	25.3
Investment	0.1	19.7	11.1	0.0
Maintenance	0.1	9.4	3.7	0.0
Communications	0.2	0.0	0.0	0.0
Total	*12.3*	*53.3*	*139.0*	*25.3*
Variable costs				
Distribution	24.5	5.7	4.5	5.5
Incentives	10.1	27.9	0.0	0.0
Credit card	3.1	17.3	12.6	11.3
Total	*37.7*	*50.9*	*17.1*	*16.8*
Total	*50.0*	*104.2*	*156.1*	*42.1*

illustrative.) Conventional wisdom in the airline was that e-commerce was by far the cheapest channel, and web sales were priced accordingly with large discounts. The channel director wanted to check out these assumptions in order to work out where to put his future investment.

What he found, after a lot of careful work with the accountants, combining information from different sources, came as a surprise. The 'trade' channel (sales through travel agents) had significant commission costs, so the variable costs per sale were far from negligible at 37 currency units per sale. However, web sales had an even higher variable cost, for two reasons: credit card charges, and the discounts that were being offered online in the mistaken belief that this would save the company money. Furthermore, the fixed costs were much higher for the online channel, owing to the high costs of IT development and equipment. Higher still were the costs of running call centres.

An analysis purely based on current channel cost might have led to the entirely erroneous conclusion that the direct sales channels should be closed. Indeed, the fact is that some segments wish to deal with travel agents, and this was still the most efficient way to serve customers with more complex requirements. However, other segments prefer to buy online, so the challenge was more one of getting the coverage map right and getting costs and prices in line.

The channel director therefore developed a new coverage map which directed the travel agent channel at the customers where it was needed. In the light of the cost data, he adjusted the online pricing so that only the price-sensitive segment would be discounted, and then only when the plane would otherwise not be full. He also reprioritised investment in website capabilities to reduce the load on the call centres when website users got stuck – an important multichannel effect which was driving up the call centres' overall costs. The whole scheme resulted in projected savings of several hundred million dollars over five years – a goal which the airline is on target to meet at the time of writing.

This example shows how important it is to get a handle on current channel costs. However, in the use of call centres by customers who then place the order through another channel, we have also seen how multichannel purchasing can skew these data. The same applies, of course, to other buying combinations, such as talking to a travel agent and then buying online. What we really need, therefore, is cost information not per channel, but per channel chain.

Costing channel chains: Infinite Innovation Inc.

Costing channel chains is a matter of detailed estimation of the degree to which different customer groups will use different channels and each channel's effectiveness at each step of the chain, such as converting enquiries into sales. The exercise generates metrics for efficiency (cost) and effectiveness (conversion or attainment of other objectives) that will enable managers to assess channel policy continually.

Table 6.2 Cost comparison – field only versus multichannel

Sales process	Field only			Multichannel		
	Customers	Cost £000	Cost per process £	Customers	Cost £000	Cost per process £
Enquiries	100	—		120		
Qualify	100	2,000	20,000	120	1,200	10,000
Proposal	70	3,500	50,000	85	3,000	30,500
Follow up	40	4,000	10,000	50	4,000	80,000
Close	10	2,000	20,000	15	3,000	20,000
Assess new opportunities	10	200	20,000	15	240	10,600
Customer development	10	200	20,000	15	240	10,600
Revenue	50M			75M		
Total cost		11,900			11,680	
Cost per order			1,190			1,160

The IT services provider Infinite Innovation Inc. compared the cost of the traditional field sales force against a team-based multichannel approach (see channel chains in Chapter 4, Figure 4.18 and Figure 4.19). As can be seen from Table 6.2, revenue increases 50 percent whilst costs decrease so that the cost per order falls by almost 3 percent. This results in sales costs, as a percentage of total revenue, falling from 23 percent to 15.6 percent.

Lead-generation and implementation costs are not affected by the channel chain in this case, so they are excluded from the cost analysis. The current channel chain generates sales of £50 million through 100 orders. The new channel chain will allow more enquiries to be processed, but there is no difference in the percentage of enquiries that pass through to proposal and are followed up. The closing success rate is slightly higher in the new channel chain because field sales people are focused on critical junctures of the sales process. The big difference is in the costs of qualifying each lead, generating a proposal and following it up.

■ The prioritisation matrix

All sorts of exciting possible strategies will have emerged by this point. As a result of the previous steps, the organisation will have a list of possible channel innovations, and for each, a summary of its attractiveness to customers via the channel curve, as well as analysis of current and projected future costs. However, as there is always has a limited budget and limited management time, it is now necessary to prioritise between the options available.

An approach that has been used in the context of internet innovations is the eBusiness value matrix (Hartman and Sifonis, 2000). This compares the ROI of an investment on the one hand with its risk and difficulty on the other, based on such factors such as the degree of innovation involved and the extent of change required. A variant on this theme was proposed by Tjan (2001), again focusing on the Internet.

Using this matrix, we plot the viability, or potential pay-off, of each proposed e-project against its fit – its potential to dovetail with a company's existing processes, capabilities and culture. The proposed initiatives can then be plotted on a map which suggests whether each should be invested in, redesigned, spun out or killed off (Figure 6.4).

The companies we have worked with on multichannel strategy like the idea of these tools, but report that both of them suffer from the same drawback: while they assess the attractiveness of an opportunity to the company, they do not measure its attractiveness to customers – clearly equally critical if the figures in the business plan are to be achieved, and a major failing of many a dotcom business plan.

Our channel curve addresses this problem by starting with customer buying criteria. However, although the channel curve summarises which approaches are likely to succeed in the market as a whole, an organisation

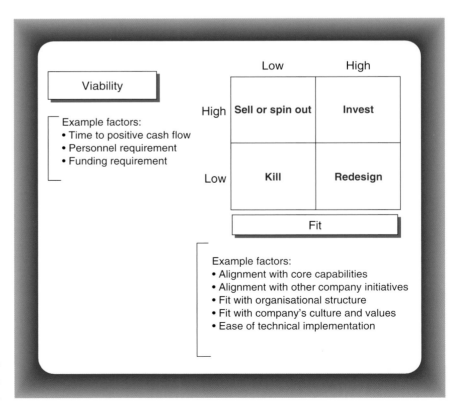

Figure 6.4
Tjan's Internet
portfolio matrix

will typically not have the resources to pursue all viable options – some of which may, in any case, deliver little value to shareholders, however welcomed by the market.

The answer is to combine these approaches in a portfolio matrix which looks both at the attractiveness of an offering to the customer, and its attractiveness to us. For this purpose, we suggest using the prioritisation matrix illustrated in Figure 6.5.

Developed by the Open University's Professor Elizabeth Daniel and the authors, this matrix compares multichannel projects against two dimensions: attractiveness to us and attractiveness to the customer. In many ways it is just like the well-known directional policy matrix we discussed in Chapter 4, which compares market attractiveness against business strengths, but this time in assessing the horizontal axis (attractiveness to the customer) we compare not rival competitors but rival channel strategies. So if, say, we are considering selling via a web and call centre combination rather than a direct sales force, how would this channel strategy compare in the customer's eyes with their current way of doing business?

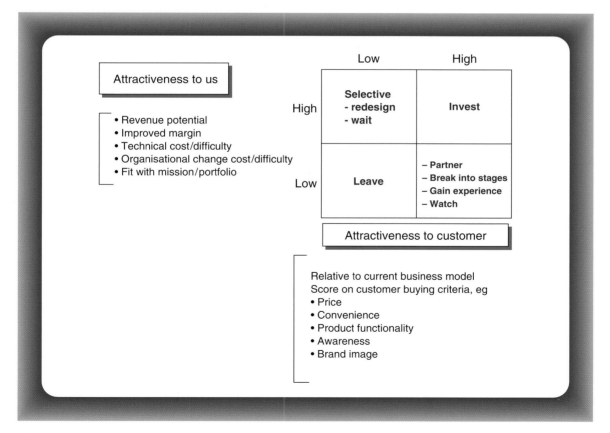

Figure 6.5
Prioritising multichannel projects

Much of the work to fill in this matrix has already been done in previous steps in the strategy process. We have compared various channel strategies against customer needs using the channel curve. Hence the horizontal axis simply corresponds to the position of the proposed route to market on the channel curve compared with the best alternative. A better curve than the alternatives will correspond to a position well to the right of the matrix. To be precise, the position on the horizontal axis can be determined mathematically using the channel curve data by comparing the weighted average score of the proposed channel with the best of the alternative channels. (If we are improving our channel offering through an existing channel, the comparison is with the curve for our current offering.) This is explained in more detail later.

The vertical axis uses a similar multifactor calculation. The figure shows some typical factors that reflect both the potential return and risk factors, such as the degree of technical and organisational difficulty, but these need to be reviewed carefully for each organisation in order to reflect its priorities. The scores can be made, as with the channel curve, on a judgemental 1 to 10 basis. Clearly this is not an exact process, but it provides a practical way of reducing the list of potential projects to a few that require the drawing up of a full investment case.

An example – insurance company

An example of the application of the matrix is shown in Figure 6.6, for an insurance company examining its distribution policy in a particular European country.

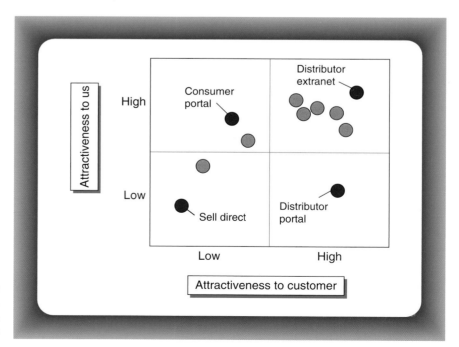

Figure 6.6
Prioritisation
matrix – insurance
company

The company drew the following conclusions about the four sample projects we have labelled in the figure:

1. A *distributor extranet* was a potential project to provide web access to the financial advisers who distributed its products, as an alternative to the call centre and account managers currently available to them. A clear win–win for the highly technical advisers, this was implemented as soon as possible, along with some of the other projects in the top right quadrant, starting with those closest to the top right-hand corner.
2. Another easy decision was on *sell direct* in the bottom left quadrant, which the company decided not to proceed with. This actually scored so low on customer attractiveness that it was off the left-hand edge of the scale. The internal team doing the scoring believed, based on the available market research, that the few customers who were yet prepared to buy long-term savings products without any form of advice would probably prefer to use a fund supermarket to compare different offerings. Its low margins and channel-conflict issues gave it a low score on the 'attractiveness to us' axis, too.
3. A *distributor portal*, a new, web-based intermediary between the insurance company and its financial advisers, was likely to reduce prices, and forming such a portal was also outside the organisation's current skill set, so this scored fairly low on 'attractiveness to us'. However, because it was attractive to customers, the company decided it would happen anyway in due course. So it decided to partner with another company offering this service.
4. Regarding a *consumer portal*, the company felt it possible that one-stop shops to buy savings products by telephone and Internet might become more attractive to consumers, in the same way as, say, car insurance has changed. The company took a watching brief, to see whether customer views would move this towards the right over time.

Constructing and interpreting the matrix

To illustrate how the calculation works, Figure 6.7 shows the data for the horizontal axis in the case of the distributor extranet. The scores for the 'present business model' of face-to-face and telephone dealings with the financial advisers are compared with the scores that are anticipated if the extranet is implemented. It can be seen that the extranet is expected to reduce costs for the insurance company, some of which can be passed on in slightly higher commission – the single most important buying factor in the judgement of the company – as well as in slightly lower charges to the end consumer (a relatively minor advantage, as its weighting is only 2 out of 100). Furthermore, it will help the financial adviser's administration, and provide some additional sales support aids such as calculators, as well as helping the insurance company's brand

CSF	Weight	-NewBusModel- C	PresentBusModel C
▶ -PorterCOST-	0		
Admin	5.	6.	5.
BrandReputInnov	8.	7.	4.
Commission	40.	8.	7.
InvestFundChoic	15.	8.	8.
PastPerformance	20.	7.	7.
PriceCostCharge	2.	5.	4.
SalesSupport	10.	7.	5.
Weighted Sum		7.46	6.55
Normalised (Avg)		1.06	0.94
Normalised (Best)		1.14	1.

Figure 6.7
Channel curve
data – extranet for
insurance IFAs

image and reputation for innovation. The net result is a weighted average score of about 7.5 if the extranet is implemented as against 6.5 at present, resulting in a relative score of +1 – a position substantially to the right of the midline on the matrix (which represents a score of 0). In other words, this innovation would be welcomed by the company's immediate customers, the financial advisers, who make a large proportion of the buying decision.

As for the interpretation of the matrix, summarised in Figure 6.5, the implications of the right and bottom left boxes are fairly straightforward (though, as usual, with portfolio matrices the cross-hairs should not be taken too literally, given the judgemental way in which the matrix has been constructed). Opportunities that are highly attractive to both the organisation and the customer are likely to be targets for investment, while those that are attractive to neither will probably be ignored.

The advice in the top left box is again fairly close to the Boston Consulting Group's original formulation for the Boston Matrix and its Directional Policy Matrix variants, in which the equivalent box was termed 'question mark'. The 'question' with these opportunities, which are highly attractive to us but less so to customers, is whether they can be moved to the right. For example, opportunities in the insurance company which scored low due to low customer connectivity to the Internet, or low current speeds of service constrained by narrowband connections, suggested opportunities which could be taken when judged sufficiently close to a point where customer take-up would become significant.

The interpretation put on the bottom right box by practitioners is perhaps surprising for those used to the Directional Policy Matrix. Some of the insurance company's projects in this box were targets for partnering

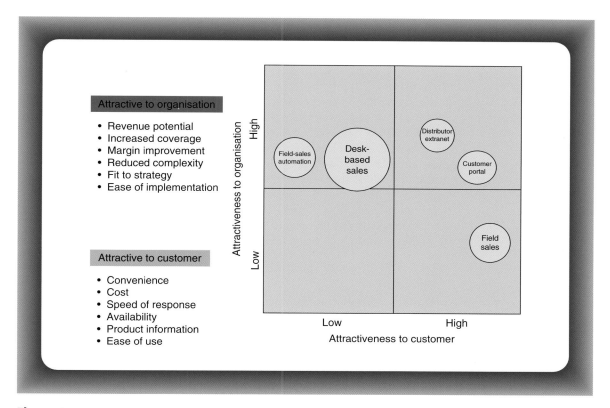

Figure 6.8
Prioritisation matrix – Infinite Innovation Inc.

strategies, in which partners would be chosen to counteract the factors which led to a low score on attractiveness to us. A poor fit with the organisation's technical and organisational skills, for example, was countered in one case by a plan to find an appropriate partner with the right skills. In another case, the opportunity was felt to be outside the organisation's mission, but leaving it to competitors would have left the organisation too exposed, leading again to a partnering strategy.

Another potential strategy in this box is to break the project into stages. This may be appropriate where the project has high risks, which could be reduced through a staged approach.

Constructing the prioritisation matrix: Infinite Innovation Inc.

We continue our worked example of Infinite Innovation Inc. with their prioritisation matrix (Figure 6.8). In a useful variation on the way we have described the matrix so far, this example varies the diameter of the circles to represent the size of investment being made by the company in channel innovations.

In this example, we can see that the largest channel investments are in chains and solutions that are least attractive to customers. The channel investment most valued by customers (more field sales people) is unattractive to the company and not receiving a lot of investment. Perhaps this is the most attractive to customers because they are not used to team-based, multichannel selling from the company. Perhaps they are not convinced that the company can implement it effectively, and are worried that service levels will fall. The two projects that are in the top right quadrant receive the smallest investment. The prioritisation matrix suggests that the company should increase investment in the portal and extranet. Field-sales automation is not what customers value, so that might be implemented selectively. Desk-based sales might be critical to making team-selling work, but it seems to dominate the investment portfolio. Perhaps it could be introduced more slowly to allow funding to be redirected to projects of higher customer priority. Field-sales investment is valued by customers, but is not attractive to the company; can investment be more selective until other channels demonstrate their value to customers?

The prioritisation matrix, then, is useful for slimming down the wide range of potential projects for improving the route to market. The insurance company found that the tool provides a welcome structure to the board's decision-making debate, and rapidly sorts out which projects are the top priorities. It also forces the proponents of a project to ask the right questions early on, thereby increasing the quality of proposals put to the board. However, it does not remove the need for a detailed financial investment case for projects which seem, on this judgemental basis, to be candidates for go-ahead. We now turn to the construction of this investment case.

■ Building a full financial case

For prioritised projects, there is a need, next, to develop a detailed investment case. This enables the project's return on investment (or net present value, according to the preferences of the company) to be assessed for funding purposes.

The means of constructing the financial case will vary according to the nature of the project and the company's conventions but, generally, some kind of cost/revenue model will need to be built for the company's marketing and distribution channels, incorporating revenues and costs for each channel as well as costs that are not channel specific. We have dealt with some of the cost issues in the previous section.

By modelling future years as well as the current year, the impact of the project on costs as well as revenues can be estimated. Anticipated revenues, particularly, will still need management judgement, but at least the channel curve means we have some kind of rational basis for making this estimate. If a large increase in market share is anticipated, for example, this should be backed up by a significant improvement on the channel curve.

One thorough approach to building such a cost/revenue model is to use customer lifetime value (CLV) (Blattberg *et al.*, 2001), assessing the impact of a project on the sum of the customer lifetime value across all customers. A CLV approach is worth working towards, but for most organisations today this is simply not possible, as they do not have appropriate data. Most struggle even to understand current profitability by customer or by channel.

A simpler model of costs and revenues will therefore often need to be constructed and used to assess the impact of a project. The model can concentrate on those parts of the overall picture that are most likely to be impacted by a proposed project. Is the project tackling fixed costs, acquisition costs, ongoing transaction costs or retention costs? Are its revenue objectives based on improving post-sales service and thereby retention rates, or improving conversion rates and thereby market share?

To start, a baseline needs to be created of the current costs and revenues across the chosen channels, as discussed earlier in this chapter. While measures will vary according to the company and channels under review, some typical measures are listed by way of example in Figure 6.9.

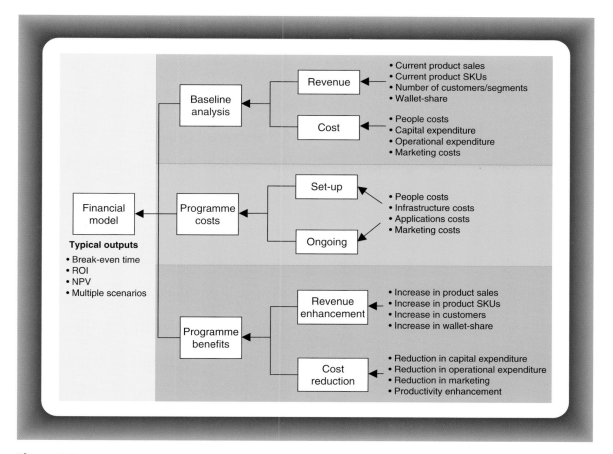

Figure 6.9
Financial impact of channel strategies

Once a baseline has been captured, it is time to consider the likely programme costs. Here, it is important to consider all aspects of the proposed project(s) identified in the prioritisation matrix. Typically, these should include any external costs to outside vendors as well as internal costs. It is important to document the assumptions made in making these estimates of both the set-up and ongoing costs.

Finally, total programme benefits should be measured in terms of cost reduction and/or revenue enhancement. Here, the specific measures will depend on the company, business unit and channel(s). However, it is often advisable to design multiple scenarios for the programme benefits, thus helping to mitigate risk and assess the likelihood of an attractive break-even and return on investment (ROI).

An example of a successful multichannel programme investment case is provided by a large, fast-moving consumer goods (FMCG) company. The company was suffering from a downturn in profitability, despite owning an excellent range of household brands. Closer inspection of its existing channel operations showed that an expensive sales force was being employed across all customers, from the corner shop to the national supermarket chain. This cost drain was compounded by a reliance on lengthy paper order-forms that needed to be re-typed, resulting in errors, delays and process inefficiencies.

The sales force was supported by a call-centre operation. However, the call-centre staff's main functions were to take '*ad hoc*' customer orders and deal with the wholesalers; fielding after-sales service enquiries originating from sales-force relationships was secondary. Moreover, the call-centre operation was not using a system integrated to back-end systems. This made it impossible to deal with real-time customer enquires about particular orders.

For this company, therefore, the cost of maintaining the channel infrastructure was extremely high in relation to best practice in the industry. Furthermore, it seemed a fair guess that the poor non-integrated customer experience across multiple channels was losing the company revenue.

A total multichannel programme was therefore initiated, split into three work streams:

1. *Deploy a field-force effectiveness solution* – the sales force was cut back and re-focused on the most profitable accounts. Their effectiveness was improved by e-enabling them with wireless field-sales devices that would allow them to enter orders, prioritise their accounts easily and give real-time 'added value' information to customers.
2. *Build and deploy an extranet* – all customers were given access to an extranet making available the full range of products, product information and order history. This enabled them to order when they wanted, and to get direct access to valuable point of sale information and of course product details. This also applied to the wholesalers. In turn, the company was able to cut costs dramatically from the sales force and back-end administration support.

3. *Streamline and re-focus the call centre* – in the old model, the call centre was generally reactive and essentially supported the administration of order entry. The call-centre applications were replaced so that they could integrate fully with the other channels and back-end systems. Moreover, the development of the extranet helped the call centre not only to support the two primary channels to market – the direct sales force and extranet – but also proactively to contribute to the 'identification', 'qualification' and 'sell' stages of the sales cycle.

The investment case was very attractive. Restructuring and process redesign meant that operational costs were slashed by 40 percent across the channel mix, while revenue increased by 11 percent. The revenue increase could be directly attributed to better segmentation and targeting, and more effective use of the direct sales force and call-centre customers.

It is instructive that the original sign-off for the investment case, though, was based on a simple break-even analysis. Often, there is a temptation to 'boil the ocean' with immense detail and pages of assumptions. However, there are dangers in making the business case too complicated, with too much detailed analysis founded on numbers which, inevitably, are mere estimates. The appearance of precision can lead to these numbers being treated with excessive reverence, and can obscure the main argument. In our experience, it is better to keep a relatively simple modular approach to multichannel projects and ensure that large projects are split into separate phases or work streams, each with their own manageable investment cases.

■ References

Blattberg, R.C., Getz, G. and Thomas, J.S. (2001). *Customer Equity: Building and Managing Relationships as Valuable Assets*. Harvard Business School Publishing.

Hartman, A. and Sifonis, J. (2000). *Net Ready*. McGraw-Hill.

Tjan, A.K. (2001 February). Finally, a way to put your Internet portfolio in order. *Harvard Business Review*, 76–87.

PART 3

Making multichannel work in practice

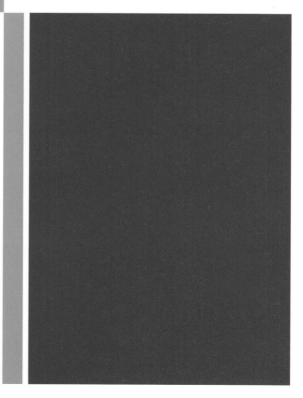

CHAPTER 7

Organising
for successful
change

It is not necessary to change. Survival is not mandatory.

W. Edwards Deming

Every time we were beginning to form up into teams, we would be disbanded. I was to learn later in life that we tend to meet any new situation by reorganising; and a wonderful method it can be for giving the illusion of progress, whilst producing confusion, inefficiency and utter demoralisation

Petronius Arbiter, 210 BC

One of the questions we get asked most frequently by clients who have identified a need to change their multichannel strategy concerns the organisational structure they should adopt to maximise their success with the new strategy. After all, it may be stating the obvious, but a new strategy is almost certain to entail at least some change in structure if it is to work effectively. At its core, strategy is simply a sustainable pattern of resource allocation. It therefore follows that a decision to change the multichannel strategy (in other words, to change the channel resource allocation pattern) means that we need to reconsider the organisational structure which marshals these resources.

At least these organisations are asking what their future structure should be, even if the answer is not obvious. Remarkably, some companies – though thankfully few – omit to consider their organisational structure at all and, curiously, expect to be able to deliver the results demanded by the new strategy without making any significant changes to their structure at all.

A quick route through this chapter

Organising for successful change is complex, and so therefore is this chapter. The reader with limited time may wish to follow the following quick route through the chapter, and return to other sections as necessary:

1. Organisational structure: see the BT and IBM examples in the section 'SBU structure and organisation', from page 146
2. Diagnosing cultural issues that need to be changed: see the cultural web tool in the section 'Resolving contradiction between stakeholder groups', from page 156
3. Managing a multichannel project to achieve the benefits you want: see 'The Benefits Dependency Network project management tool' from page 168
4. Successful piloting of new channel models: see 'Positive piloting – Vauxhall's two way communication pilot', from page 172.

■ Fundamentals of organisational structure

In Chapter 4, we looked at what our different channels need to deliver to different customer groups. When considering how the organisation will achieve that, the fundamental rules of business apply concerning how resources (both human and capital) are structured, how the flow of information, goods and services is enabled, and how the necessary changes are managed and enabled. However, at the same time as we urge readers to remember the overarching rules that apply to structural reorganisation generally, it is also worth noting that, in our experience, there are some ways of approaching this question that work better than others for multichannel organisations.

So what is the 'right' structure for a multichannel organisation? It is unfortunate but true of academics and consultants that we cannot answer simple questions like this one with a simple answer, as each organisation is unique. However, we can reduce the answer to two key areas about organising for successful change that are worth covering specifically in a book about multichannel marketing:

1. *SBU structure and organisation*. We will share some factors that need specifically to be addressed by multichannel organisations, and some examples of companies that have used their insight successfully.
2. *Change management*. It is in the management of change that we have seen some of the most stark contrasts between those companies who exhibit good practice with resultant success and those who fail to recognise the unique aspects of multichannel strategy change which need to be addressed as part of the change management process.

SBU structure and organisation

As with any major corporate decision, structure is, by necessity, situation-specific and contingent on the organisation itself. This means that most organisations face the usual challenges that crop up not only with structural reorganisation but with any significant change. They are faced with the need to create a new organisation that will suit the requirements of the new strategy but with which the organisation will feel internally 'comfortable', and which will not be obstructed by politics or lack of management ability to implement the change.

We will therefore start with two successful examples, but with the caveat that we suggest these not so that others can precisely emulate the structure that they have adopted, but rather in order to understand why their structure works *for them* and to emulate the process they used to design it.

Fitting structure with strategy and culture: BT and IBM

BT and IBM both redesigned their organisational structures as part of moves towards a new multichannel strategy. The structures they chose are widely different from one another, and yet each is successful for the organisation that designed it.

The BT Major Customers division, whose coverage map we described in Chapter 5, has mastered the art of creating an integrated channel structure whilst maintaining the role of account managers and leveraging their intimate knowledge of the customer and ability to customise BT offers. BT manages the multichannel strategy with two governance boards that meet monthly. The Account Management Governance Board sets policies and manages the progress of the technology enablers needed. The Multichannel Governance Board sets business policies and operational strategies that drive multichannel marketing throughout the business. This latter board comprises the head of the Major Customers business unit, heads of marketing, channel heads, and heads of the account management groups. They manage the development and changes to coverage maps and policies, make sure that channels integrate, decide which accounts are better managed by partners, and so on.

Account Management is still responsible for account development but, instead of this being a single channel responsibility for the sales force, they are now responsible for the account regardless of channel (see Figure 7.1). The new channels are managed by Channel Marketing, but they are

	Account Management			
	Government	**Financial services**	**Commercial & brands**	**Corporate mid-market**
Channel marketing	Field sales Government	Field sales Financial services	Field sales Commercial	Field sales Corporate
Desk-based resource	DBAM DBTS	DBAM DBTS	DBAM DBTS	DBAM DBTS
BT.com				
Partners				

Figure 7.1
BT Major Customers structure

managed on service-level agreements, with each 'vertical' leader responsible for a set of accounts. Every month, the Head of Channel Marketing has a review with each vertical leader to ensure that channel performance meets expectations and continues to support the future plans of that vertical group.

The Desk-Based Account Managers (DBAMs), and the Desk-Based Technical Specialists (DBTS) who support them, are located within three major offices of BT in the UK. Each desk-based person works within a specific vertical business unit (e.g. Government, Finance) and participates in his or her account teams' weekly sales meetings (normally by telephone). They are recruited, paid and performance-managed by Channel Marketing to promote the spread of best practice, maintain resource flexibility, and provide a strong sense of identity and cooperation with other DBAMs. Nonetheless, each account team has its own working practices and, whilst some DBAMs are dedicated to one account, some can support the work of three or four accounts. This requires considerable flexibility and maturity on the part of DBAMs.

Conversely, we see the comparative fluidity of the IBM model, which, as we described in Chapter 5, involves seven overlapping routes to market for different types of client need and different priority and scale of accounts (see Figure 5.3). The IBM model is driven by metrics, and relies on good internal communication. This model works to match the immediate nature of the customer need with the best channel through which that need can be fulfilled, and an explicit recognition of the fact that the same account will want to work through different channels for different needs.

The presence of a client manager, based in the sales and distribution arm of IBM and covering one or many accounts, provides a coordination and information point that clients can use for escalation and direct dialogue. A strong emphasis on communications, a common and structured sales process and a shared base of information helps to smooth what might otherwise be a complex model.

IBM has seen many benefits in terms of access, cost to serve, and the provision of integrated offers. One of its strengths is its fluidity. It has continued to evolve over the last decade, most notably as the web has continued to increase in importance as a medium in all channels, and as many of the partners' own business models have blurred and the shape of their offerings to customers and partners has changed.

In many respects the choice of how to engage is made by the customer, although dialogue between the different parts of IBM and the client manager informs the way that a response is handled, and a close working relationship between the client manager and IBM services plays an important role in managing the larger customers who draw on the widest range of IBM's capability. As a result, the IBM organisation can be very fluid in its contact with customers. This works in an organisation that is as large and complex as IBM, where it would be extremely difficult for a single client manager to understand all the different product and service areas that a customer might require. The client managers seek to focus their energies on understanding their particular customers and what their issues and requirements are, what they are trying to achieve. The client managers can then act as a kind of 'filter' or 'platform' through which other areas of IBM pass to reach the customer, offering the specific solutions and products that are required. Importantly, contact between different areas of IBM and the customer may be either indirect (through the client manager) or direct (informing the client manager), as this ensures that such a complex and multi-faceted relationship does not become clogged or bottlenecked.

Reconciling the existing with the new

Redesigns of a new structure rarely occur without having some kind of legacy structure that needs to be taken into consideration. Most large organisations have not just one structure to consider but several. It is not uncommon for a single organisation to go through a series of structural reorganisations. For example, from starting with a European structure, a company might have moved to a structure based on centres of excellence, then a European structure with some kind of matrix overlay. Many companies change their structure every few years and since, in our experience, none of these structures works intrinsically any better than the others, the net result is simply that people within organisations become mistrusting of and resistant to another structural change.

We do not suggest, therefore, that wholesale structural change, designed around the multichannel strategy, is the answer. Indeed, our research has shown that doing this often results in an 'ivory tower' syndrome, where employees regard the multichannel activity as disconnected from other parts of the business process, with negative consequences and a feeling of functional insularity.

However, it is important that the organisation is enabled to deliver the strategy. One way of considering organisational design is to think of it as a way to reconcile three sets of interests that at best differ from – and in some cases completely contradict – each other. From this perspective, there are three parties involved, each with their own agenda:

1. *The owners and leaders of the organisation.* In a commercial organisation, the core interest of this group is to optimise risk-adjusted return on investment. This means maximising the revenue and minimising the costs, and doing so in a way that does not take an inappropriate amount of business risk. In non-profits, the terminology is different but the principles remain the same. A charity, for instance, might want to optimise its donated income, and the positive outcomes it gets from spending that income, whilst minimising administrative and fundraising costs and without contradicting any of its core values. To make life more complicated, the goals of the owners of the business may be coherent at a high level (e.g. optimise the share price) but more complex at lower levels (e.g. grow one business area, 'milk' another).

2. *The executives and employees of the firm.* Those tasked with implementing the actions that flow from an organisation's strategy will, hopefully, share the goals of the organisation. However, they may also have other

functional or individual goals. Marketing, finance, research or any other department may be seeking to drive the company in a direction they see best. Commonly used labels like 'product led' or 'sales led' are often used to describe firms that have succumbed to factional interests in this way. Similarly, individuals may have explicit or implicit goals to maximise their benefits (e.g. a salesperson on commission) or minimise their personal 'costs' (e.g. a customer-service representative wanting to avoid difficult customers). It is not hard to see that the agenda of those who implement business plans is not one agenda but often many, and why, in any exercise to implement channel change, the interests and responses of the frontline staff and their managers can make or break an initiative.

3. *The customers.* At the simplest level, customers can be thought of as behaving like Adam Smith's rational economic man (Smith, 1776). They simply seek to meet their needs as best they can ('maximise utility', in economist terms) at the lowest possible cost. In reality, however, customers' needs and costs are both complex.

In all markets, customers have basic needs that must be met (for example, the service must be legal, the product must perform its technical function, the service needs to be accessible to the customer). However, in most markets with a surfeit of choices these needs are often well fulfilled, and higher needs include personal fulfilment, image, and association with values-drive behaviour (e.g. green, efficient). Similarly, what customers regard as 'cost' is not simply the direct price cost of the product or service; it also includes indirect costs, such as running costs, and the time and hassle to source and set up a product. Anyone who has switched office software or mobile phones is familiar with the hidden time costs of the new acquisition. To complicate matters further, of course, there is not a single, homogeneous group of customers. In mature markets, customers segment into many different groups driven by different needs.

Looked at from the multiple stakeholder perspective, organisational design is more complex than sketching out an organogram. Failure to address the needs of any owners, implementers or customers will result in their 'opting out'. Owners can withhold resources and replace executives. Employees can (usually tacitly) withhold commitment or, in extreme cases, sabotage implementation. Customers can, of course, go elsewhere.

Organisational design therefore starts with understanding the complex, fragmented and conflicting needs of these three stakeholder groups.

Customers

Customers are almost always the best place to start in the consideration of stakeholders. They are ultimately the source of continuing value through sales revenue, and they often provide the most compelling reason to change, as their behaviour and response is so independent of the interests of the organisation.

In Chapter 2, we discussed the value drivers that underpin your company's need to change its multichannel approach. These are the factors which will drive the response of customers to your overall proposition compared to that of your competitors. Value drivers fall into three key areas: access, cost and customer experience. These are not mutually exclusive, of course, but to be valid they must always be considered from the customer perspective. A common mistake made by many companies is that they treat their own drivers (e.g. cost reduction) as though they were a matter of customer preference, and indeed often assume that they can reduce their costs and not the customers and expect the customer to appreciate it.

These value drivers should also be considered when you look at customers as a stakeholder group when you are designing your future multichannel structure.

Access

How convenient and easy is it for customers to buy your product in a way that suits them, or to answer their support or account queries? Customer behaviour and preferences vary not just segment by segment but also by mode (e.g. the difference between a major family food trip and a quick visit to buy forgotten items in the lunch hour). Given the choice, different customers will choose to contact you or to purchase in different ways. As one regular book-buyer we know put it:

> I am usually quite happy to purchase a novel or business book sight unseen over the Internet, simply based on the description and reviews or recommendations. However, when buying children's books, I prefer to visit a bookstore to browse. Since a child's book is likely to be a gift (which, in my case, probably means that time is a greater consideration than cost) I am also more likely to purchase my chosen book there and then, whilst a book I might come across for myself on the same visit, I am more likely to add to my Amazon wish list or purchase online later in order to avoid carrying it home.

Designing the internal structure in such a way as to support the channel chains that evolved out of our discussions in Chapter 4 is important. This may mean internally creating communication links across multiple channels to ensure that the customer experience is seamless as customers access different channels at different times. It may mean opening up different channels to different groups of customers to give them greater control over which channels they use for which part of their decision-making or purchasing process.

Cost reduction

If customers perceive the proposition to be expensive compared to that of competitors – if, in other words, they are looking for increased value through a reduction in the price of goods or services – then it is worth encouraging customers as much as possible to use lower-cost alternative channels in order to reduce cost to serve.

When designing an organisational structure, it is worth considering the stages in the purchase where customers might use lower-cost channels without detracting from their overall experience. BT successfully achieved this with their redesigned channel structure (previously discussed). Their Desk-Based Account Managers were able to deliver a level of service that matched customer needs and expectations at least as well as – and in some ways better than – the previous model, which relied on heavy use of a direct sales force. The fact that customers of all sizes also had access to the web channel for uncomplicated, routine purchases and simple queries gave them added value through greater control. Above all, though, this new model significantly reduced the cost to serve these business customers, allowing BT to keep its prices competitive in the eyes of customers comparing the value of a BT proposition with that of competitors.

Customer experience

Customer satisfaction appears high on the list of factors that companies use to measure their performance and to benchmark themselves against competitors. However, as we have already outlined, customer experience in a multichannel environment is particularly important because customers perceive channels as simply different parts of the same organisation or brand, whether or not that organisation has integrated the channels at the 'back end'.

Thus, one of the first (if not the easiest) steps in terms of reviewing an organisational structure to improve the overall experience of a multichannel customer is to remove channel silos and integrate different channels across the structure. For the fortunate, this may have the happy consequence that your customers will more readily move to a lower-cost channel of their own accord (e.g. using the web rather than call centres if they feel more in control and know that they still have access to a 'real person' should they get into difficulty). However, the fact that the *organisation* may well be faced with the two (often conflicting) goals of improving the customer experience and reducing cost to serve does not mean that the *customer* will associate the same two behavioural activities! Too many managers fall into the trap of convincing themselves that their strategy will necessarily achieve both aims. In most cases, improving the customer experience adds cost – at least initially – and which goal takes precedence is a matter of strategic decision.

Once again, this means understanding customer segments well and knowing where they derive value from the channel chains they use. Is a small increase in cost to serve justified by the improved experience? Or is the company's aim to streamline and reduce costs to serve (even at the risk of a reduced customer experience) because customers place higher value on knowing they receive the lowest possible price?

Lands' End prominently displays its toll-free telephone number on its website to allow online customers immediately to access helpful call-centre staff, and offers real-time chat and personal assistance. Its investment in both online and offline channels as an integrated channel choice is aimed at providing a better customer experience rather than reducing costs. Conversely, the Amazon website attempts to anticipate all likely questions in its online help menu but makes it impossible to find a telephone number (at least as far as we've found), and the closest an online customer will get to a real person is 24-hour email response. These very different approaches are equally valid. Although the Lands' End and Amazon online channels are quite different in their approach, both are successful. The reason? They have each designed their channels to deliver value *as their target customers would define the term.*

The customer point of view

Understanding the customer's point of view really is the key to understanding the value drivers that should influence structure. In order to gain insight into where customers are seeking greater value, we suggest the reader should consider one or several of their own customers with whom there is an 'issue' – for example, where the company is not currently meeting the customer's value needs. Value drivers generally apply to a specific group of customers, so it should be possible to look at customers either as individuals (for a relatively small company) or by segment (for a larger company with good segmentation), and understand where value is derived from their point of view.

The channel chain analysis tool we discussed in Chapter 4 is an excellent way to uncover the value drivers that the organisation needs to accommodate. In turn, those value drivers form the basis for design of an organisational structure that will resolve or improve the delivery of customer value.

Leadership of the company

It is, of course, all very well to focus on the customers and understand what their needs are. However, ultimately most managers are accountable not to the organisation's customers but to its leaders, whether the board of directors, the shareholders or another group. The company's leaders generally have a very clear idea about what they want the company to achieve, and it can almost always be drilled down to a succinct goal of financial growth in either profit or turnover, or both. This is the ultimate goal to which a multichannel strategy is expected to contribute.

It is also the case that the company will have some kind of strategy in place to achieve these financial goals. There may or may not be an explicit strategy document detailing the overall way in which the company's leaders expect to meet their financial objectives, but in every company we have worked with there is an understanding amongst those leaders about how the profit is to be delivered.

At an operational level, the number of possible strategies a firm might employ to deliver its profit or other goals might seem bewildering. However, Porter's work on competitive strategies clarified this by recognising that almost all strategies fall into one of three 'generic' types (Porter, 1980):

- *Cost leadership,* in which resources are focused on being the lowest-cost producer in the market and the offer to the customer being based around low price – Wal-Mart or Ryanair typify this approach

- *Differentiation*, in which resources are focused on being the 'best' in some dimension of product or service performance – Sony and IBM provide examples of this approach
- *Niche*, in which resources are focused on meeting the needs of a tightly defined (but not necessarily small) group of customers – V-tech applies this strategy to the children's computer market, as does IMS in the field of pharmaceutical market intelligence.

Which of these generic strategies is adopted has huge implications for the role of channels. This is perhaps best understood by considering the ideas of Treacy and Wiersema (1995), who adapted Porter's generic strategy ideas and took an internal rather than customer perspective.

According to Treacy and Wiersema, successful firms choose to concentrate their resources on being operationally excellent, or being product excellent, or being customer intimate. These correspond approximately to cost leadership, differentiation or niche generic strategies. The central premise of Treacy and Wiersema's work is that being excellent (i.e. significantly better than the competition) in any dimension requires resources, and no firm has the resources to be truly excellent in more than one dimension at any one time. Even if it did, the culture and philosophy of each approach is contradictory. Imagine Ryanair trying to care about a customer's needs, or Ferrari trying to be cheap and cheerful. As a consequence, successful firms allocate resources so as to be excellent at different parts of their value chain. Operationally-excellent firms focus on operations and supply-chain management, product-excellent firms concentrate on innovation and product development, and niche firms focus on understanding customer needs. The corollary of this focus is that these firms accept being merely adequate or acceptable in the two areas they chose not to focus upon. Treacey and Wiersema's ideas provide a good explanation of how firms succeed and also how firms fail. Their explanation of failure is that firms lack the discipline to focus and, as a result, spread resources too evenly. The consequence is that they are better than adequate but not excellent in any of the parts of the value chain. Such firms fall victim to more disciplined, focused competitors.

The work of Porter and of Treacy and Wiersema is important to multichannel marketing. Consider the primary role and design implications of the three approaches:

- Operationally-excellent firms need multichannel strategies that deliver acceptable value and experience to the customer at the lowest possible cost. This pushes them towards customer-facing operations that are large scale and automated (e.g. web-based), and away from personal contact.
- Customer-intimate firms need multichannel strategies that deliver a highly personalised and high-value experience to the customer at an acceptable cost. This pushes them towards personalised customer-facing operations that are smaller scale and relatively expensive.
- Product- (or service-) excellent firms need multichannel strategies that deliver greatly superior customer value at an acceptable cost and

with only an acceptable level of tailoring. This pushes them towards customer-facing operations that are somewhere between large scale, automated and small scale, personal contact.

It is likely that the issues uncovered in Chapter 4 that your multichannel strategy needs to address will correlate with the company's overall strategy, whatever that may be. For companies whose multichannel organisational structure needs to provide an improved customer experience, we would expect this to tie in with a company-wide objective to win in the market through customer intimacy, through the ability to deliver an overall proposition to target customers who are of high value to the organisation and for which the company is willing to pay more. Alternatively, if the multichannel goal is to encourage the use of lower-cost channels in order to deliver a product or service more cheaply than competitors, we would expect this to fit with a generic corporate strategy of being the lowest-cost provider in the market.

However, in our experience this is not always what happens. Very frequently there is some conflict between what a company's leaders *say* they want to deliver (e.g. a technically superior product and more customer-focused service that a clearly defined group of selective customers will be willing to pay more for) and *how* they expect to achieve increased profit (e.g. by large-volume supply of a non-customised product through low-cost channels to maximise volume and minimise the cost of delivery). Alternatively, the fit between the overall positioning of the brand and the strategy provides very little compelling reason for the customer to respond in the way intended.

There is an important link here to a wide base of academic research and strategic fit. At the risk of being simplistic, strategy is about alignment to the market. Strong strategies are those that obtain a good fit between the organisation and its market environment. This view, however, contains an obvious contradiction or dilemma. Do we fit the company to the market, or *vice versa*? At one extreme, purist marketers might think that rebuilding the company to meet the needs of the customer is the only choice. After all, we control what the company is, but we can't control the market, argue the marketing fundamentalists. At the other extreme, research or operations evangelists might argue that a firm is what it is, and it is easier and more efficient to persuade customers to buy what we can do well. Both ends of this polarised thinking encapsulate practical thinking. Neither markets nor organisations are perfectly malleable.

As with most dichotomies of this type, the real answer lies in synthesising these two extreme views with the specific facts of the market situation and company position. Arguably the most dominant strand in current academic thinking about strategy began in 1991 with Jay Barney's ideas about resource-based advantage. Barney argued that whilst the marketing purists had a point, so too did the opponents. Firm success and competitive advantage, he contended, could be explained best in terms of firms trying to meet customer needs but doing so *based on what kind of firm they are*. More specifically, this explanation of firm success argued that firms have innate resource advantages that stem from their history and market position (Barney, 1991). These resources might be tangible, such as intellectual property or some physical assets, or they might be intangible, such as tacit knowledge about the customer or some aspects of the firm's culture. The central point of this theory, however, is that firms succeed when their strategy makes use of any innate, distinctive resource advantages that a firm has over its competitors.

The generic strategy selected by a company's leaders (whether implicitly or explicitly) is usually driven by its resource base. In other words, the underlying driver behind how the company intends to achieve its financial goals is largely that of what the company is actually capable of. Consider BMW – its strategy of delivering vehicles with superior design and performance to a discerning group of drivers is designed to fit the fact that, as an organisation, they have a comparatively high cost-base. That is not to say that they will not, like other companies, seek to keep their costs under control; simply that the leaders have recognised that the business will never be in a position to be the lowest-cost manufacturer in the market. They therefore choose to compete on a different field altogether. Whilst keeping costs within industry-acceptable levels, they ensure that their product performance meets or exceeds that of competitor vehicles and, most importantly, that they deliver an overarching brand proposition that appeals to their target customer group. They do not promise the 'most affordable' or the 'safest' car; they offer 'the ultimate driving machine'.

Wal-Mart, on the other hand, with its promise of 'Always Low Prices' makes no other promise to customers than to keep prices low. It does not suggest that it will stock the widest range of goods or provide a personalised customer service. The generic strategy of being the lowest-cost provider ties completely with the company's goals to keep channel costs to a minimum.

There is an important point to make here about strategy coherence. Strategies are patterns of resource allocation decisions. They usually cascade from the top of the organisation downwards. At the highest level of corporate strategy are those decisions about which industries to be in. Those decisions usually define the existence of the different strategic business units that make up the firm. Each of those units will have a marketing strategy, which Smith defines as 'that set of management decisions about which customers to target and what to offer them' (Smith, 2005). The marketing strategy has to be coherent with the generic strategy, and consistent with the firm's resource advantages. Flowing from the marketing strategy are functional strategies such as marketing communications (the choices of media, messages and audiences) and supply chain strategies (choices regarding how to supply the product or service.)

Clearly these strategies must be coherent, and they must reinforce rather than contradict each other. In practice, however, multichannel strategy is too often disconnected from the overall market strategy. Consider HSBC, which targets high-value customers with a 'Premier' offer, but makes those time-poor customers go through a low-cost automated phone system. PC

World is another example; its positioning as a helpful and knowledgeable access point for bemused technology users is too readily undermined by poorly-trained shop assistants.

The key point here is that your multichannel strategy is part of the value proposition the customer sees. It must therefore fit with your choice of customer and offer (i.e. your marketing strategy). It is horribly easy when making well-intentioned decisions about, say, telephone systems or staff training, to actually contradict the intent of the marketing strategy.

Implementers

The third stakeholder group we need to consider is those who will be responsible for delivering the strategy. This includes employees, and perhaps also third-party partners who will provide part of the multichannel delivery. At the extreme, this may mean partners such as franchised retail outlets (frequently seen in telecoms or vehicle retail). Less extreme (but no less important) examples might be an outsourced call centre or offshore technical support team.

If you plan to change your multichannel strategy, and therefore your structure, you need to consider how this will impact on those who will implement the strategy and work within the new structure. In many cases, employees or other partners see the changes as having a negative impact on their own role, importance or benefits. For example, in the pharmaceutical industry, the direct sales force traditionally has a lot of customer contact and, as a result, generally holds a high degree of political power within the organisation. As pharma companies increasingly move toward multichannel structures, we might anticipate some resistance from employees. Members of the sales force may anticipate a reduction in their political sway within the organisation; some individuals might feel disempowered by the reduction in customer contact time or by the increase in contact time that other colleagues will have with customers.

It is vital to anticipate and manage the frequent divergence between the goals of the organisation and the goals of individuals. This challenge is considered in academic circles by 'agency theory' (the academic term for an employee is an 'agent').

Agency theory starts from the premise that employees act in their own best interest and that, like customers, they seek to maximise their benefits (status, social and financial) and minimise their costs (time and effort). Problems arise when the employees' interests and actions do not coincide with the interests and actions of the firm.

This can be a common challenge in multichannel change. Ask a sales representative to capture customer data on his laptop for the tele-agent or web to refer to, and he may see this only as increasing his effort and undermining his importance in serving his customer. Similarly, the decision to prioritise and offer better service to high-value customers on the basis of their income is not lost on the frontline contact-centre staff, who frequently earn less than the 'deprioritised' customers and yet their commitment and skills will be essential to execute the strategy successfully. With customer commitment heavily dependent on frontline employee commitment, this is a vital consideration in thinking through the multichannel change.

These situations can easily lead to poor outcomes for the firm – and the customer – and outcomes that close management may ameliorate, but only at high cost with a suboptimal experience for the customer.

As far as possible, the interests of the firm and its employees need to be aligned through the change. This requires more than simply changing reporting structures and incentives. The factors to be managed can be summarised in the acronym PARC (Roberts, 2004):

- People, including recruitment, training and retention practice
- Architecture, the structure of the firm
- Routines, covering all of the explicit processes used by the firm
- Culture, including the firms underlying beliefs and values.

■ Resolving contradiction between stakeholder groups

It's easy to see that, in considering the needs and drivers of these three stakeholder groups, there are likely to be some contradictions. The objective therefore is to find a structure that either resolves or circumnavigates those conflicts and offers a solution that is acceptable and workable for the implementers, delivers the results the company's leaders require, and helps to resolve the value-driver issues identified as being important to customers. The right structure for the organisation will be one that works, taking the needs of all those stakeholder groups (and the inevitable contradictions between them) into consideration, along with the priority areas for performance in the multichannel arena.

So, how can we build a structure to do that? Before considering the recommendations that arise from our research, it is worth taking a reality check here. The problems of aligning the needs of multiple stakeholder groups, of aligning different levels of strategy and across multiple channels are not trivial. There is never a panacea that can be expected to work perfectly in all cases. Any answer (or set of answers) is normally as complex as the problem it solves; it will be context-specific and subject to change as the firm, the market and the strategy change. That said, our research and experience suggest some general principles of good practice.

Structure is more than just boxes in a chart

We think it may be safe to assume, at this point, that our readers have identified a number of 'problem areas' where the priorities of different stakeholder groups differ. The next thing for us to do, therefore, is to suggest how it might be possible to develop a structure that will work around those problems and provide a realistic solution.

The impact of any new structure on the existing systems and structures that exist in an organisation will generally involve both 'hard' and 'soft' systems and structures – those that are explicit and those that are implicit.

What will be the impact of the proposed new structure on the incentive systems in the organisation? Are project systems set up to deliver the multichannel strategy through this structure, or do they need to be reviewed? Are the physical infrastructure and IT systems conducive to the new multichannel structure, or is it necessary to review, revise or upgrade them?

Will the organisational culture be accepting of the proposed change? Will employees adapt easily, and adopt the new structure and systems that are required? Do people need to change their normal patterns of behaviour, who they deal with and how, where they source information, how they are rewarded or incentivised? For example, will customers have to change their usual behaviour, to stop calling a free telephone number and start using the Internet to solve their problems? Is the plan to stop rewarding call-centre staff for handling a maximum volume of calls per hour and to start an incentive scheme linked to cross-sales and problem-solving?

Do people trust those with whom they will be expected to work in the future? Again, this applies to customers, employees and partners. It could be, for example, that the plan reduces sales-force contact time and increases customer reliance on the call-centre and web channels – do customers trust those channels? Do they feel confident that the call-centre staff can offer an appropriate level of service? Is the web channel designed to make the customer feel confident that an order will be delivered when and where it is required?

Similarly, if there is to be a new internal structure with closer links between channels, do employees trust those with whom they will, in future, be working closely? If the members of the sales force will be expected to pass a valuable customer sales lead to an external retail channel, are they confident that the retailer will handle the customer well and not damage the customer relationship? If someone on the desk-based sales team needs to promise the customer that a member of the direct sales force will return their call within a certain timeframe, do they trust their colleague in the direct sales force to make that call?

These types of questions can be investigated, illustrated and explained using a tool called the cultural web (Johnson *et al.*, 2006). The cultural web is a tool for uncovering and understanding the central paradigm or view of the world from which a company or function operates. In essence the tool is simple, although it requires skilful application. The inputs into the cultural web are the observable aspects of the company culture. These include structures, stories, myths, legends and symbols (see Figure 7.2).

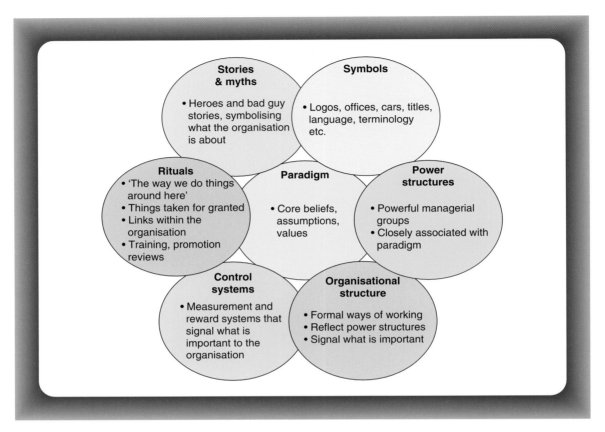

Figure 7.2
The cultural web

The cultural web takes these and assembles them in a way that unveils the usually implicit beliefs at the root of the corporate culture. Often these are surprising and, when made explicit, unsupported by evidence.

An example of this occurred in a private hospital group, with the espoused value of being patient-oriented. The cultural web revealed many things, like car-parking priorities and appointment-booking systems, that in fact pointed clearly to the organisation's paradigm that the consultant surgeons were the most important stakeholders and the hospital fitted patients' needs in around them.

The cultural web can be applied at the level of the whole organisation, or for parts of it. If two silos have to work closely to deliver an effective multichannel experience, for example, it may be advisable to use the cultural web to diagnose the culture of the two organisational units, and work out how any differences can be overcome or managed. You can ask members of the unit to assess themselves, or you can ask their colleagues to assess them! Figure 7.3 shows how a group of senior non–marketers feel about the culture of the marketing department – they are always at

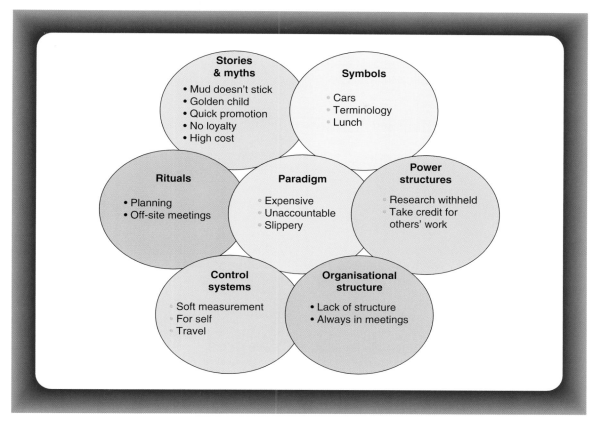

Figure 7.3
How marketers are perceived by senior non-marketers

lunch; they take credit for all revenue, irrespective of how it is generated; they are promoted fast – in sum, they are expensive, unaccountable and slippery … A few little cultural issues to overcome here!

A successful multichannel structure needs to be aligned with the types of changes that being a multichannel organisation is likely to throw up. This means viewing each of the different stakeholder constituencies in the structure and how they interrelate. In particular, it's important to make explicit some of the issues that are frequently implied or assumed.

One of these is third-party responsibility. Where third parties are involved in the channel chains, it's important to be explicit about their role, their responsibility, and how this relates to in-house capabilities and channels that rely on in-house rather than third-party, external teams. Making the requirements, systems and matters of communication and trust explicit helps to answer the question of whether it is truly possible to outsource certain channels and still maintain an adequate level of control. Similarly, this process of making the links and systems more explicit can help to highlight potential problem areas. For example, if incentives are offered to third-party channel partners, how are these the same as (or different from) the incentive systems and remuneration or rewards that are in place for internal staff? Is the difference workable and does it benefit the organisation, or will it potentially lead to difficulties, with different channels are pursuing different objectives in order to achieve the best personal rewards?

This, of course, is closely linked to the matter of trust we touched on earlier. Trust needs to be dealt with openly. When faced with the proposal that they will work with certain groups, teams or individuals, people are most unlikely openly to tell their manager that they don't trust those they are expected to work with. However, the lack of trust will shape their behaviour. They may try to work around the new system, they may simply continue to 'do things the way that has always worked', or they may actively try to sabotage the system in order to prove to themselves (and others) that so-and-so cannot be relied upon to do what is required, thus promoting a different solution or 'proof' that the old system worked better. Raising trust overtly as a legitimate aspect of working across teams makes it easier to address any problems and issues that may underlie people's attitudes and behaviours.

Reconciling the differences

The fact that each organisation and market situation is unique means we cannot recommend a single 'best' way of organising a company to deliver optimal multichannel success. Companies organise around channels (as BT has done for its major business customers), customer segments (as Dell does with its business-to-business, business-to-consumer and various sub-segments), product groups (as pharmaceutical companies do when they organise by therapeutic areas) or geography (like many major construction companies). Most end up with some kind of matrix, hybrid or overlay structure that allows them to deliver a consistent customer experience through a number of different channels. The important thing to note here is that no structure works inherently better than any other. The key is in finding a model that fits the target customers and can be reached from the current starting point, from the structures and systems already in place.

Any successful organisational model will anticipate and address the challenges that any solution is likely to present at the boundaries. For example, being organised around channels often results in internal problems when customers hop between those channels – thus, if the company plans to be organised around channels, managers need to focus on linkages and 'bridges' between different channels. BT achieves this by making the channel structure only one dimension of its organisational structure, and by placing emphasis on cooperation and teamwork to ensure that employee behaviour does not undermine the corporate goals. Another example is the UK bank First Direct, where the emphasis for the contact centre is placed on helping customers to use the web channel, talking them through the process and helping them become familiar with the new channel.

When Legal & General partnered with the supermarket J. Sainsbury to deliver insurance products through a retail channel, they anticipated a potential problem because legal regulations required them to 'shift' the customer relationship from the supermarket (where the customer would first begin the decision-making process) over to the insurance company, which would be responsible for delivering and managing it within FSA guidelines. Using carefully crafted communication tools and appropriate messages at each stage of the decision-making process, Sainsbury and Legal & General developed customer communications that effectively 'break' the relationship so that customers move seamlessly from Sainsbury to Legal & General as they move from in-store communications (e.g. leaflets, posters and banners) to the website.

Finding the best structure for your company

Our conclusion, then, is that there is no 'best' multichannel structure to be recommended. The best structure for any particular company is contingent on its situation, culture, and existing systems and structures. However, by means of reviewing what we have covered in this chapter and in an effort to guide those readers who are looking for guidance in this area, we can boil it down to a small number of key questions. The answers to these questions will help determine the optimal structure for the organisation:

1. What's your generic strategy? How does the organisation intend to compete in the market and create shareholder value and profit? This will filter through to the multichannel strategy and affect decisions about the resources available for structure and organisation.
2. What is your customer strategy? How does the company aim to create value for the customer? The answer to this question will help to determine the level and type of service needed, and which channels will be most effective in delivering it.
3. What would your employees and delivery partners do if they were left to their own devices? Understanding what is in the best interests of this stakeholder group helps to identify potential difficulties in some possible structural options. Ensuring that employee goals and corporate goals are well aligned ensures that the structure is one that employees and partners will strive to follow instead of combat.
4. How much does value creation depend on your channel strategy? If the answer to this is 'a lot', the structure probably needs to be more channel-oriented than if value creation relies more heavily on, for example, product performance.
5. How granular is your market? Understanding customer segments well will help you to understand how customers are likely to use channels. Having customers that are likely to hop frequently between channels, or operating in a market that is fast developing and where customer

channel behaviour is likely to change rapidly or frequently, increases the need for more robust communication systems and linkages across channels to ensure consistency of customer experience as customers hop and switch from channel to channel less predictably.

■ Change management

Once the new structure has been designed, the other important area to consider is how to make this happen within the organisation. Companies that are successful in this respect are those which recognise that change is something that needs to be managed and directed. Change is not instinctive. In most organisations, employees do not follow their leaders like a flock of sheep. There are boundaries that exist between functions and different business units, between suppliers and customers, between different channel partners. These all need to be aligned in order to achieve a corporate change.

Prosci presented comprehensive findings from 411 companies on their experiences and lessons learned in change management (Prosci, 2005). Two key findings in that report were that:

1. The primary contributor to success of any change is active, strong and viable sponsorship
2. The top obstacle to successful change is employee resistance at all levels.

Successfully achieving change in an organisation's multichannel approach is no different from any other change. It requires long-term planning, education, attention to detail, and good management processes. Depending on the situation, there are different approaches the management team can take to making change happen. Some adopt a highly directive approach, others a more step-by-step approach; all encounter different reactions from different stakeholders.

Our experience is that the most common mistake is to identify the new 'vision' and present it to employees without first gaining their buy-in and involvement. Whilst this can occasionally work in situations where employees and partners are already committed to change and where the change is not urgent or imperative, the approach more usually results in a lack of commitment and understanding amongst the teams required to deliver the change. This is compounded when the senior team, having presented the change, expects it to be implemented and happen without further input. The team then moves on to a different strategic activity, and the required change, now lacking both commitment *and* senior management sponsorship or involvement, simply founders and fails to materialise.

There are plenty of books already written on the theory and practice of change management, and we certainly don't plan to cover the same ground here. However, there are three key areas of change management that, in our view, are particularly relevant to a multichannel context and these are worth mentioning:

1. Project management
2. Communication
3. Piloting

Project management

This, more than any other aspect of change management, is the one area where we have seen companies succeed or fail most dramatically. The need to treat change as an overall integrated programme was cited as a significant success factor whenever we carried out research through the Cranfield Customer Management Forum, and we therefore make no apologies for discussing the subject now in a little detail. However, this hardly touches the surface of the research findings or their far-reaching conclusions for multichannel organisations, so we invite any readers with more than a passing interest in this area to contact us to find out more and get a full copy of the relevant research reports.

By treating the change as a project, it becomes recognised as an important factor in the success of the multichannel strategy. It is not enough simply to 'paint the picture' of how the future needs to look, to issue a new organisational structure chart and expect the company to gravitate towards that future. Similarly, announcing the new structure as a kind of *fait accompli* is insufficient – we need to identify and recognise the series of incremental steps that it will take to reach the ultimate goal.

For example, when Heineken Ireland wanted to initiate a series of wide-ranging changes in their sales, logistics, customer-service and trade-marketing operations at the end of the 1990s, they created a programme plan that ran over 3 years and incorporated actions across many functions coordinated by their board. This helped to provide momentum, the essential integration for multichannel operation, and a forum that was able to resolve the inevitably conflicting interdependencies involved in such a major exercise.

Self-evident as this is, it would be unrealistic to expect a sudden change or transformation. Just as customer behaviour has evolved over time, so must the organisation look for incremental change in the direction of seamless multichannel structure. That evolution needs to happen gradually and in tandem with the continued changes in customer behaviour, and will require companies to develop step-by-step, inventing and adopting new capabilities to add value to both customers and the business.

Research by Cranfield's Customer Management Forum (Clark *et al.*, 2004) shows how important project governance and stakeholder management are in a CRM context, and this applies equally to the management of change where multichannel structures are concerned. This work gained important insights into the management of such change projects by comparing different stages of project implementation.

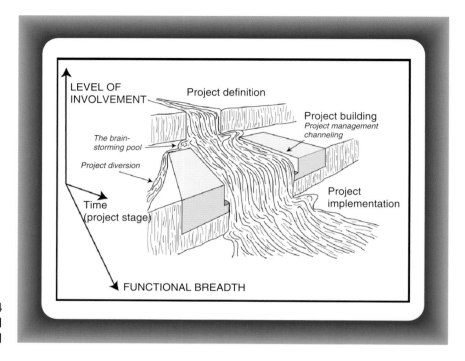

Figure 7.4
The Waterfall
Model

It is important to have both senior management support and cross-functional involvement in the project. However, there are practical limitations to this – involving all levels of management and all functions for the entire project would be unworkable. Cranfield's research with companies that have made this work for them reveals a pattern of management and functional involvement that is deliberately managed. The metaphor of a waterfall taken from this research report illustrates the different levels of involvement across the organisation over different project stages.

This model (Figure 7.4) suggests that the implementation of change be divided into three stages, each with an optimal level of senior management involvement and breadth of functional involvement.

Strategic definition

At this strategic stage of the project, its scope and scale is defined. By now, the inputs are the strategic context of the project (its drivers and relationship to organisational objectives); the process is one of reconciliation with other activity; and the outputs are broadly defined objectives for the project, initial resource allocation and, significantly, senior team consensus about commitment to the project. The task of strategic definition is limited to the senior management team of the strategic business unit. Best practice seems to involve the exclusion of lower levels of functional management and external partners – this helps to avoid the situations outlined earlier, where different stakeholders may have conflicting agendas; it also avoids the risk that the project may be diverted away from strategic goals or perhaps designed to fit the capabilities of an existing structure or existing implementation team.

Failure to consider the strategic definition as a separate and valuable step has proved a stumbling block in a number of organisations that we have worked with. One, a retail bank, struggled to find a way to bridge the existing essentially product-division silos. Another, a pharmaceutical company, struggled to launch an e-detailing multichannel initiative because of the challenges of aligning different functional areas.

In a multichannel situation, resolving this step and securing an optimum definition is about benefits realisation. Prior to the Internet, most companies worked within the limitations of a single-channel model. Even though this made some activities more costly, it was difficult to make any significant change to performance within the constraints of a single channel. With their initial introduction of an online channel, many companies simply saw this new channel as a bolt-on to their existing channel structure. For example, one public services organisation we worked with had the aim of making 'all services available via the web'. However, this did not actually provide any benefit to customers (the public) or to the organisation itself. To compound the problem, because the objective was defined as making the services available via the web and there were no targets linked to customers actually using the new channel, there was no measurement of the extent to which online services were being used or accessed.

Project-building

This is the transitional phase between the conceptual design and execution of the project. Project-building operates most effectively within the clearly defined parameters (objectives and resources) defined in the strategic definition stage. At this stage the involvement of the senior management team remains important, but can now typically be limited to a single senior executive acting as a sponsor and link to the executive team. At this point, a small group of functional middle managers can develop the specific objectives, and clarify the key milestones, inputs and outputs of the project. This stage may involve the selection of one or more channel partners and the subsequent involvement of those partners. It is also at this stage that dedicated resource becomes significant. The outputs of the project-building stage are quite detailed, including task delimitation, resource allocation and scheduling for subsequent stages of the project.

Project execution

This is the final, ongoing stage of the change-management project. It operates within the detailed task delimitation, resource allocation and scheduling set in the prior phase. Senior management involvement becomes less – usually restricted now to monitoring, control and political lubrication. Middle management involvement changes in its nature from definition to management of execution, and is now supplemented with more involvement from functional staff, who gradually take ownership of the project. The outputs of this stage are the operational project and its benefits and, as with any project, the feeding back of lessons from implementation into the process for reiterations or developments of the project.

The Benefits Dependency Network project management tool

We recommend the use of a tool called the Benefits Dependency Network to ensure that, by introducing new channels and creating a multichannel approach, you deliver some defined benefits to the customer and the organisation. 'Being multichannel' is not simply about introducing a new channel or migrating customers from one channel to another. Those who do it successfully use the points of leverage between different channels to support the dominant channel with other channels, and create valuable benefits that attract and retain customers.

The Benefits Dependency Network (BDN) tool (Ward and Daniel, 2005) does not simply list project elements and track their resourcing and timescales, as most project management tools do. The BDN tool works backwards from the project's objectives to ensure that all necessary business changes are made. It then shows the chain of causality between IT systems, business changes and project objectives in a graphical format.

A simplified example of the BDN for one project, a sales-force effectiveness programme within a pharmaceuticals company, is shown in Figure 7.5. The company is the UK subsidiary of a US-owned multinational, and is essentially a sales and marketing organisation to distribute predetermined products. As its biggest cost is the direct sales force, optimising the effectiveness of this channel is the main lever it can pull in order to improve financial results.

The main elements of the network, which, in general, is built from right to left, are as follows:

- First, the *drivers* of the project are defined. A driver is a view by top managers as to what is important for the business, such that the business needs to change in response. In this case, the drivers (which are not shown in the figure) were a group directive for 'a CRM system'; the need to replace an inadequate customer-contact and representative reporting system; and the perceived need to improve the customer experience.
- The *investment objectives* are then a clear statement of what the project is trying to achieve. Originally, the project team in this example had listed 'increase shareholder wealth' as an objective, but after discussion it was agreed that this represented a corporate objective rather than the objective of this specific project. A revised objective of maximising sales force effectiveness was set.
- In order to achieve these objectives, some *benefits* will need to be delivered to different stakeholders, including customers. These are now

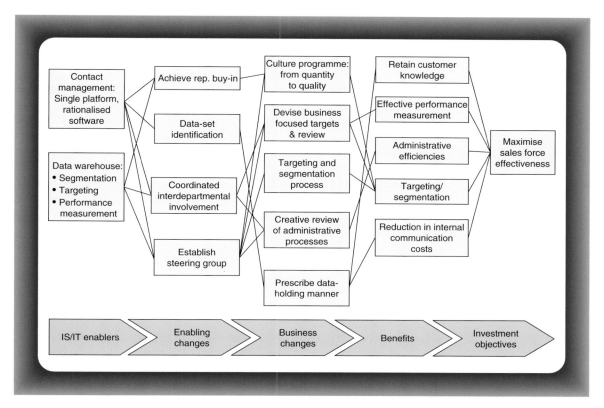

Figure 7.5
The benefits dependency network – a pharmaceutical company

explicitly identified and quantified. In this case these included, for example, the retention of customer knowledge when representatives leave the company, the institution of effectiveness-oriented measures of sales-force productivity (such as call rate per segment and prescribing rate per segment) rather than the previous input-focused measure of overall call rate, and administrative efficiencies that save representatives time.

● In order to achieve these benefits, it is necessary for organisations and people to work in different ways, and it is these permanent changes that are captured in the *business changes* part of the network.

● Other one-off changes may also be required before the project can go live – for example, to define new processes which are needed, and to establish organisational roles and skills sets. These are termed *enabling changes*. Here, these included the establishment of a steering group and other mechanisms to ensure cross-functional coordination, such as cross-functional data flows on profit by segment.

● When this analysis has been carried out, the specific role which technology will play in project's objectives can be defined in detail. These technology changes are listed under *IS/IT enablers*. Here, they were an integrated contact management system and a data warehouse to run analyses such as targeting and performance measurement.

The tool was originally designed to flush out the business changes needed to make the use of new technology effective if an IT-enabled project is to succeed. However, it has since been used successfully on a variety of other projects at the customer interface which may or may not have a significant technological component, such as channel change and CRM projects. By clarifying the benefits sought, the project can be monitored and measured effectively. This avoids the common problem we have all experienced of 'project drift' where, as a project progresses, the benefits it will deliver gradually shift towards those which employees (or the IT enabler) can deliver instead of those which the business requires as payback for its investment.

This type of tool is valuable in both consolidating and focusing the upfront step in realising the change and in managing the change through subsequent steps. However, sadly, the evidence is that most firms do not perform this kind of pre-planning and measurement. Back in 2003, even after the peak of the CRM investment boom, less than one in five companies put the processes and tools in place to assess and guide the capture of business benefits.

The Benefits Dependency Network (and similar tools) is useful for selling the change internally. Not only does it ensure that project objectives align with the business objectives, but its clear, graphical illustration also encourages clarity of logic for a project which allows earlier rejection of projects which are likely to fail. The fact that it is developed collaboratively helps achieve consensus on the project and makes communication of the necessary business changes easier. At the same time, ensuring that those business changes are identified and made explicit contributes significantly to the change-management process; it determines the appropriate metrics and assigns clear responsibilities for different elements of the network. It also helps to avoid falling into the common trap of managing a project 'to specification' rather than by tracking the outcomes that are required.

Communication

When looking to implement a multichannel strategy, most companies underestimate the level of customer communication required – especially if the strategy requires customers to move from one channel to another, as it often does. For example, the strategy might require customers to move away from using a face-to-face channel and towards using a 'remote' channel or channels, such as a telephone call centre or the web. Very frequently, in our experience, there are processes, policies and information that are critical to the provision of the customer experience and which are not documented, especially in a face-to-face channel or local environment.

These type of issues can only be addressed by careful assessment of the current procedures, meticulous pre-planning for a move, and careful and sustained communication with customers to help them understand the nature of the change and the exact details of the transition.

Many companies underestimate the extent of external communication to customers and channel partners that is required. This encompasses comparatively 'small' details, such as making sure that the right people in customers' organisations know a new telephone number and who will be handling their call. The paper supplier we referred to in Chapter 2 encountered just such a problem. The management team made the mistake of leaving it to their sales force to communicate informally to the customer the new information about the centralised, office-based sales team who would be handling routine orders and enquiries. The sales force passed on the necessary information to their immediate customer contacts, but failed to ensure that the same information was disseminated within the customer organisation. The result was that whole teams within customers' companies simply did not have the necessary information when the changeover happened. Customers became irritated and felt undervalued by the supplier, and a great deal of time was wasted when people continued to try to communicate through the old 'tried and tested' channels, being reluctant to switch to the new office-based centre, which they perceived to be disorganised and disinterested.

As important as external communication is its internal equivalent – accessible and shared customer information. Usually this relies on some form of IT enablement, and the range of such systems is wide and varied. We have seen companies succeed (and fail) with multimillion-dollar CRM systems, with simple Microsoft spreadsheets, and with everything in between.

When companies underestimate the amount of communication that will be required, they often don't plan it properly. Because they don't plan it, they fail to spot processes and elements of the customer experience that are likely to drop through the cracks. Careful planning raises the opportunity to introduce customers to their new contacts; this is particularly important in a business-to-business environment. It's vital to ensure that adequate support systems are in place, both for the changeover period and subsequently. For example, calls to a telephone call centre may take slightly longer while people become accustomed to the new process of ordering by telephone; if this results in long telephone queues, customers will quickly form a poor impression of the call centre, even though the 'problem' is only a temporary one. With careful planning and thorough communication come opportunities to shape expectations – both those of customers and those of employees and channel partners.

Piloting

Piloting is widely used in marketing communications to measure the effectiveness of communications campaigns, but it is also one of the tools that we recommend most strongly for companies looking to adopt a new multichannel strategy. Piloting helps to identify where real behaviour differs from perceived behaviour, to see how people actually carry out certain tasks – very often not in the same way as they say or believe that they do!

Piloting uncovers vital information, especially in business-to-business situations. It often exposes issues like customers who do not telephone or fax their routine orders to the office as the sales force said they do, or a pricing structure in use that is not the one that the Sales Director believed it to be (both real examples!). In fact, many customers have special pricing deals or ordering arrangements that are not well documented and have developed historically over a period of time, perhaps due to a large order placed years ago or as compensation for a customer complaint in the past.

At the outset of its relationship with Sainsbury's supermarket, Legal & General was concerned that customers would not buy a comparatively complex, high-involvement product such as insurance on the web. It initially designed its channel chains to take customers from in-store communication (e.g. a leaflet or poster) through the decision-making process, expecting that approximately 40 percent of final purchases would be generated online. This figure had been surpassed by the end of Year 1, and by Year 3 more than half of purchases were generated online. What Legal & General had discovered was that that customers were, in fact, very comfortable making such a purchase online. The 'issue' had not been the web, but the fact that with other, similar purchases the online customer experience had not met customer needs, thus driving customers to other channels where they would ultimately complete their purchase. When customers could find the information and reassurance they needed online, they were happy to buy via that channel. Legal & General took advantage of this new knowledge, and now actively seeks to drive its Sainsbury's online business through in-store marketing activity, direct mail campaigns, links to the Sainsbury's and Sainsbury's Bank websites, pay per click advertising and search-engine optimisation.

These are just two examples of where early live experience uncovered the 'reality' of processes and systems, both formal and informal, that were not as expected. Often it's best to conduct a formal pilot rather than learn these lessons from early mistakes that are made across the entire customer base. GM's Vauxhall brand provides a good example of a well-designed pilot.

Positive piloting – Vauxhall's two way communication pilot

During the 1980s, the Internet opened up new possibilities for car manufacturers to move from a one-way to a two-way communication model. Instead of simply advertising through broadcast media and, to a lesser extent, using direct mail to try to drive customers to the dealership channel, the web offered an inexpensive channel through which customers could respond to and interact with car manufacturers. The prospect of gaining feedback from consumers, to distinguish between individual model preferences, purchase intention and perhaps even sell vehicles online, was an exciting one for car manufacturers. However, selling directly via the Internet inevitably set alarm bells ringing among dealers, and forced the manufacturers to think carefully before upsetting the distribution channel they were so dependent upon.

As long ago as 1996, GM's vehicle manufacturer, Vauxhall, initiated a pioneering two-way communication programme in the UK. The programme was founded in the observation that there is a characteristic lifecycle to buying a new car – the timescales vary, but the process remains very similar. The gap between successive purchases is, on average, every 3 years, but this varies widely from customer to customer; some customers replace their car every year, others every 10 years. The Vauxhall pilot took the crucial step of asking people their purchase intentions, and directing a communications programme around that information. The aim was to encourage existing and potential customers to enter into a dialogue with Vauxhall, to ascertain when they intended to replace their vehicle, and to send them an invitation to test drive at the critical moment.

Vauxhall ran a 6-month pilot to gauge the impact of the programme. The pilot included isolating a control group drawn at random from both existing customers and prospects. These people – 10 percent of the total – were excluded from the communications programme. This would mean some lost sales during the course of the pilot, but this was considered worthwhile in order to demonstrate the benefits. The control group received no communications from Vauxhall, but their level of purchase was monitored through collation of owner sales certificates.

Vauxhall recognised that its programme had to win the support of the dealership channel. A 6-month pilot followed by quantitative research demonstrated that a significant majority of dealers were prepared to recommend the scheme and were confident it would produce sales results. At this point the programme was rolled out.

In 2001, the programme generated over 8,000 incremental new car sales, representing a return on investment of 120 percent. An attitudinal tracking survey also showed that prospects involved in the programme were 25 percent more likely to put Vauxhall at the top of their shortlist, and twice as likely to consider Vauxhall, as those who were not involved.

Clearly, the programme was valuable and well thought out. However, the important thing to note here is that the pilot exercise taught Vauxhall several key lessons that they might otherwise have missed:

- Many consumers were willing to respond to the manufacturer if they were interested in the incentive and/or the product
- Many were also willing to provide a reliable estimated repurchase date, as well as other information about their profile and preferences
- Crucially, a one-to-one, tailored dialogue using this information provided better financial results than the traditional mass-market communications alone

This pilot informed the design of GM's larger Dialogue programme, which followed in much of Europe and is described in Chapter 4.

Operating in multiple channels has become a permanent part of the business landscape. Companies that excel can make it easier and more enjoyable for their customers to purchase by providing a multichannel environment that meets the needs of those customers, thus potentially gaining customer preference over competitors with inferior channels or poorly developed multichannel capabilities.

However, organising for a new multichannel strategy is neither quick nor easy. We can all but guarantee that managers will never feel they 'got it right'. Along with the inevitable process of constant iteration and improvement, therefore, comes the imperative of using data to track, measure and understand the performance of the organisation. Doing this in a multichannel environment brings its own unique challenges, and this is covered in the next chapter.

■ References

Barney, J.B. (1991). Firm resources and sustained competitive advantage. *Journal of Management*, 17: 99–120.

Clark, M., McDonald, M.H.B. and Smith, B.D. (2004). *Understanding the Devil: Uncovering the Detail of How Effective CRM is Implemented*. Cranfield School of Management.

Johnson, G., Scholes, K. and Whittington, R. (2006). *Exploring Corporate Strategy*, 7th edn. Prentice-Hall.

Porter, M. (1980). *Competitive Strategy*. Free Press.

Prosci Benchmarking Report (2005). *Best Practices in Change Management*. Prosci.

Roberts, J. (2004). *The Modern Firm*. Oxford University Press.

Smith, A. (1776). *An Enquiry into the Nature and Causes of the Wealth of Nations*. Edinburgh.

Smith, B.D. (2005). *Making Marketing Happen*. Elsevier.

Treacy, M. and Wiersema, M. (1995). *The Discipline of the Market Leaders*. Harper Collins.

Ward, J. and Daniel, E. (2005). *Benefits Management: Delivering Value from IS and IT Investments*. Wiley.

CHAPTER 8

Tracking and measuring effectiveness

The only man I know who behaves sensibly is my tailor; he takes my measurements anew each time he sees me. The rest go on with their old measurements and expect me to fit them.

George Bernard Shaw

The importance of measuring the effectiveness of any project or business activity is something we all recognise. As discussed in the previous chapter, making sure that the multichannel strategy delivers the benefits that the business requires and being able to quantify and justify to investors and stakeholders that the benefits are real and advantageous to the business is essential. The right measures of effectiveness also help to steer the project as it is being developed in the first place, highlighting where reality may be different from perceived reality, and they are critical in the ongoing implementation and forward iteration as the multichannel strategy is developed over time. In short, if there are no metrics in place to measure effectiveness, how can you possibly know for certain if your multichannel strategy is succeeding or failing?

■ Measuring strategically

Although 'metrics' always appears boldly on the 'how to' model for any project, it is perhaps unfortunate that it usually appears at the end – a kind of postscript to project management or strategy development – 'Oh, by the way, you should put some measures in place to make sure your strategy works'. Whilst this is better than failing to measure at all, it is not the most effective way of working, and it doesn't instil us with confidence. As our Cranfield colleague Dr Brian Smith puts it, it is rather like waiting to test an aircraft until it's loaded with passengers and then seeing if it takes off without crashing (Smith, 2005).

Metrics need to be in place before, during and after your new multichannel strategy is launched. Before the proposed multichannel structure is finalised, it is possible to use metrics to substantiate what is believed to be true so that the structure can be planned according to real metrics – in other words, a plan made based on reality and not just a perception of reality. During strategy development and implementation, metrics can be used to inform a pilot exercise and then put in place to benchmark during roll-out – monitoring whether customers are 'migrating' to the new structure as the pilot suggested they would. After implementation, metrics are used to plan the new structure and to measure the performance of channel chains and their contribution to the business.

■ Measuring in a multichannel environment

The problem, and the reason it's worth including a chapter on metrics in a book about multichannel marketing, is that the complexities of multi-channel marketing are such that traditional approaches to tracking and measurement are generally inadequate. Traditional metrics have been aligned to channels, measuring resource input or leads in at one end and the value of sales generated by the channel at the other end. For companies that have been operating in a single channel environment, this might have been relatively efficient – but it no longer works when the organisation diversifies to a multichannel approach. Even in companies with strictly delineated channel structures – siloed working, if you like – customers still hop from channel to channel so that it is impossible simply to measure the performance of a channel according to a 'sales generated per dollar resource input' model. With a truly multichannel organisation such as we are working towards, this becomes even more the case. A multichannel model is not built around customers using single channels, but around them using channel chains that cross boundaries and use different internal resources at different stages in the buying process. There is no longer a clear demarcation between the input of effort from, say, the sales team and the benefits (sales) delivered on, say, the website.

So clearly we need to measure effectiveness – and clearly measurement needs to be accurate and useful. However, traditional methods don't work. This is the dichotomy faced by many multichannel organisations. And what we learn from the failure of those traditional metrics is the importance of three steps:

1. Choosing the right things to measure
2. Understanding and measuring channel crossover
3. Gathering the correct data

Achieving these three steps will provide sufficient data to gain meaningful information about the company's multichannel operation. It leaves us in a position to pull together an accurate measure of the effectiveness of channel chains and of their contribution to overall business performance.

■ Choosing the right things to measure

Choosing what to measure is one of the most powerful means organisations have of making their strategy happen. EasyJet never ceases to look for ways to reduce costs, continually pushing cost per available seat kilometre – now an extraordinary 3.91 pence (down 7 percent in 2 years) – and celebrating every small improvement in the contributing drivers, such as the Internet sales percentage and advertising spend, and turning the tables on the airports who determine substantial chunks of the cost base by engaging them in competitive tendering for EasyJet's new business. By contrast, Sears Canada, basing its differentiation on quality of customer service, tracks employee satisfaction, customer retention and revenue, and models the relationship between these key variables, so it knows that a 5 percent rise in employee satisfaction delivers a 1.7 percent increase in customer loyalty and a 3.4 percent increase in profits. 3M famously maintains its reputation for product innovation by tracking the percentage of sales deriving from products released in the past 5 years.

Conversely, when metrics are out of kilter with strategy, behaviour will be too. To start with, operational people spend their time – or the customer's – doing the wrong things. The UK directory enquiries facility 118118 received very bad publicity in 2003 for driving its call-centre staff so hard on average call duration that many were deliberately cutting callers off before providing the right information. Furthermore, without clear metrics aligned with corporate strategy, evaluating the business case for major projects can be a random, political affair, with the proponents of a project choosing the metrics that most support their case.

Most fundamentally, the wrong measures can lead to the company being strategically blindsided. British Airways was slow to spot the change in structure of the airline market, believing that corporate travel was immune to the low-cost model long after an analysis of its own internal data might have told it otherwise.

In general, then, a changing world can leave our metrics lagging dangerously behind. This is especially true as customers have moved to use multiple channels in their dealings with suppliers. This fundamental change has left many organisations measuring on principles still founded on separate channels. When the sales force achieved a sale on its own, it could be tracked, managed and remunerated on the percentage of leads it converted, the sales revenue it generated and so on. But how does this reflect the complementary role of the website in providing information about the product range, or the role of the service centre in cross-selling? And how about sales in which the sales force plays a part but which are fulfilled by remote channels?

Similarly, the success of a business-to-consumer Internet channel cannot be assessed purely on the basis of sales made on the website. One department store has found that for every pound of revenue it takes on the web, three pounds are spent in the store after browsing online – so it works equally hard to help these customers, through such facilities as store locators and information on the nearest store with a particular product in stock (McDonald and Wilson, 2002). The renewed growth of interest in the web channel over the last couple of years has demonstrated this again and again, with firms focusing on using the web in conjunction with their offline channels, valuing the catalogue and the store and enabling the movement between channels. All these are responses to customer demand and the higher value of the customer who uses multiple channels.

Thus, particularly where the organisation is structured around channel silos, ways must be found of ensuring that the channel barons who head them up are motivated to act in the best interests of the customer and the company, rather than maximising the sales and minimising the costs of that particular channel. This means developing a single set of metrics for the multichannel customer interface as a whole.

Developing a driver tree

At this point, one might ask: 'So what is the best set of metrics for a multichannel company?' Unfortunately, this is a bit like asking 'What is the best car?' – which all depends on whether you are a family of four with a dog looking for the right vehicle for the weekend, or an image-conscious single person looking to impress. If what you measure is a key lever for achieving strategy, then good metrics sets are as individual as the strategy itself – and no-one ever tells us that their strategy is identical to that of the competition. So there is no way round the time-consuming process of determining the right metrics set for the circumstances. Although the end result we are looking for is a reasonably parsimonious set of key measures by which to steer the customer-facing parts of the business, to arrive at this important choice correctly takes a fair amount of work.

We can, though, give a flavour for how this process might work, based on some of our research at Cranfield and IBM Global Business Services. To illustrate the process, we will use a fictional example that is based upon a composite of our experience with several multichannel organisations.

This well-established company comes from a bricks-and-mortar background, but over the past few years has added a transactional website as well as traditional catalogue-based home shopping. While its target segments vary in their price sensitivity, its positioning can be broadly described as value based rather than price focused. Its switch to a multichannel strategy was accordingly driven by the desire to provide a convenient set of options covering a range of purchase situations, and thereby to increase share of wallet, rather than by any hope of reducing costs through a switch to lower-cost channels.

The process draws on IBM's long experience of the 'systems thinking' tradition that provides the best underpinning to metrics design. It involves the creation of a 'driver tree' showing cause-and-effect relationships between the objectives of the multichannel strategy and the key drivers influencing them. The nature of such a tool is such that it would be impossible to include it in a readable form in a book, so it is included here (Figure 8.1) purely to illustrate how it is structured. As we can see, the driver tree shows a complete picture of all the potential metrics, flowing from the key objectives (to the right of the tree). A subset (for example, 'channel attractiveness to customers' – Figure 8.2) can then be selected to focus on in a multichannel balanced scorecard.

The model begins with the key objectives of the multichannel strategy, which are mainly towards the right-hand side of the diagram. These objectives can be identified using the Benefits Dependency Network (BDN) that we discussed in Chapter 6. You may choose to select drivers

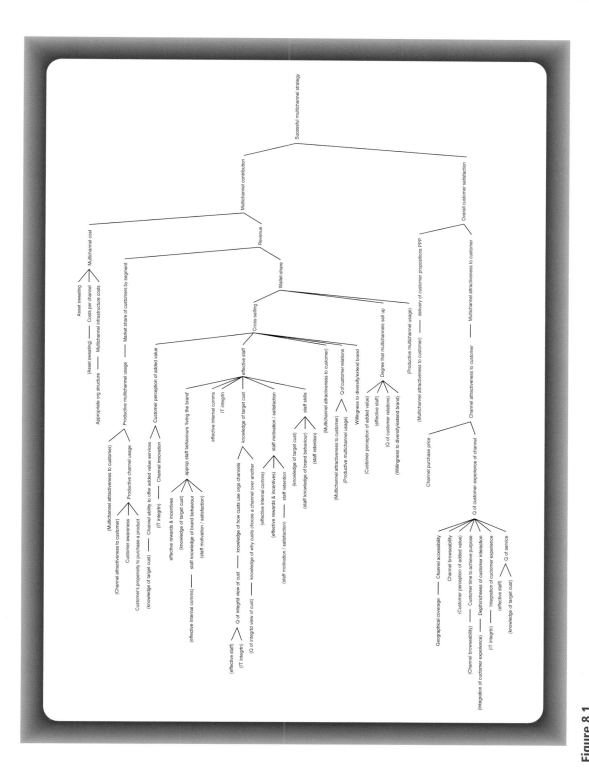

Figure 8.1
Cause and effect model – large UK retailer

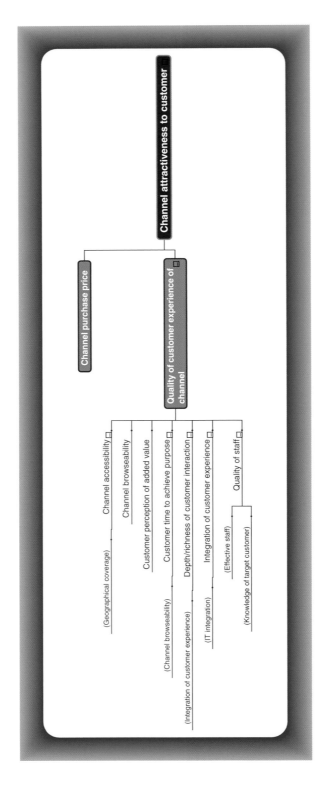

Figure 8.2
Channel attractiveness branch from Figure 8.1

from any 'stage' of the BDN, depending on what stage you are at in the strategy development process. This data flow usually works in both directions and can prove immensely useful for the BDN as well, by helping to substantiate and populate it with accurate data which either support the planned strategy or prove it to be unstable and requiring revision. It also helps to identify the individual change projects that will have the most fundamental, far-reaching or valuable impacts, so that resources can be directed accordingly.

For this retailer, these were primarily focused on customer satisfaction and revenue generation and protection – for example, extending the share of wallet by extending the product line and the range of shopping occasions (as Tesco Express has done for shopping when filling up with petrol), as well as increasing customer market share by improving geographical coverage. The retailer also set an objective of 'sweating the existing assets'; it makes more sense in terms of return on capital for the retailer to serve home-shopping customers through existing stores rather than invest in dedicated picking centres. This formed part of the small area of the network concerned with cost (at the top of the tree); we would expect a price-focused retailer, by contrast, to have a particularly well-worked cost-focused branch. The overall financial objective was of 'multi-channel contribution' – a measure of revenue minus channel-related costs. The company considered the use of customer lifetime value here, but concluded that this would leave flighty, low-spending 18-year-olds at the top of the pile and anyone much over the age of 45 at the bottom – the result would be excessive 'robbing today to get tomorrow'.

As well as the objectives themselves, the model includes the key drivers of these objectives, which are defined as variables with a high impact on one or more objectives and over which the organisation has high influence. Their direct or indirect impacts on the objectives are shown with lines on the driver tree. Some of these drivers relate directly to the customer experience, such as 'customer time to achieve purpose' – which, in the case of placing an order, is around 5–10 minutes for an experienced web customer, compared with 20–25 minutes to place a telephone order. Others are enablers of this experience, such as IT integration – a crucial influence on such variables as the customer's perception of an integrated experience across channels, and the quality of the company's integrated view of the customer. IT integration also, perhaps surprisingly, aids channel innovation rather than being in tension with it; consider the ways in which Tesco uses its Clubcard information on its website to personalise the service – a differentiator it could not deliver without integration of customer data across channels.

Choosing key metrics for a scorecard

This driver tree looks complex, and we suspect such tools generally will be. The fact is that successful multichannel strategies depend on many factors, relating to people, processes, technologies and customer perceptions as well as products and physical assets – and this complexity needs to be understood if we are to choose the right metrics to follow.

However, if we were routinely to track every variable on the tree, we would be in danger of creating a measurement industry and burying ourselves in complexity. What is more, this complexity of metrics would be quite unnecessary. At its simplest, if A influences B which in turn influences C, it will probably suffice to measure just A, or perhaps A and C. So, by adopting this kind of thinking, we need to define a sensible subset of the variables by which to steer our strategy. We want a small list or scorecard which will, with sufficient confidence, enable us to track progress towards our strategic objectives.

Breaking down conversion metrics by the buying cycle

It is good practice to develop staged metrics to evaluate the efficiency of the sales process at each stage of the buying cycle, and many organisations do this to a greater or lesser extent. Figure 8.3 shows an example for the call-centre channel, taken from a British Gas service centre which

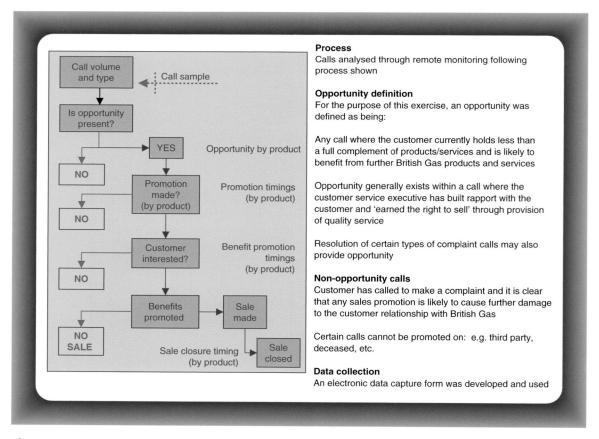

Figure 8.3
Tracking conversion ratios – British Gas

also has a cross-selling role. The process and the metrics which support it are focused on this issue of cross-selling efficiency.

However, metrics design becomes more complicated when multiple channels are involved in the customer relationship. This is illustrated well by a particular high-street chain's website, the channel chains for which we described in Chapter 4. You may recall that by selling pure play on the web, it was costing £1,600 to recruit each customer to make an initial purchase of, say, a £25 kettle.

Clearly, much needed correcting. With some help from the web designers and the search engine hosting the banner ads, the company calculated the ratios shown in Table 8.1 to help it analyse what was going wrong (data and strategy details have been amended to protect confidentiality). This breaking down of conversion metrics by the stages of the buying cycle was essential to diagnose and fix the problems, and to evaluate the various solutions. The company found, for example, that more careful placing of advertisements, to attract surfers who were looking at related material, made some difference to the locatability/attractability ratio, but not enough. Promotional emails to the customers of a related business (being careful to ensure that the email came from the business on whose website the customers had already registered, to avoid accusations of spamming) provided a much better ratio, as did reciprocal arrangements with other online retailers with complementary product ranges, providing links to each other's sites in one case and a co-branded site in another.

Table 8.1 Efficiency of a banner ad campaign

Ratio	Calculation	Notes
Awareness efficiency (aware customers/target market size)	40,000/200,000=20%	Banner ad campaign increased from 15% to 20%; cost £50,000
Locatability/ attractability efficiency (visitors/aware customers)	3,000/40,000=7.5%	3,000 unique visitors to website during campaign (from 1m page impressions); cost per visitor £16
Contact efficiency (active visitors/visitors)	600/3,000=20%	600 visitors stayed beyond home page
Conversion efficiency (Purchasers/active visitors)	30/600=5%	30 purchases from click-throughs from banner ads; cost per purchase £50,000/30=£1,600
Retention efficiency (Repurchasers/ purchasers)	Not known	Not known at time of evaluation

Most successful of all, though, were offline promotions. The company made a big difference (at virtually no cost) through prominent displays of the website address on stationery, store signs, vehicles and so on. It tried handing out promotional leaflets in shopping centres, finding this a much more cost-efficient approach than banner ads, and it tried offline press advertising with a promotional code offering a discount on the first purchase, to ensure trackability. For the first time it could compare advertising costs online and offline, as it had worked out the impact of its banner ads not just on sales but also on awareness levels. It found that offline ads were little better.

The company also paid attention to achieving a higher conversion rate once leads had been generated. Some simple changes to the home page improved the 'contact efficiency', while continued usability testing ensured that customers weren't needlessly lost through user-interface glitches.

Annotating the channel chain with metrics

The resulting strategy involved a mix of promotional approaches, and is constantly evolving. As we discussed earlier, this strategy involved much closer working between channels than the company had initially antici-pated. Therefore the company began to develop cross-channel metrics, which can be annotated on a channel chain diagram (Figure 8.4).

Figure 8.4 shows which channels are available for each stage of the cus-tomer relationship, supplemented by lines indicating the common routes

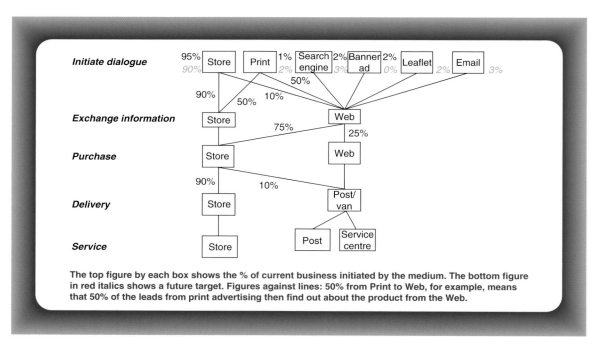

The top figure by each box shows the % of current business initiated by the medium. The bottom figure in red italics shows a future target. Figures against lines: 50% from Print to Web, for example, means that 50% of the leads from print advertising then find out about the product from the Web.

Figure 8.4
Channel chain and metrics – high-street chain

from one channel to another. For example, on the whole, customers who first spot an item in the store will continue to buy it from there. However, as we mentioned earlier, the company was surprised to discover that, of those customers who looked at an item on the website and went on to buy it, only a quarter did so online, the rest going into their local store.

■ Understanding and measuring channel crossover effects

This presents the problem of tracking this cross-channel customer behaviour. How can the impact of a paid search campaign with a search engine be measured if it is as likely to generate traffic to a store, sales force or call centre as to a website? How can the impact of a direct mail campaign be tracked if it generates website traffic as well as direct responses?

Broadly, this choice involves making a selection of variables which:

- cover the driver tree horizontally, incorporating a mixture of objectives, their immediate drivers and the enablers of those drivers
- cover the driver tree vertically, so important branches of the tree (such as the branches relating to 'effective staff' and 'quality of customer experience of channel') are represented
- can be viably measured

Figure 8.5 shows an example scorecard that divides into the standard sections of Results, Core processes, Customers and stakeholders, and People and knowledge – though these are not set in stone.

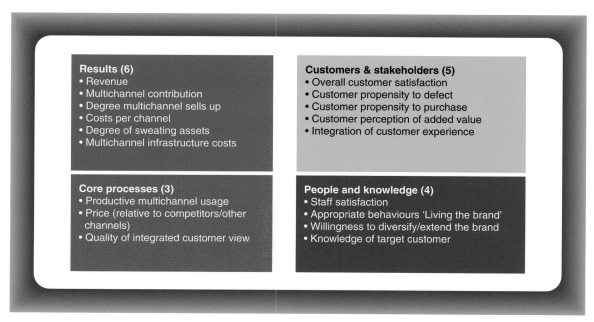

Figure 8.5
Multichannel scorecard for retailer

Many of these items might equally appear in a single-channel organisation – for example, revenue, customer satisfaction, price and staff satisfaction. Others, though, reflect the multiple means by which customers achieve channel chain effectiveness through a multichannel approach – for example, multichannel contribution, degree multichannel sells up, costs per channel, productive multichannel usage and quality of integrated customer view.

Consider, for example, 'degree multichannel sells up' in the results quadrant. A major driver of profitability in the low-margin retail sector is the proportion of sales of higher-margin products, such as Tesco's *Finest* range. So a key benefit of new channels sought by this retailer is increasing this proportion – through higher-margin top-up shops, perhaps on the Internet.

This emphasis on upselling contrasts with that in much of the retail financial services sector, where, because of the high cost of customer acquisition, cross-selling can be the key to getting more lifetime value from the customer. First Direct says that those of its customers who use both online and telephone channels have double the number of product holdings of those who only use the telephone – and have lower defection rates, too.

Defection rates are an issue for our retailer, too, so early warning of the customer's propensity to defect is polled regularly and included in the scorecard. Another vital customer measure is their 'perception of added value' – whether customers feel the multichannel proposition provides something that they want or need that they cannot get from the previous model. Amazon's book and CD recommendation facility based on past purchases is a case in point.

Achieving a channel mix which provides this added value and increased customer revenues is not cheap, however. From new formats such as metropolitan mini-stores to heavy investment in its web channel and supporting logistics, our retailer has been incurring significant capital expenditure as it rolls out its channel strategy, as well as ongoing maintenance costs to keep this infrastructure up to date. To keep an eye on this, the results quadrant includes a measure for 'multichannel infrastructure costs'. These can of course go down as well as up, through outsourced or consolidated call centres, for example. In the case of loyalty cards, we are seeing movement in both directions; some retailers are outsourcing to save costs while, conversely, Tesco has taken a controlling stake in its key supplier Dunnhumby.

'Productive channel usage' is a key variable driving market share. With an essentially stand-alone channel such as a traditional direct sales force, we can measure how well the channel contributes to market share by monitoring its rate of conversion of leads to customers, and hence its cost of acquisition. If, however, the role of the channel is to take the customer on to the next step in the buying cycle and hand them over to a different channel for the purchase itself, we need to monitor more specifically the conversion efficiency and the cost of moving the customer along that specific step. Thus the whole buying cycle might involve several efficiency ratios and corresponding costs. We cover this in more detail in Chapter 9.

■ Gathering the data

How can we measure the impact of multiple sales and marketing initiatives which cut across multiple channels? There are two broad cases to consider:

1. *Where the individual customer's journey can be tracked.* The ideal approach is to follow individual customers or prospects as they hop from one channel to another. Techniques for observing customers as they channel hop include different telephone numbers on different advertisements, special web pages as different entry points to a website depending on the promotion, coupons and special-offer codes linking to a specific advertisement, asking website visitors to register, and so on. Loyalty cards, and the business-to-business equivalent of encouraging customers to identify themselves and 'register', whatever the channel, can also be extremely useful here. By integrating loyalty card data across both stores and the web, Tesco can track when someone has browsed online and then purchased the same product in store.

2. *Where the individual customer cannot be identified.* The problem with many situations, though, is that we cannot directly tell what stimuli the customer is responding to, or which channels they have looked at prior to purchase. Here, use of control groups, or methods such as econometric modelling that look at the impact of overall spend across different channels or media, may be the only option. At US mobile telephony business Nextel (now part of Sprint), callers are tracked as they pass through all stages of any transaction, whatever the voice channel. This enables their response to dealing with an automated channel – as opposed to an agent – to be monitored, and Nextel to put in place appropriate strategies for both high- and low-value customers.

The relevant techniques to support these different situations have flourished in pockets of marketing practice – such as direct mail and television advertising – for quite some time, but their usefulness extends far beyond these areas. We will therefore explain the basics of two approaches, control groups and econometric modelling, and illustrate their applicability to the evaluation of multichannel effectiveness.

Using control groups

A very useful technique for measuring the ROI of individual activities within a complex multichannel route to market is *control-group measurement* or experimental design (Almquist and Wyner, 2001). Control groups or control cells are used to track the impact of any specific activity over and above all the general noise the customer may hear. They are used to identify the specific impact, for example, of a direct mailshot. Instead of mailing all of the target customers, a subset of the customer base or 'control group' is set aside at random and not mailed, with the remaining 'action group' receiving the mailing. The only difference between the action and control groups is the receipt of the mailing, so any difference in the two groups (such as different purchasing rates) can be attributed to the mailing (once random variation has been accounted for statistically).

As an example, a retailer evaluated the impact on sales of a new customer magazine for its loyalty card holders. It compared the performance of the mailed customers with a control cell of customers who were not sent the mailing. The results, shown in Table 8.2 (with amended figures and some figures omitted to protect confidential data), showed a significant increase in sales in the mailed group.

The company also wanted to know whether an email campaign targeting the loyalty card holders was effective, so it subdivided its customers further, with one group receiving emails as well as the magazine and another receiving just the magazine. Another control-cell analysis, shown in Table 8.3, teased out the additional sales that were being generated by the email campaign as against the magazine alone. When compared against the costs of media production, mailing and emailing, this analysis enabled the company to conclude that both the magazine and the email campaign were well worth maintaining.

Table 8.2 Control cells – customer magazine impact. Customer behaviour pre- and post-mailing period was analysed to understand the impact of the magazine selling

	Performance pre-mailing*		Performance post-mailing**		Increase vs pre-mailing period (%)		Out-performance of mailed members
	Mailed members	Control cell	Mailed members	Control cell	Mailed members	Control cell	
Active members							+6.8
Spend							+23.7
Visits							+7.4
Transactions							+15.1
Average transaction value							+11.8
Average spend per visit							+16.8
Average spend per member							+19.8

*25 September–13 November 2002
*20 November 2002–9 January 2003

Sometimes, a campaign or set of activities naturally falls into a sequence of stages, in which case a multistage control-group design can be used. A business-to-business service provider tracked the effectiveness of a direct mail campaign by looking at both the effect of an initial mailing and also the incremental effect of a follow-up mailing, as illustrated in Figure 8.6.

While the technique is mostly applied to marketing communications activities, it is equally useful for assessing different sales channels. British Telecom's Major Business Division used control groups to evaluate the effectiveness of its pilot programme introducing Desk-Based Account Managers (DBAMs). The action group had a small team of DBAMs supporting field-based salespeople, while the control group continued to use just field staff. The experiment found that the action group had a considerably lower cost of sale and achieved higher customer satisfaction, as well as generating incremental revenue.

Another example of the use of control groups to evaluate the success of a whole programme is General Motors' multichannel CRM initiative, described in Chapter 7. General Motors set out to build long-term relationships with prospects through direct mail, emails and magazines, constantly tailoring these communications by asking for customer data on expected car renewal date, models of interest and so on. By setting aside a control group who were not included in this programme, General Motors was able to assert with some confidence that its pilot programme with the launch of the new Vectra generated over 8,000 additional car sales.

Care is needed, though, to get the design right. A European services company evaluated a promotion to its loyalty card holders using control groups, and this seemed to show that the promotion was generating an

Table 8.3 Control cells – impact of email campaign

	Performance pre-mailing*		Performance post-mailing**		Increase vs pre-mailing period (%)		Out-performance (members receiving magazine + emails)
	Magazine only	Magazine + emails	Magazine only	Magazine + emails	Magazine only	Magazine + emails	
Active members							+4.7
Spend							+5.9
Visits							+0.3
Transactions							+2.2
Spend per active member							+1.4

*25 September–13 November 2002
*20 November 2002–9 January 2003

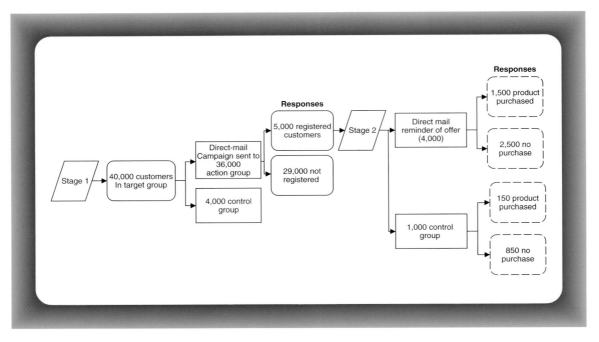

Figure 8.6
Multistage control groups

extra 10 percent of revenue from the action group. On closer inspection, the control group was actually bringing in up to 5 percent more revenue than the action group before the promotion even started, so the uplift was probably less than the company initially thought (see Figures 8.7 and 8.8). This kind of problem is often caused by an allocation into action and control groups which is not truly random.

Econometric modelling

When trying to disentangle the effect of several different marketing initiatives, another approach is to look simultaneously at the impact of all of them through econometric modelling. This uses the statistical technique of linear regression to tease out the relative impacts of several 'independent variables', such as advertising spend across a number of media, on a 'dependent variable' such as sales. Used extensively to evaluate the efficacy of TV advertising, the technique can be used across a range of other applications.

As an example, a major website used the technique to evaluate its promotional spend across a number of media. Values for a range of independent variables, such as promotional spend in TV, radio, newspapers and online, were entered for each month over the last few years, along with the dependent variable of the number of visitors to the website that

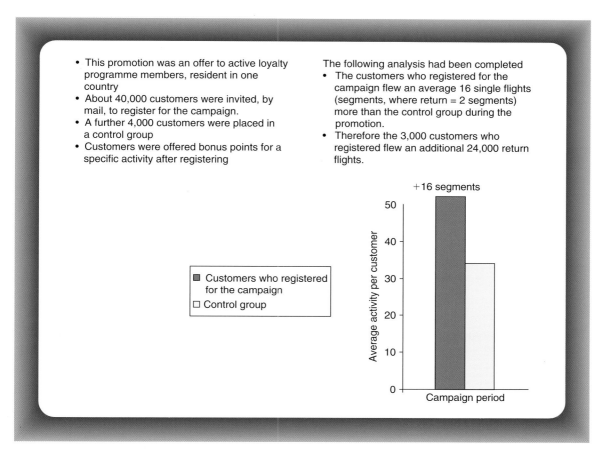

- This promotion was an offer to active loyalty programme members, resident in one country
- About 40,000 customers were invited, by mail, to register for the campaign.
- A further 4,000 customers were placed in a control group
- Customers were offered bonus points for a specific activity after registering

The following analysis had been completed
- The customers who registered for the campaign flew an average 16 single flights (segments, where return = 2 segments) more than the control group during the promotion.
- Therefore the 3,000 customers who registered flew an additional 24,000 return flights.

Figure 8.7
Control group evaluation in services company (1)

month. (This example shows that econometric modelling can be applied to any stage of the sales process, and not just the bottom-line sales figure.) Independent variables were also entered for such other factors as the level of competitive advertising (see Figure 8.9). A statistical package then separated the impact of these various variables and produced the conclusions shown in Figure 8.10.

This showed that each pound of advertising spend was generating 2 visitors from television advertisements and 4 from online spend, but 5.5 from radio and 13 from press advertisements (while competitor advertising spend had a negative effect, as expected). The company naturally adjusted its spend towards greater weighting on press coverage.

This technique, which is in use mainly in some FMCG markets, could be much more widely applied to other sectors; in particular, it offers the potential to evaluate the effectiveness of some multichannel campaigns that cannot otherwise be properly assessed. It does require a fair amount of historic data, though, which often rules it out.

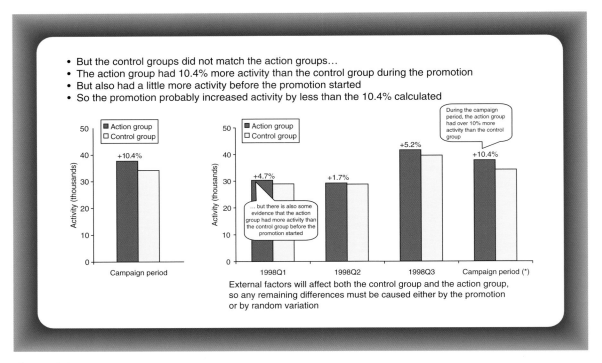

Figure 8.8
Control group evaluation in services company (2)

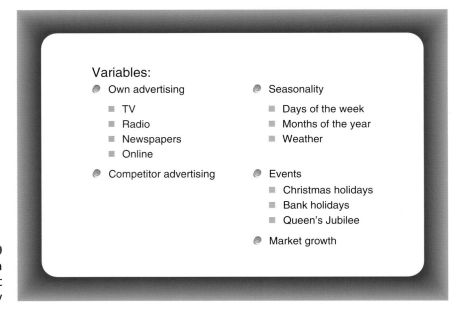

Figure 8.9
Variables in an econometric modelling study

Channel	Unique users	Half-life	Unique users per £ spent
TV	12,000,000	10 weeks	2
Radio	250,000	1 week	5.5
Press	3,000,000	3.5 weeks	13
Online	1,200,000	3 days	4
Competitor activity	−1,000,000	5 weeks	—

Figure 8.10
Econometric modelling to assess drivers of web visits

■ Pulling the data together

Techniques such as control groups and econometric modelling can be invaluable for assessing the contribution of specific activities, but how can we assess the overall performance of the multichannel route to market?

The British Telecom pilot of the introduction of DBAMs which we referred to earlier is a good example of how to do this in a holistic way, as it incorporated not just revenue and profit measures but also customer satisfaction and employee satisfaction ones. However, there is one metric which deserves some specific further attention: how to measure the profitability or contribution of marketing channels. It is common for organisations to track channel performance, and to reward channel management, on the basis of the contribution of each channel, typically measured in terms of revenue minus channel expenses – or, to put it another way, the 'expense-to-revenue ratio' of expenses as a percentage of revenue.

This works well if each channel operates independently, but if more than one channel is involved in the purchase process then the measure is clearly imperfect. If the high-street chain's website which we discussed earlier generates four times as much revenue for the stores as it takes online, then its overall contribution to the business is clearly greater than its own expense-to-revenue ratio would suggest.

There are two ways round this problem. The first is to allocate a financial value to the leads being passed to another channel. However, it may prove impractical to track all of this channel-hopping behaviour in detail. Another interesting approach (adopted by BT and IBM, amongst others) is therefore to focus on the overall expense-to-revenue ratio not for a single channel but for a group of customers irrespective of channel.

Figure 8.11 illustrates this for BT Business, the part of BT Retail which sells to small and medium-sized companies. BT calculates the expense-to-revenue ratio for each channel – field sales, desk-based sales, two categories of intermediary and BT.com – comparing these

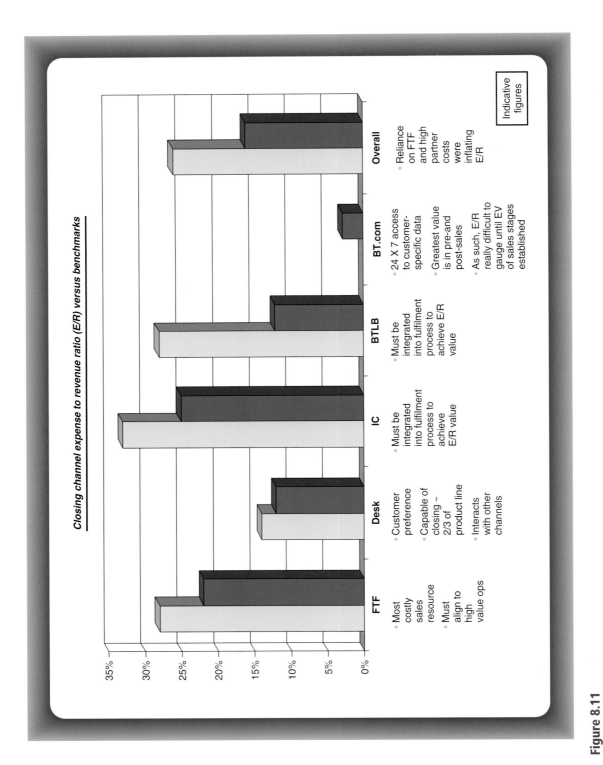

Figure 8.11
Expense to revenue ratio – BT Business

with benchmarks representing a best-practice organisation. However, it focuses primarily on the overall expense-to-revenue ratio across all channels, seen on the right of the chart. By targeting sales managers on this overall ratio for the set of accounts for which they are responsible (as well as on account revenue, of course), the managers are motivated to make sensible use of lower-cost channels and to get the channels working together effectively, while leaving them empowered to work out exactly how this can best be done in each account. Because profits ultimately come from customers and their lifetime value, this represents one of the most successful models we have seen for motivating behaviour in sales channels that aligns with the organisation's interests.

Measuring the effectiveness of marketing and sales was never easy, and today's multichannel, multimedia world makes it even more complex. Techniques such as control groups and econometric modelling are not new, but their application throughout the buying cycle, across multiple channels and outside the control of marketers within areas such as sales is comparatively recent. With a bit of forethought, marketing campaigns and changes to the sales approach can be evaluated rigorously – a great bonus when the case for a wider roll-out of a new approach needs to be made.

One company is currently using control groups, for example, to assess whether a field-based sales force or a call centre is most appropriate for various categories of sale. By allocating 1,000 leads at random into two piles, one going to the sales force and one to a call centre, the company will soon have clear data to confirm or, if necessary, modify the managers' intuition. Meeting the accountants halfway has to be better than retreating behind the half-truth that the value of a happy customer cannot be measured.

If future channel decisions are to be more rational than those we saw in the dotcom boom, the choice of metrics plays a crucial role. Most organisations have reasonably developed metrics for individual channels, but extending this metrics set to allow for today's channel-hopping customer requires some fundamental rethinking. It is essential, however, if we are to steer by the stars and not by the light of passing ships.

Thus far, we've focused on internal success factors in multichannel marketing. This is appropriate, since there's little point in driving customers to our channel options if they're not in place and working well. In Chapter 7 we discussed how we might organise ourselves for multichannel marketing, and in this chapter we have looked at how we might measure and control the activity once it begins. The next chapter considers how we might drive customers to use the right channels at the right time and for the right reason. Before going on to that, however, be aware that our work has illuminated a fundamental characteristic of this part of the process; namely, that effective multichannel marketing is about creating value. This might seem obvious, but many firms make the mistake of thinking that it is simply about cutting costs. The difference is that, whilst cutting costs may create value, this is not identical to value creation, which may involve improving customer satisfaction and hence preference. And, of course, cost reduction and customer satisfaction need not be mutually exclusive. In short, changing the way customers use your channels is best initiated by thinking about the value you intend to create, rather than just the money you want to save.

■ References

Almquist, E. and Wyner, G. (2001). Boost your marketing ROI with experimental design. *Harvard Business Review*, October.

McDonald, M.H.B. and Wilson, H. (2002). *The New Marketing*. Butterworth-Heinemann.

Smith, B.D. (2005). *Making Marketing Happen*. Elsevier.

CHAPTER 9

Encouraging customers to use channels effectively

That's the secret of entertaining. You make your guests feel welcome and at home. If you do that honestly, the rest takes care of itself.

Barbara Hall

In Part 2, we worked through a detailed process for developing a multichannel strategy. In Chapter 7, we moved from strategy development into implementation. We discussed the careful handling of structure, and how to avoid a good strategy being undermined or damaged by poor or inadequate organisation. In Chapter 8 we discussed measurement and metrics, what to measure and some of the methods that have been found to work well in a multichannel environment.

However, ultimately, any amount of work on multichannel strategy and implementation serves no purpose if customers do not change their behaviour and use the new channel chains. There would be no point in understanding the market and company, devising and implementing a potentially ground-breaking strategy and ensuring that all the metrics were securely in place to measure improved performance and success, if customers continued to behave as they always did, using the old (less effective) channels.

Sadly, unlike Kevin Costner's *Field of Dreams*, it is rarely enough simply to 'build it and they will come'. Customers will not gravitate towards a new channel or change their behaviour simply because we have made it possible or even cheaper for them to do so. Our experience is that customers are 'sticky' and self-serving – the majority prefer to continue with their habitual channel usage unless and until they perceive there to be some personal advantage in changing those habits.

On top of this, in terms of customer behaviour, certain marketing principles apply here, and it's worth reminding ourselves of those before we begin talking about encouraging changes in that behaviour.

First, the principles of segmentation operate strongly – all customers do not behave in the same way. We should not expect different segments of customers to follow the same behavioural patterns when they are driven by different needs and desires. A strategy needs to be based on good, solid segmentation (not simply product groups or customer descriptor groups) and channel chains need to be created to suit those segments. In the same way plans to encourage changes in customer behaviour, to convince customers to move into new channels, should be based on the segmentation that helped us to understand their needs and drivers in the first place.

Secondly, the innovation diffusion curve operates in this situation. Some more innovative customers will adopt new channels relatively quickly, and generally relish the opportunity to try out new channels and channel combinations. The majority will look to see how well others get on using new channels, or they will wait for those channels to become more 'established' before they begin to use them themselves. Inevitably, there will also be another group that sticks religiously to their established patterns of behaviour, resisting any channel change regardless of benefits

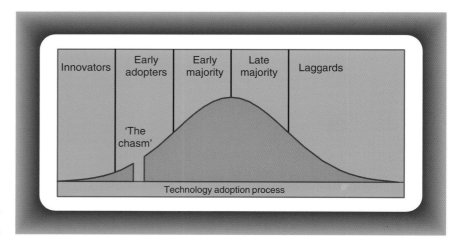

Figure 9.1
Technology
adoption process

or cost-savings, simply because it is different and new. There are, of course, techniques and mechanisms to manage the introduction of new channels and encourage customers to try to adopt them.

Thirdly, customer behaviour is influenced by product lifecycle. Product lifecycle is the result of the different levels of innovative behaviour of different customers and the natural tendency of competitors to copy a successful product idea. In fact, the model refers to all products of a certain form (for example, the lifecycle of the floppy disc is now almost over) rather than to an individual company's product. Typically, product lifecycles exhibit the classic embryonic/growth/maturity/decline pattern (see Figure 9.1).

Importantly, the stage of a product lifecycle can be gauged by measuring certain factors, such as growth rates and number of competitors. For more detail on the subject of product lifecycle management generally, we refer the reader to McDonald's book on marketing plans (McDonald, 2002). The important point for multichannel marketing is that the significance of innovators and the size and nature of segments often varies over the term of a product lifecycle.

In short, then, this is not simply a case of one size fitting all. Our approach to encouraging customers to move between channels needs to be contingent upon our specific situation. Which segments are we trying to encourage to adopt new channels? How innovative are they in other aspects of their behaviour? Are they likely to 'suck it and see' when a new channel is introduced, or do we need to 'prove' the value of the new channel and how it will improve the customer's buying experience before they will even trial it?

In other words, the marketing objective may change with context, from penetration to differentiation to harvesting cash. Multichannel marketing is capable of contribution to all of these objectives, but we need to start from a clear understanding of what we are trying to achieve.

■ What's in it for the customer?

We also need to remember that this is not simply a case of moving customers from channel to channel to suit the organisation's cost-saving or other goals. We are asked far more frequently than we would like: 'how can I persuade my customers to move to a lower-cost channel?' But this question makes an implicit assumption that we want or can reasonably expect all customers to use the lowest-cost channel. This is almost never an appropriate objective, and certainly not a realistic one.

The change needs to address the fundamental challenge that if we want customers to change channel usage behaviour, we have to make sure there is something in it *for them*. As we said before, it's about creating win–win situations, channel opportunities that give both the customer and the provider greater value – and these will rarely be universal, with one solution fitting all customers and all transaction types.

In practice, it means encouraging customers to use the lower-cost channels such as the web in situations where their needs are simple, but still allowing them access to higher-cost channels when they feel they need help. This may mean encouraging a business customer to use the web for routine purchases and ordering – giving them greater control, with 24-hour access to their account information and a home page they can personalise with immediate listings of their most regular product purchases, and the opportunity to compare different products and services. But it also means continuing to have available the call-centre support or a direct sales manager for when they have questions – for example, when they need advice about different products and services, have questions about their account or want to discuss the possibility of a bespoke package offer.

In a business-to-business context, imagine an office equipment supplier whose regular customers are happy to place routine orders over the web. They could be offered additional value from this service by having a link through to their own employee intranet that offers pre-agreed items for individuals or teams to 'place an order' using a department reference or internal authorisation code. These 'orders' could then automatically be collated by the supplier into a single order that maximises the overall price discount, and sent to the customer's purchasing team for confirmation before despatch. However, if the customer plans to open new office premises, we would not necessarily expect the same behaviour – at this point, the same customer might want to talk on the phone about products that are not regularly purchased, or a special discount for a large order, specific delivery requirements, or a visit from a sales person to the new premises to help design and recommend what will be required.

In a consumer context, think about your banking. In all probability, routine contact with your chosen financial services institution is a matter of you reading automatically generated printed statements, accessing your accounts via the web, receiving information as a text message on your mobile telephone, and perhaps occasionally calling the call centre to set up a new standing order or request a replacement bank card. However, the day that you win half a million on the lottery, you will more likely expect to talk to someone face-to-face about the options available. You may then want to go and compare these recommendations with suggestions from other financial institutions and to follow up with additional questions – for which you would reasonably expect to talk to the same individual as you originally met, and not someone in a call centre.

As we can see, moving all customers exclusively to lower-cost channels in these situations would not satisfy customer needs. Importantly, doing so would also not bring the maximum benefit to the supplier – maintaining the higher-cost, direct-contact channels as an option for the customer actually benefits the supplier greatly by leaving those channels open for sales opportunities.

So how can we go about creating the kind of win–win situations that encourage customers to change their channel behaviour? Having designed and built channel chains that we believe to be more valuable for the customer and for ourselves, how can we persuade customers to move through the new channel chains we have built? As we said in Chapter 1, customers are like water – they will 'flow' through the routes that they find easiest and most convenient. Thinking about *why* customers behave in a certain way will provide the answer to those questions.

■ What makes people migrate to a new channel?

As with so many areas of marketing, it's easy to be misled by what customers tell us about why they do what they do. People may say they want something, when they actually want the result that comes from that. The classic examples, of course, are Henry Ford, who said that if he had listened to his customers he'd have built a faster horse, and Sony, which, if it had asked its customers what they wanted, would never have built the Sony Walkman.

We frequently hear, for instance, that customers want personal service and to deal with a 'real person'. But that's not necessarily true. Think about the most successful large retailers. They are all self-service outlets where customers browse the store or website, selecting the goods they wish to purchase and then going to the checkout to make the purchase. These self-service retail outlets sprang up and took over from the old-fashioned grocery shops that had personal counter service. Customers made the choice to use the new self-service shops because it gave them more control over the goods they purchased, cheaper prices, and a better and wider choice of goods. Despite what they said, the fact that they deal less with real people is irrelevant.

This example also illustrates how a binary view of channels is not very appropriate. If we go to a large supermarket, it's self-service – but only inasmuch as we push a trolley around the store and go round, picking up what we want to buy. It's not entirely self service, though; customers do still have contact with people. At critical points in the shopping process, there is still a need to have people. At the moment, it's for things like complaint resolution, return of unwanted goods, help with navigating the store, assistance with checkout and validation that people are paying for what they're getting. In future, of course, we may not need people to do those things. Indeed, already some supermarkets use some type of 'self-service checkout' that allows customers to scan barcodes on goods as they put them into their trolley and then check themselves out with a credit or debit card when they have completed their shop. For the time being the success of these systems relies on random occasional checks and the availability of staff for when customers have a problem or query. The important thing is to see the trends that are developing and to realise by looking backwards at where we have come from how and why this self-service format has completely overtaken the old personal-service format. This serves to illustrate the rapid shift in the way that people buy not just groceries but also most consumables and consumer services.

Understanding innovation

There has been a similar customer behaviour shift with companies who have a direct mail channel. Those of us who remember the 1970s can recall buying products by post. We responded to an offer that came with our mail, or which we saw and cut out from a newspaper. The goods were then delivered by post and, if necessary, returned by post for a refund. Gradually, we became accustomed to buying things 'remotely'. We gained confidence in the idea that it was not necessary to see and touch the product before purchase, and that mail order was a reliable, secure and convenient way to buy goods. After that, we began ordering by telephone instead of completing an order form; we became used to the idea of call centres and buying things over the phone. In the late 1980s, this channel extended beyond goods and products such as clothes, and our confidence in the telephone as a channel grew so that we would buy services such as banking or insurance. The success of companies like First Direct and Direct Line in the late 1980s and early 1990s is testimony to a significant change in the customer's relationship with the telephone as a channel. People began to use telephone in a different way – to resolve queries, to purchase, to find out information. As the phone became ubiquitous, consumer behaviour changed.

We are currently seeing a similar shift regarding the Internet. When the web 'arrived' in the mid-1990s, it was new and exciting and relatively rare. People used to ask 'do you have email?' rather than 'what's your email address?' Do you remember when there was only one computer in your organisation with access to the Internet, and it was a privilege to use it because the culture was still 'afraid' of anything that could apparently link in to company systems? The Internet is now a high-growth medium in many sectors, not just travel, books and entertainment (when was the last time you checked out a cinema schedule any way other than online?), starting to represent over 10 percent of sales in many categories and with little sign of a slowdown in its share growth (and this underestimates its impact in facilitating sales across other channels). Already there is a significant amount of business generated through the Internet, either at point of purchase or as a supporting channel. As broadband becomes more widespread, we will see a rapid shift as the channel grows and becomes more and more the channel of choice.

Interestingly, these examples demonstrate both the growth of a specific channel and also the growth of multichannel. Retail self-service is complemented and supported by the face-to-face channel. Most people using the Internet use it in combination with other channels – for example, by researching a product or comparing prices from different companies before purchasing. The same is true of the telephone as a channel – many mail-order clothing companies thrive on the fact that people browse a catalogue or the Internet and then telephone to place their order or seek further information before ordering online. The point is this: people like to have the option to use different channels for different parts of the transaction or different types of transaction. The success of each channel relies of the customer being able to choose when to use it and when not.

Before we move on, let us touch on mobile telecoms as a channel. There is a great deal of hype about this being the next likely big channel shift – will it or won't it? This is a matter for conjecture, and in our work over recent years we have not seen anything that makes us say conclusively that mobile will be the next 'big channel' or that it won't. What we are seeing is a lot of customers using the phone and web channel combination, and a blurring of the distinction between mobile and other telephones. Mobile operators, of course, already envisage ways that people might be able to pay for things other than mobile services and related products through their existing mobile billing system. Already it is simple to buy a mobile phone 'top-up' through a bank ATM. It doesn't seem to be a great leap for the phone to become a method to purchase other goods.

From a communications point of view, using mobile phone text messages as a medium has undergone huge growth in the last 3 to 5 years – for example, with banks providing a text message update service to customers. Even so, we've barely touched the surface of mobile text as a medium for business-level communication; even less so for business-to-business products and services. The reason for this is unclear, but using this medium does require some significant investment, so it may simply be that only few companies have yet made that investment.

Having the right proposition

If we understand why customers choose different channels, then, it becomes clear that the first step in encouraging them to use an appropriate channel is to get the proposition right. It's about creating a win–win situation. In Chapter 4, we discussed the customer value through channel chains – the need for the customer to find value in using a particular channel or combination of channels. Of course, financial incentives can be put in place to encourage trial or ongoing use of a particular channel, but the only sustainable way to ensure that customers use a channel is to increase its value to them, to create a preference for that channel. Financial incentives only work on an ongoing basis if they are necessary to 'balance the value' and make a particular channel more valuable to the customer without undermining their cost-effectiveness for the company.

As always, the essence remains customer choice. Take away customer choice to use a particular channel and they will see its value as lost, regardless of how much more value is added by alternative channel options. However, give customers the choice of channels and they will move to the channel chain that genuinely offers most value.

Making it easy for the customer

When it comes to encouraging customers to switch channels, another key factor for success is to make it easy for the customer to choose and use the channel we want them to select. Improving the user experience on both the IVR and web channels can have dramatic effects on the willingness of the customer to use a channel to fulfil a particular requirement. This can simultaneously transform the customer experience and the economics. IBM.com found this to be true when it re-launched its online channel some years ago after reviewing the customer usage. With a specific focus on user engineering they not only increased site traffic by over 100 percent but also, and perhaps more significantly, increased sales off the channel by 400 percent – in the first week! When this sort of experience encourages customers to use a new lower-cost channel for a high-frequency need (e.g. balance enquiries, bill payment or information), then the business can often dramatically reduce the cost of service.

In a multichannel situation, the need for ease applies not only to each channel but also to the handovers between channels. It is vital to ensure that the linkages are in place between the various channels in a channel chain, and that customers can move from channel to channel with ease. In an ideal situation, customers will not even be conscious of a channel switch. When placing an order online, customers do not think about channel linkages when they telephone to ask about delivery schedules; they simply perceive the online service as being inadequate if they are unable to book delivery to suit them or if they are held in a call queue for too long. It is therefore critical to make sure that the effectiveness of one channel is not undermined by the failure of others to deliver.

One of the authors recently encountered precisely this problem. Dell's otherwise excellent technical-support channel (outsourced to a call centre somewhere in India) established within an hour that the DVD drive was faulty and promised despatch of a replacement – which day would be preferred? Sadly, they didn't realise the part was out of stock and consequently failed to deliver on the day agreed. Finally, a week later, they despatched the replacement drive … to an old address. To be fair, Dell's technical-support team did subsequently rectify the problem, but the fact remains that the telephone support service, which would otherwise have received 'full marks', was let down by the failure of linkages between channels.

A more successful example is provided by Legal & General, which supplies insurance services to consumers through Sainsbury's supermarkets. The benefits are communicated in terminology and using media intended to appeal to specific target customer groups, and the whole package, from the start of communication through to delivery of the policy, is planned to make it easy for customers to buy online. From the moment customers pick up a leaflet at the supermarket till point to the moment they purchase online, the process is seamless and easy.

■ Speeding up the process

If we want to move customers from one channel to another, the answer, in a nutshell, is to steer them rather than force them, to give them choice and to make it easy to use the new channel. But what will make them move to a new channel more quickly?

As we have said before, customers take the easy route. Give people ease of access to a new channel, make it easy to use and allow them to educate themselves, and very quickly, by word of mouth, the innovators will educate others and people will learn about new channels. A good example of this is the plethora of social network websites which rely on personal communication to increase their usage. This kind of 'viral impact' can be used to describe the way that people adapt to use new channels. As long as it is easy, people will educate themselves and each other, and a classic innovation diffusion curve develops.

Incentivisation and differentiation

Of course, using a 'carrot and stick' approach can work and may make channel change happen more quickly. However, as with anything that removes customers' channel choice and forces them down a particular route, this can be risky. As we said before, when, in the UK, Abbey started to charge people for using their more expensive counter-service channel in the mid-1990s, it led to uproar; customers expected to be able to use the service free and complained that they were being charged to access their own money. Similar fees for card usage and ATM access have met with customer resistance; however, a more positive example is the way in which some ATMs located in places other than on the wall of the bank now charge a usage fee, justified by the additional cost of maintaining an 'off-site' machine and supported by offering additional services through the ATM. By differentiating and offering more (more convenient location, added value services), the usage fee becomes acceptable.

Incentivisation can simply mean making a channel much more attractive to one or several customer groups, and thus much more attractive to use. In Kolkata, the Standard Chartered Bank has created an all-woman bank branch (including the security guards) with the explicit aim of attracting more female customers. In the USA, probably the leading initiative in this regard has been the rollout of the 'Occasio' branches since 2000 by Washington Mutual. These focus on the user experience, with a concierge and a much more retail and open ambience. Not only have they eliminated the transactional image set by teller windows and replaced it with a much more accessible feel; by effective handling of the customer for routine transactions and the provision of this within the branch they have also enabled the dialogue that helps drive customer recruitment and cross-sell in branch.

Offering a discount for using a particular channel is one option, and can be useful if it encourages people to trial a new channel. However, it's important to be sure that discounts encourage the behaviour you want and not the behaviour you don't want. We came across a business-to-business example of this in one of our research interviews. The company operated in a medical devices market in which there were only two significant players and 400 customers, each of whom held an 'exclusive' contract with one of the two suppliers. Interestingly, the supplier we interviewed discounted heavily when customers who were not 'on contract' placed occasional, small-quantity orders. They justified this by saying they wanted to win these customers. In fact, those small orders were expensive to fulfil, and the customers were not trialling but making a distress purchase when the competitor was out of stock. By discounting around 15 percent of their business with about 40 percent off the list price, the firm was throwing money away.

Another way to speed up the migration of customers from one channel to another is by surcharging for the use of the old channel. This needs to be carefully managed so that it is not seen by customers as a negative incentive or a penalty for using a familiar channel. However, in general terms, it becomes acceptable to customers when it is easy and accessible for them to use another channel. EasyJet used this technique successfully by charging people for telephone booking – but they only instigated this surcharge when the Internet had become sufficiently widespread that the majority of customers had access to the free online channel. In this case, too, it was accepted by customers who were familiar with the brand's low-cost focus and who deemed it appropriate that the company would pass on the additional cost of a different booking channel. (This, of course, is also an example of EasyJet successfully breaking the normal rules – they clearly communicated and separated the different channels instead of merging them seamlessly. This works for EasyJet only because their 'low-cost' ethos is so intrinsic to the brand. Not only do they save the cost of integrating multiple channels, but their brand values actually make it acceptable and even expected by customers!)

If a negative incentive or surcharge is to be used, it needs to be deliberate and carefully managed. In almost all cases where we've seen this method used, we have also seen it as damaging to the overall brand. Backing out of an existing channel – for example, by removing the account management team – is fine, but it's important to make sure that the new channel chain is secure first. Giving customers ample choice over a period of time and encouraging their use of your preferred channels allows them to shift themselves into the new channel chain. The company may then find that an existing (perhaps expensive) channel becomes obsolete and can be removed – or it may be that, although scarcely used, it remains valuable as a support for other channels.

Ultimately, it comes down to knowing your segments. If the offer is appropriate for a particular segment, then people are more likely to adopt it. SkyPlus provides a range of benefits to different customer segments. For those of us who struggle to programme our own video recorders, it gives the ability to record and watch television programmes with ease. On the other hand, its slightly funky positioning means that the innovators in society perceive it as novel, quirky and generally better than the 'old way' of recording TV. It also acts as a fully automated contact centre with Sky, so there is no need to have phone contact with the customer-service centre because almost everything can be done through Sky Plus.

Plan for migration

Those companies that we have seen successfully move customers from one channel to another do seem to have one thing in common. Rather than building the new channel and then allowing customers to move at their own pace, they have a plan for migrating customers. A good plan looks at the long term rather than the short term, leverages customer attitude and behaviour, and provides incremental steps with customer 'milestones'. For example, with EasyJet the plan was to surcharge telephone bookings *once the Internet was well established and a majority of customers would have access to online booking*.

A good plan is to start with the most responsive customers – those that are most incentivised to move. This could be because the new channel is more valuable to them, or because the old channel is less appealing. In general it's a matter of looking at people who have a relatively innovative mindset, and so it may simply be that a new channel is exciting or trendy. The new channel needs to be attractive to those customers – novel and easy to use. Once those customers are confidently using the channel, others are more likely to find it acceptable and try it themselves. And don't underestimate the power of word of mouth – people talk about what they do and what they find useful or interesting. Were you somebody who tried using telephone banking when it first became available just because it seemed like an interesting thing to try? Or did you begin using it after other people you know told you they had used it and found it easy and convenient?

Of course, when it comes to moving customers from one channel route to another, the usual barriers to the adoption of new innovation are likely to occur. If the innovators trial it and find it lacking, it will be an uphill struggle to get them to continue using it, let alone persuade others to shift. For example, if we want people to use the web, our website needs to be fast and easy to use. If we want people to switch to a call centre, we need to be certain there are enough telephone lines and enough staff so that customers don't wait too long for their call to be answered. If we want people to buy online and have goods delivered, we need to make sure our logistics system allows them to choose a delivery slot. A budget is a must, but just because we want people to move to a cheaper channel that doesn't mean the channel can be built cheaply. The budget needs to be sufficient to build a channel that meets customer needs, or it will become a white elephant.

It is also helpful to see multichannel marketing in a time-related context. Over a period of time, markets change as new ideas (technological or commercial) emerge, competitors enter and grow or exit … and customers learn. The time-related evolution of markets entered the management argot with the idea of the innovation diffusion curve (Rogers, 1976) – the idea that any new idea is adopted first by innovators, then by early and later adopters, and finally by laggards. When one considers this in the context of a certain product form, it leads to the concept of the product form lifecycle (Figure 9.2), in which the same need is met first by one product form then by another, each waning and waxing over time. The currently voguish example is the recent demise of the floppy disc in the face of flash memory sticks, but longer-term examples can be seen in areas such as music recording (e.g. 78s, LPs, cassettes, CDs, MP3s, etc.) and printers (ribbon, dot matrix, laser, inkjet). Most sectors exhibit product form lifecycle effects, albeit the reality is messy because old products linger and some, like the eight-track cartridge or the minidisk, fail to get past the embryonic stage.

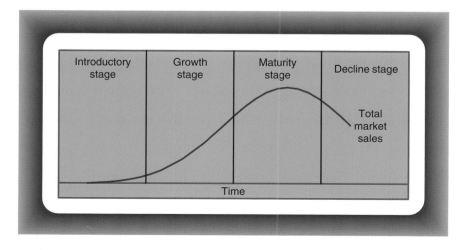

Figure 9.2
Product form
lifecycle

The key point is that product lifecycles form a context for multichannel marketing. This is because the lifecycle stage of a product is a reasonably good guide to how to manage that product and what marketing approach to take. In embryonic phases, advantage usually flows from simply communicating awareness and superiority over the previous product. In the growth stages, the battle is mostly about demonstrating differences between a particular offer and one or two different approaches (for instance, the format war in video-recording). Increasingly, however, embryonic and growth phases are over in a flash and most of the market-share struggle occurs in a mature phase, where several large, well-resourced competitors fight it out with offers in which the core product or service is pretty similar. One only has to consider the purchase of consumer products such as white goods, or services such as insurance, to see that, without intelligent differentiation, it is easy to move from the embryonic stage to commoditised decline so fast that little profit is made.

It is in the context of mature markets in which differentiation is difficult but essential that multichannel marketing is most often used. The creation of value by tailoring the offer in a way that is impossible through only one or two channels, the delivery of a more pleasurable experience, accessibility, convenience or lower cost through the thoughtful combination of complementary channels, lies at the heart of multichannel marketing today and, increasingly, of all differentiation in mature markets.

Using existing channels to help

The change that most companies want to make is to migrate their customers to increased use of online facilities, away from personal contact such as in-store sales staff, a field-based sales force or a call centre. In this case, basic human psychology applies: a personal link works better than pure technology, and people are more likely to adopt new technology if the personal link is already in place.

For example, JetBlue, the highly successful US low-cost carrier founded in 1999, places a strong emphasis on customer service and designed their check-in process to make the process as easy for customers as possible while at the same time economic. One way that they did this was by using kiosks.

First, they positioned the kiosks where customers would walk past them – much closer to the front of check-in, rather than hidden on one side or the back of the airport. Secondly, they included the highest possible level of functionality to maximise what could be done at the kiosks, so that more people could use the kiosks instead of needing to go to the check-in desk. The kiosks also included reassuring confirmation when actions (such as seat selection) had been completed. In fact, the entire self-service experience was made as smooth and easy as possible. The result was a reduction in the number of staff required to process the same number of passengers, leading to a reduction in costs and an increase in customer satisfaction, since passengers felt more in control of the process.

With the basic transactions handled effectively it was possible then to place emphasis on other aspects of the service without compromising profitability – such as encouraging the use of the call button!

The attractiveness of the economics and speed of kiosks is one of the reasons that airports are now starting to encourage the development of multi-use kiosks and the choice of these as the default route for passengers who have not checked in online.

Another way to encourage trial of new channels is by effectively using the existing channels to teach people how to use the new channels. This was the approach that many airlines took to increasing the use of kiosks at airports when they were first introduced. Similarly, a number of Canadian banks successfully use this approach by having telephone support staff offer to talk customers through using the website for the first time, and retail banks have increased the use of their automated machines for bank deposits and other services by having a member of staff in the bank lobby to help customers use the machines and become familiar with the technology and services available.

The evidence suggests that this is a powerful way of encouraging a change in customer behaviour, especially in a move from a human to an automated channel. A change in behaviour, especially one that is well established, needs not only an incentive (speed, cost, etc.) but also some way to de-risk the transition, and this kind of coaching from a trusted frontline staff member can provide that. This is confirmed in studies by others who have looked at the effectiveness of different approaches to encouraging channel migration (for example, Forrester).

■ The final challenge

As we said before, customers are self-serving and inherently creatures of habit. If you want them to change channel, you need to make sure that the new channel is easy to use and provides more value to them than the old channel. By applying the right mix of generic lessons, you can make it both. Achieving a real shift in behaviour requires creative thinking. It involves designing a proposition and incentives that encourage the desired action on the part of customers.

This chapter and this book as a whole have tried to give the reader a practical insight and approach to realising multichannel marketing. Multichannel marketing is simultaneously evolutionary and revolutionary – evolutionary in the sense that it builds on established principles of marketing that have created and will create value for most successful firms; revolutionary in the sense that technological developments and management innovation have made possible value creation in a way unimaginable to earlier generations of marketers.

In Part 1, we attempted to ground multichannel marketing in the context faced by almost all firms. Globalisation, increasing customer expectations, hypercompetitive markets and ever more demanding shareholders mean that markets have to square the circle of simultaneously creating more value for customers whilst maximising risk-adjusted return on investment. Fortunately, multichannel marketing creates the opportunity for doing this, and the diagnostic provided in Chapter 3 is intended to allow readers to begin applying this thinking to their own business.

In Part 2, we began to apply the concepts of multichannel marketing to the real world. Clearly, this begins with developing a strategy, but it also includes integrating that strategy across products, customer segments and channels. Importantly, this is a non-trivial, resource-intensive task, so we paid special attention to the issue of justifying such investment.

Finally, Part 3 concerned itself with the critical issue of implementation. This begins with organisational change, enabled and directed by tracking and measurement. Ultimately, it involves timely customer migration with minimum disruption whilst creating maximum customer and shareholder value.

We hope that this book, based as it is on extensive real-world research, carries many useful and insightful lessons from firms that have learned best practice to those that wish to emulate them in their own sector. However, because multichannel marketing involves change, perhaps it is appropriate to end this book with one last lesson about successful change. We observed this lesson in all of the successful companies we studied, but it is most succinctly expressed in a quotation from Warren Bennis, arguably one of the best value creators of the modern era:

> If there is one generalisation we can make about leadership and making change it is this: NO change can occur without willing and committed followers.

■ References

McDonald, M.H.B. (2002). Marketing Plans: How to Prepare Them, How to Use Them. Butterworth Heinemann.

Rogers, E.M. (1976). New product adoption and diffusion. Journal of Consumer Research, 2: 290–301.

Index